The Path of Handsome Lake

A Model of Recovery for Native People

The Path of Handsome Lake

A Model of Recovery for Native People

by

Dr. Alf H. Walle
Erskine College

INFORMATION AGE PUBLISHING
80 Mason Street • Greenwich, Connecticut 06830 • www.infoagepub.com

Library of Congress Cataloging-in-Publication Data

Walle, Alf H.
The path of Handsome Lake : a model of recovery for native people / by Alf H. Walle.
p. cm.
Includes bibliographical references and index.
ISBN 1-59311-129-0 (hardcover) – ISBN 1-59311-128-2 (pbk.)
1. Indians of North America–Alcohol use. 2. Indians of North America–Counseling of. 3. Indians of North America–Rehabilitation. 4. Alcoholics–Treatment–United States. 5. Alcoholics–Rehabilitation–United States. 6. Handsome Lake, 1735-1815. I. Title.
E98.L7W35 2004
362.29'286'097–dc22

2004008232

Printed in the United States of America

DEDICATION

In a most basic way, this book is dedicated to all those Native leaders, typified here most forcefully by Handsome Lake, who have provided their cultures with the ability to confront and overcome adversity. Numerous resourceful individuals who have lived in eras ranging from the early 19th century New York State of Handsome Lake to the contemporary world of Alaska where a new generation of individuals (such as Harold Napoleon) carry on the process of cultural renewal. They are the real thinkers who made this book, not myself. I, in the final analysis, am merely their "Boswell."

From a personal perspective, I would like to dedicate this book to those who most influenced me. Listed in alphabetical order, they include: Ray Barnhardt, Marcella Brimo, Oscar Kawagley, Michael Salzman, and Joe Smith. Thanks so much to all of you.

CONTENTS

APPENDICIES

PREFACE

In recent years, a transformation has been taking place in the way that we perceive alcoholism and in the ways that alcoholics are encouraged to restructure their lives. In the past, a "one size fits all" perspective reigned. According to such a vision, although various people suffering from alcoholism may be different in many ways, they are viewed as being unified by their malady. As a result, the logic goes, it is useful to focus upon this similarity instead of splintering people off into innumerable subgroups, based on this or that area of distinctiveness.

Due to the fact that there is a strong tradition of recovering alcoholics entering the field of alcohol counseling, furthermore, many practitioners have embraced what they knew best and what worked for them in their own lives. In a majority of cases, that tended to be the 12 Steps program initially developed by Alcoholics Anonymous. As a result, programs of recovery and therapy have historically tended to adopt the 12 Steps model.

At times, it has appeared that a major role of residential treatment facilities for alcoholism has been to prepare clients to attend Alcoholics Anonymous meetings and to practice the 12 Step Program after returning from institutional life. Although Alcoholics Anonymous' iron grip on treatment and self-help options is now beginning to be relaxed, a strong legacy of proposing universal methods has long dominated the field of alcohol therapy/recovery. That tradition is far from being eclipsed today.

In recent years (happily, in my opinion) other strategies of therapy and self-help have arisen in order to more effectively deal with the needs of spe-

The Path of Handsome Lake: A Model of Recovery for Native People, pages ix–xi

cific individuals and groups. These alternatives have ranged all the way from small local enclaves (such as Pagans in Recovery, which once functioned in Washington, D.C.) to programs that embrace a particular psychological slant, to groups that position themselves to serve circumscribed groups such as women, etc. Native strategies that build upon the Native cultural heritage of Native people are one aspect of this movement.

This group of essays is written to provide a series of suggestions to Native people who seek to deal with alcoholism from the perspective of their unique heritages and with an understanding that the pressures to which Native traditions and societies have been subjected may trigger dysfunctional behavior, such as excessive drinking. In doing so, I link the work, life, and example of Handsome Lake, an Iroquois leader of the 18th/early 19th century to strategies of recovery that are geared towards contemporary Native people.

The book is divided into three distinct sections. Chapters 1–3 provide some general discussions, including an overview of the "cultural configurations" method to be used in the analysis, a brief overview of Native American history, and a discussion of Native alcoholism. The purpose of these discussions is to provide the background material needed to fully benefit from what will follow.

Chapters 4–6 focus largely upon social theories of addiction culminating in a further discussion of the dilemmas that Natives often face. The goal here is to provide perspectives that can be used to deal with the fact that Native alcoholism may be distinct in some respects from the alcohol problems faced by other people. Key to these discussions is the fact that Native cultures tend to face profound stress and even decay and/or extinction. These pressures can be terribly hurtful to people because peoples' cultures and ways of life tend to be the bedrock underlying their existence and psychological health. When cultures are under attack, dysfunctional behaviors such as alcoholism are often both a symptom of cultural stress and change and an artifact of the pain people feel, as a result. Mainstream people, in contrast, seldom face this kind of stress to the degree that it routinely impacts Natives.

Chapters 7–11 deal in more detail with the strategies of recovery that were proposed by Handsome Lake, an 18th/early 19th century Iroquois leader and visionary. This section culminates with discussions of what I call the "Path of Handsome Lake" (a six component operationalizing of Handsome Lake's teaching) and another formulation that I call "Landmarks of the Path" (a means of evaluating progress and guiding therapy and/or self help). The goal is to provide a useful set of tools and perspectives regarding Native people and their dysfunctional behavior, such as alcoholism. This section concludes with discussions of how the method can be used in both therapy and in self-help groups.

I present this book as one way in which Native people may be able to embrace their cultural heritage as they seek to recover from alcoholism. Inspired by the example and teachings of Handsome Lake, I have updated his perspectives and explained them in terms of modern sociological and psychological theories. By doing so, a strategy of recovery for Native people living in the 21th century is offered.

Part I

A THEORETICAL AND EMPIRICAL GROUNDING

It has long been known that Native people are especially vulnerable to alcoholism. And increasingly, we recognize the cultural stress faced by Native societies and its impact upon individual people, are primary triggers for this terrible problem. As a result, the first section of this book deals with issues related to the Native cultural heritage that must be considered when developing strategies of recovery that are geared around the specific needs of the Native American population.

In Chapter 1, "Avoiding Counselor Bias: A Cultural Configurations Approach," the basic model of culture to be used in this book is presented from a theoretical perspective. In essence, the "cultural configurations" approach centers upon the fact that different societies embrace a wide range of traditions, beliefs, attitudes, and solutions that are unique to them and that they form a longstanding pattern of response to the challenges of the world. As a result, individual peoples must be viewed on their own terms and not from the perspectives of outsiders. Only then can the counseling profession and self-help groups adequately tailor strategies of recovery around the way people really think, feel, grieve, and celebrate. The cultural configuration approach is a classic method of social analysis that provides a useful set of techniques that make the mainsprings underlying cultures more assessable.

While Chapter 1 deals with social theory, Chapter 2, "The History of Native Americans: A Relevant Overview," provides a brief overview regarding various Native American cultural traditions. So depicted, various Native American societies are portrayed as distinct and not merely as part of a large homogeneous group. Thumbnail sketches of the basic cultural areas of the Native America facilitate this vision.

Although a proud and robust cultural diversity continues to exist among different Native American societies, however, today's strategies of coping are encouraging a greater cooperation between various indigenous groups. This trend has resulted in the diffusion of tactics and attitudes among various Native American groups. While specific Native cultures remain distinct, increasingly they feel united with other indigenous people. Thus, while specific traditions continue to be important and cherished by specific Native American groups, similarities between the plights of various Native cultures are being recognized and, where appropriate, collective actions and identities are being established.

Although this book focuses around Native Americans, the experiences of many Native people parallels the American experience. As a result, thumbnail sketches of Native Hawaiians and the Maori of New Zealand are offered to broaden the perspective.

Chapter 3 focuses upon the problem of alcoholism among Native Americans. In doing so, both genetic and social theories are discussed. Far from being mutually exclusive, these different impacts are seen as being complementary and building upon each other to create the hurtful environment in which Native Americans exist.

The goal of these chapters is to prepare the reader for Section 2 that focuses upon the social and cultural stress faced by many Native Americans. This (often unmitigated) stress is a major contributor to the patterns of alcoholism exhibited by many Native people.

CHAPTER 1

AVOIDING COUNSELOR BIAS

A Cultural Configurations Approach

There was a time when the counseling and social work professions tended to view themselves in "generic" ways and, as a result, they did not forcefully deal with the issues of race and ethnicity as a central concern. As an alternative, counselors tended to intuitively assume that all people afflicted by maladies (such as alcoholism) were suffering in, more or less, identical ways. Following from this assumption is the corollary that universal "one size fits all" treatment plans and self-help strategies are approriate for all people.

As late as 1962, when Gilbert Wrenn published his influential "The Culturally Encapsulated Counselor" (1962) there existed a chronic need to remind members of the counseling profession that the world view they brought to the helping relationship might be so narrow that minority clients risked being under-served by professionals who lacked an ability to interact effectively in cross-cultural or trans-cultural encounters. Since Wrenn voiced his warning, there has been an increased emphasis upon recognizing cultural differences and affirming that counselors need to tailor strategies around the specific needs, wants, and attitudes of their culturally diverse clients. Indeed, many observers and advocates for minorities have depicted culturally insensitive treatment as a covert (if not actually overt) form of oppression that is forced on ethnic and racial groups by the domi-

The Path of Handsome Lake: A Model of Recovery for Native People, pages 3–19

nant culture. As a result of such concerns, developing and deploying the cultural skills and perspectives needed to effectively and sensitively serve diverse client groups has emerged as a major component of social work and substance abuse counseling.

Unfortunately, oppression can result from well-meaning intentions. Thus, Michael Salzman (1995) complains that counselors run the very real risk of making inappropriate attributions regarding the problems faced by clients who happen to be members of an ethnic group that is significantly different from that of the counselor. In such situations, the risk of being mis-diagnosed and saddled with inappropriate therapies loom as real possibilities. Salzman concludes:

> Culturally derived attributional differences and the biases inherent in counselors' attributions represent a veritable minefield of potentially dehumanizing error in work with those who are culturally different (Salzman, 1995)

Today, of course, great strides have been made in the way counselors are trained in order to make them more aware of cultural variation. And there has been a call for the American Counseling Association to phase in multicultural standards (See, Arredondo & McDavis, 1992). While these advances are applauded, future strides remain to be made.

One basic key to understanding lays in acknowledging that special types of trauma are faced by members of ethnic and racial minorities as they confront the mainstream world. Looking at a wide variety of cultures, (ranging from Alaska Natives to Native Hawaiians to the Navajo) a familiar pattern occurs and reoccurs. When cultures are under attack, their members tend to suffer from a wide variety of psychological maladies that occur when cultures face stress. Thus, in cultures under attack, pychological problems can easily result (Salzman, 2001).

Even with the progress that has been made, cultural and ethnic distinctiveness continues to be a significant impediment to the effective treatment of cultural and ethnic minorities. Since the artifacts of misunderstanding typically insinuate themselves in covert ways, however, counselors are likely to be unaware of their impact and, therefore, ill-equipped to guard against them. In spite of well meaning the intentions, the subtleness of misunderstanding can lead professional counselors to rely upon preexisting attitudes, beliefs, and yardsticks of evaluation (1) when analyzing culturally diverse clients and (2) when designing, implementing, and facilitating strategies of recovery. As has been emphasized in recent years, culturally insensitive tendencies, unconscious though they may be, can silently undermine the therapeutic relationship.

Due to a broad-based emphasis upon diversity within our country, the impact of intellectual "blinders" has been increasingly discussed within the literature of social work and alcohol abuse therapy. Thus, far, such discussions have been largely been focused around strategies of intervention. Following this tact, issues involving cultural diversity are translated in terms of the counseling profession. Much productive dialogue has resulted from dialogues that embrace this perspective

Here, however, the opposite orientation is briefly discussed: this chapter deals with counseling in terms of social theory, not with reference of the internal traditions of the helping professions. Nonetheless, relevant perspectives are discussed as they relate to counseling and therapy. By providing this alternative strategy of organization, discussion, and analysis, a more robust understanding of the impact of social theory upon alcohol abuse therapy results.

One way of understanding the influence of social theory upon practitioner disciplines (such as counseling) is to briefly consider the impact of the "social structural model" within the social sciences as well as alternatives to it. When doing so, it is worthwhile to recall that social structural models focus explicitly upon the overarching culture and are not intended to explicitly deal with the individual. This focusing upon the "macro" culture, of course, is somewhat different from the typical perspective of alcohol abuse counselors who are primarily concerned with helping individual people face specific problems. Although counselors focus on individuals, however, they often need to embrace key aspects of the social structural paradigm. As a result, the underlying logic of this approach has great value to the counseling profession.

It is important to re-emphasize that the classic social structural model deals with the culture, not the individual. Nonetheless, the social structural paradigm and its view of "abnormality" has exerted a strong influence upon the social sciences and strongly impacted practitioner disciplines (including counseling) that are strongly influenced by social theory. These approaches are of profound value to members of the helping professions, such as alcohol/drug therapy.

Since the classic social structural paradigm, as most commonly deployed, tends to tightly focus upon some sort of "overarching" cultural tradition represented by the macro society; it is not ideally suited to deal with distinctive sub-groups within society. Thus, it is easy for the classic social structural model (if carelessly applied) to de-emphasize the uniqueness of specific ethnic traditions.

Because this book centers upon the distinctiveness of specific segments of society (such as various Native American peoples), my discussions often transcend the general tendency of social structural models to concentrate upon similarities between various parts of a large society (such as the modern, industrial United States). By embracing a more micro focus, I can more effectively deal with the distinctiveness of specific parts of society (such as particular Native cultural groups). In dong so, the uniqueness of various Native communities can be better appreciated and more appropriately addressed.

Since the 1970s, a popular means of overcoming the limitations of the classic social structural method has been linked to some form of "poststructural analysis" that, stemming from the existential tradition, focuses upon the distinctiveness of a specific person or a restricted group. Strategies of poststructural anlaysis will not be dealt with here, although I acknowledge that poststructuralism has many useful applications and that it can often be used as an alternative to the structural method.[1]

The alternative that is recommended here, stems from the "cultural configuration" tradition of social anthropology (as adjusted so it can effectively analyze specific groups). This adjustment is accomplished through the incorporation of perspectives that stem from disciplines such as folklore. As in the case of poststructural analysis, the cultural configuration method (as refined to deal with circumscribed groups) provides a useful means of overcoming the limitations of classic social structural analysis and its emphasis upon large/overarching social groups and how their members think and act in parallel ways. By adapting the cultural configuration method in order to deal with the distinctiveness of specific groups, this well-established method can aid alcoholism counselors who seek to avoid covert cultural biases; this goal is achieved by accepting clients on their own terms and by embracing strategies of recovery that are of particular value to specific clients.

THE STRUCTURAL METHOD AND INDIVIDUAL ADJUSTMENT

As has been briefly indicated above, social structuralism is concerned with the universal or macro aspects of a culture, its needs, and its priorities. Classic social structural analysis is not designed to deal with individual people and/or circumscribed groups. Another way of coming to grips with this fact is to recognize that (1) classic social structural analysis evaluates individuals/circumscribed groups in terms of the "mainstream culture" and (2) mental health is typically equated with reference to the degree that individuals conform to the circumstances/norms, provided by the dominant culture.

Although social structural researchers may, informally, be curious about human nature or the dilemmas that are faced by individual people and/or circumscribed groups, and even though social structurally oriented researchers may embrace some fairly detailed view/theory of the essence of mankind, their work and thought revolves around the corporate/collective nature of the mainstream culture, not the plight or perspectives of individual people and/or circumscribed groups. As a result, the social structural model focuses upon the larger, overarching culture/society, its needs, and how it functions. Other, more "individualistic"/circumscribed considerations (even though they may be of significant interest to the helping professions and its clients) fall largely outside of the universe of discourse that social structuralism pursues.

According to such a mainstream focus, the needs and behaviors of society at large (not those of individual people) emerge as the paramount topic under investigation. When pursuing this course of analysis, the culture is viewed as an overarching entity and people are fit into it accordingly. In addition, the culture is viewed as possessing distinct needs, rules, and vulnerabilities. Accommodating these pressures typically takes priority over the needs of specific people. As a result, a classic social structural approach views individuals in terms of how well they fit into their cultural milieu and if they (and their actions) enhance or undermine the health, strength, and effectiveness of the larger culture. The mental health of specific people, furthermore, is often viewed as being contingent upon painlessly meshing with the mainstream culture.

From a therapeutic point of view, the social structural approach assumes that what people want (and how they hope to achieve their goals) fall into the realm of learned behavior that is dictated by the macro cultural tradition. While studying these phenomena from a social structural perspective is useful, the resulting analysis tends to be skewed towards the macro society and not the individual or the circumscribed group. Indeed, one of the classic critiques of the social structural method is that individuals and their needs tend to be left out of the analytic equation. As a result, the society, as a corporate entity, receives the bulk of attention and people and groups are evaluated merely as parts of a larger whole who should act in ways that are consistent with it. This focus upon the larger culture (and the blindspots that such a vision institutionalizes) eventually led to the decline of the classic structural model and its eclipse as the dominant paradigm of the social sciences.

It is important to remember that the classic social structural model draws an analogy between a culture/society and a living organism. So analyzed, the culture emerges as the over-riding structure and all its parts (individual people included) are viewed in terms of how well they accommodate and reinforce the larger social organism by adhering to its needs, wants, and priorities. Those individuals/circumscribed groups that do not act in ways that are consistent with the dictates of the larger cultural entity tend to be viewed as sick. Thus, the mental health of individuals is often equated to a successful merging with the macro culture and feeling comfortable when doing so. Just like cancer is a sickness because it is characterized by a cluster of individualistically-oriented "rouge cells" responding in ways that are with odds with the guidelines provided by the larger organism, people who deviate from the needs, wants, guidelines, and priorities of the macro social system are also viewed as sick, perverted, and in need of re-channeling their activities in ways that are consistent with the ethos and the priorities of the larger society.

Since deviance however, is a basic fact of life that social structuralists cannot totally ignore. In acknowledging significant variations in response and orientations, the classic social structural view equated deviance with abnormality. Much of the theory of deviance that evolved within social structuralism is related to the concept of anomie. Anomie, as a distinct concept, initially stems from the early work of pioneering French sociologist Emile Durkhiem and it was introduced in Durkhiem's *Suicide,* a classic account of how social change can result in unhappiness, despair, and (as a result) lead to a growing suicide rate (Durkhiem, 1893). Discussed in layman's terms, anomie has sometimes been equated with "normlessness," although a more theoretical definition indicates that it:

> signifies the state of mind of one who...has no longer any sense of continuity, of folk, of obligation. The anomic man has become spiritually sterile, responsive only to himself, responsible to no one (MacIver, 1950).

As a result, individuals who experience anomie become alienated and cut off from their heritage. As Dressler observes:

> To put it allegorically, the anomic individual has lost his past, foresees no future and lives only in the immediate which is virtually nowhere (Dressler, 1969).

According to Robert Merton, a major 20th century American social theorist, a key cause and source of anomie is a disparity between the goals that society gives people versus the means by which these goals can be achieved. When people cannot achieve socially lauded goals in "legitimate" ways, anomie is the likely result (Merton, 1957). In specific, Merton argues that the mores and norms of the macro society provide individuals with goals to which they should aspire, on the one hand, and the socially acceptable methods of achieving these goals, on the other. Over time, however, the culture may change to such a degree that some people are no longer able to achieve sanctioned and honored goals in socially acceptable ways. Merton suggests that if this unhealthy situation impacts people, the propensity for deviant behavior increases.

Building upon the theories of earlier social structuralists, Merton provides a typology of responses to anomie that includes (1) conformity, (2) innovation, (3) ritualization, (4) retreatism, and (5) rebellion (Merton, 1957). Basically these different categories of response can be defined as:

1. "conformity" is the situation in which the person embraces both the goals of the society and seeks to achieve these goals in socially acceptable ways.
2. "Innovation" is a situation where the person embraces the goals of society but employs methods of achieving these goals that are not socially acceptable
3. "Ritualization" is a situation where the person acts according to the norms of society but loses track of the goals to be achieved.
4. "Retreatism" is a situation where the person rejects both the cultural goals and the institutionalized methods of achieving them.
5. "Rebellion" is a situation where the person rejects the goals and means of achieving them and substitutes an alternative.

Of special interest to us here is the fact that Merton tends to view drug and alcohol abuse as a specific form of retreatism. Although these retreatist behaviors may be at odds with the norms of society, they resonate from the social structure because they are chosen as an alternative when "normal" goals cannot be realized in socially acceptable ways. Thus, although retreatism and other responses to anomie are viewed as abnormal responses (because they do not mesh with the prevailing social system), they are viewed as artifacts of the priorities of the dominant social structure.

Developing a somewhat similar model, Alexander Leighton (1968), drawing upon his anthropological fieldwork, argued that social disintegration and the resulting decline in social cohesion can be a catalyst for stress that results in dysfunction. Specific triggers that Leighton mentions include (1) low or unstable income, (2) conflicting social values, and (3) fragmented communication networks. He concluded that the resulting stress often lead psychological disorders.

While the perspective of Durkhiem, Merton, and Leighton seems to be sensible enough, it tends to view all people as being part of the larger macro social system and it assumes that people are profoundly under its influence. Thus, the social structuralists tend to view the "mainstream" society as providing the yardstick by which the behavior of all social groups can be evaluated. The social structural view also assumes that all people are strongly influenced by this "mainstream" society. Counselors (typically members and products of this mainstream society themselves) may be prone to covertly embrace the basic belief structure of the mainstream culture and view any significant deviance from it as "abnormal." It is easy to see how the needs and differences of individuals and circumscribed groups can be overlooked under such a set of circumstances. Nonetheless, the theory of anomie, as adjusted to deal with Native people, has value and will be used as required.

These tendencies to view dysfunction from the perspective of the mainstream culture are not merely an artifact of the counseling profession. In addition, the traditions of the alcohol and drug abuse counseling industry largely evolved from and have been nurtured by self-help organizations such as Alcoholics Anonymous that were formed by lay people. Alcoholics Anonymous tends to look at all participants as being basically similar (by virtue of the fact that they are alcoholics seeking recovery). On many occasions, furthermore, the norms of the mainstream culture are also covertly embraced by those embracing the program. As such, similarities between a wide range of recovering people are emphasized. Making this observation, Thombs (1999) complains:

> Probably the single greatest barrier to the integration of theory, research, and clinical practice is the treatment community's strong tradition of relying on personal experience, clinical anecdotes, and testimonials. These sources of knowledge are limited because they assume all addicts or alcoholics are alike. (p. 18)

Thus, the perspectives of the social structural approach combine with the traditions of the self-help groups and the alcohol counseling profession by viewing alcoholics and recovering people in homogeneous ways and in terms of the prevailing social structure. When this happens, dealing with the distinctiveness of individuals and circumscribed groups becomes increasingly difficult.

Having provided this thumbnail sketch of (1) the impact of the social structural method and (2) the fact that this model tends to discourage a full analysis of cultural diversity, it is useful return to the professional literature in order to see how our profession seeks to transcend these limitations.

BEYOND NARROW SOCIAL STRUCTURAL VISIONS

As mentioned above, Wrenn's pioneering work (1962) pointed to the fact that the counseling profession of his era tended to view the world from a rather limited cultural perspective. Due to the problems inherent in this myopic view, he advised his readers to broaden their intellectual horizons in appropriate ways. We also saw how the social structural model, that had long dominated social theory, de-emphasized cultural diversity. Since the time when Wrenn wrote, however, the strangle hold of the social structural model has been broken and a recognition of the power of cultural diversity has been recognized by the counseling profession. Hand in hand with these developments has been a forceful acknowledgment within the professional literature that counselors are are likely to have cultural biases that can undermine their effectiveness as practitioners (Katz, 1985; Pedersen, 1987). While some progress has been made in overcoming ethnocentrism and culturally biased perspectives, however, Sue (1997) has observed that achieving a more multi-cultural approach to counseling has been spotty and, she can express only a guarded and qualified optimism regarding the effectiveness of culturally sensitive strategies within the counseling profession. Nonetheless, providing a brief overview of the growing interest in cultural diversity is useful.

Since Wrenn's seminal work, the counseling profession has increasingly recognized the significance of culture as well as the difficulties of understanding how specific cultures operate. Counselors, furthermore, increasingly recognize that the generalizations that derive from working within the "Western" cultural tradition cannot always be usefully applied cross-culturally (McFadden, 1988; Vontress, 1988; Richardson & Molinaro, 1996). Indeed, a specialized professional journal (*The Journal of Multicultural Counseling and Development*) deals specifically with such issues.

In contrast to "monocultual" perspectives that do not adequately account for cultural differences, social sciences, such as anthropology, emphasize that the human species is very adaptable and moldable and, as a result of an inherent ability to adjust, people can learn to accept varied situations and to embrace them with relative ease. This is especially true when people are young and going through the socialization process. Due to this flexibility of human nature, what is "normal" in one culture may be "abnormal in "another".

This crucial fact was recognized as early as the 1930s; thus in Ruth Benedict's "Anthropology and the Abnormal" (1934) she emphasizes that what is "abnormal" is defined, as such, by the culture and, therefore, the category is not an "objective" and universal measure to which all "normal" people will inevitably agree. As a result of this ambiguity, if counselors bring any arbitrary view of what is "normal" to their work, they are likely to deal in inept ways with a wide range of clients. Such a tendency exists because people come from diverse backgrounds and, therefore, behavior that is "abnormal" to members of the mainstream culture may be "normal" for others.

In recent years, the counseling literature has come to conclusions that mirror Benedict's classic work. Thus, Pederson (1987) observes:

> what is considered normal behavior will change according to the situation, the cultural background of a person or persons being judged, and the time during which a behavior is being displayed and observed.

As a result, the counseling profession is paying increased attention to the social and cultural context of the client.

Christopher, on the other hand, focuses upon the worldview of the counselor. He, for example, uses the term "moral vision" (1996) to identify clusters of cultural values and assumptions that people make regarding life. He goes on to observe, furthermore, that specific cultures and individual people have their own distinct moral visions that may conflict with those held by the counselor. When this occurs, counselors are likely to be ineffective because they may evaluate their clients' behavior as abnormal even though their actions may appear to be "normal" when viewed within an appropriate cultural context.

While this emerging literature stream is of immense value, it can be profoundly strengthened by linking it to the work of pioneering anthropologists such as Ruth Benedict who (as discussed above) viewed normality and abnormality from within a cultural context. Here, this goal will be accomplished with reference to the "cultural configuration approach" of social anthropology. Although somewhat dated, the cultural configuration approach will be adapted and rehabilitated because it clearly provides a way for counselors to deal with the issues of diversity raised by Wrenn, Christopher, Pedersen, et al. and do so in a robust and holistic manner.

THE CULTURAL CONFIGURATION APPROACH

When the discipline of anthropology emerged in the late 19th century, the era of evolution was profoundly impacting the intellectual world. As with many "dominant paradigms" evolutionary theory was widely embraced and, in some cases, abused. Consider, for example Sigmund Freud's rather outlandish musings about the nature of religion, the impact that a naive embrace of social Darwinism exerted upon the Freudian chain of thought, and how this thinking became subtly intertwined with an evolutionary approach.

Franz Boas, the father of American anthropology, was not as unsophisticated. Trained as a physical scientist, Boas clearly believed in biological evolution, but he hesitated to apply such a model to the analysis of cultures. Instead, Boas argued that cultures evolve independently and in response to the specific pressures that are faced. As a result, Boas reasoned, specific cultures tend to be unique and they cannot be easily fit into some general model of cultural evolution with "primitive" and "complex" cultures as opposite poles.

The Boasian school of anthropology is typically referred to as "historical particularism" because it focussed upon specific and isolated developments of distinct cultures/societies, not with universal evolutionary patterns that effected all cultures and mankind as a whole. This type of analytic strategy closely parallels the current research stream within the counselling profession that emphasizes the distinctiveness of cultures, not universal patterns of behavior. As a result, this model has much to offer alcohol counsellors who seek to understand the specific kinds of responses that can be expected from the members of certain cultures; in so doing, analysis can transcend examining universal patterns of behaviour and more effectively deal with the uniqueness of specific cultures.

Bringing a scientific bent to the study of culture, Boas was a stickler for details and he emphasized gathering voluminous empirical evidence. Indeed, anthropologists often use the term "Boasian" to describe (in disapproving terms) the tendency to spend so much time collecting facts that the resulting empirical evidence is never adequately synthesized into a coherent interpretation of the culture. Nonetheless, Boas' work does have a theoretical underpinning. Members of the historical particularist school tended to believe that (1) circumstances impact specific cultures, (2) cultures, therefore, evolve in particular ways, (3) due to the flexibility of human nature, people and cultures can embrace innumerable patterns of behaviour as "normal," and (4) focussing upon the distinctiveness of specific groups is essential component of the social sciences.

While historical particularism offered a useful alternative to general evolutionary theory, some of the movement's leaders eventually began to realize that Boas' preoccupation with material culture left gaps that potentially compromise his method. Noted anthropological linguist Edward Sapir, for example, complained that historical particularism did not deal with the emotional lives that people experienced. To overcome these limitations, a school of anthropology that is usually referred to as "culture and personality" was established. This sub-discipline builds upon Boas' paradigm by combining the theories of anthropology with those of psychology in order to develop a more robust theory of mankind and social life (and one that acknowledges people's emotional and spiritual lives). In essence, this method combined psychology with social structural perspectives in a substantial, robust, and useful manner.

Sapir emphasized that different cultures are truly distinctive and that translating the feelings of people from one society to those of another is no easy task. Thus, Sapir once observed:

> The worlds in which different societies live are distinct worlds, not merely the same world with different labels attached. (quoted in Opler, 1967.)

As we shall see, the method that Sapir advocated (as it was further developed over time) has much to contribute to practitioners involved in alcohol counselling; this is especially true when dealing with circumscribed ethnic groups.

Eventually Benedict (a student of both Boas and Sapir) developed a sophisticated and eclectic method in which social structures and psychological responses are usefully intermingled. Benedict, incidently, came to anthropology late in her intellectual development and she had previous training in writing and literary criticism. As a result, Benedict possessed a rich and diverse perspective and one that was profoundly influenced by the broader humanistic tradition, not merely by the social sciences. Indeed, Benedict's approach is strikingly similar to that of modern alcohol counsellors who seek to merge their profession with the humanities in order to bring a "spiritual" perspective to their work. Thus, Benedict is a "kindred spirit" and many avant garde alcohol counsellors will feel most comfortable with her and her approach.

A key premise unifying Benedict's method is the emphasis that the human spirit is very adaptable and pliable; she argued that due to this flexibility, successful cultures could emphasize a wide variety of orientations; thus, what is "normal" in one context, may be "abnormal" in the next. Nonetheless, Benedict affirmed, each culture could be fully embraced by its members. Thus, "normality" must be very broadly envisioned and it should be evaluated with reference to the cultural constellations in which the client exists.

Those concerned with alcohol counselling will be especially interested in Benedict's assertion that specific people tend to respond according to the dictates and conventions of the culture of which they a part. Thus, by understanding the ins and outs" of a specific culture, the alcohol counsellor can better anticipate how members of that culture will react to circumstances and what is likely to impact or influence their behavior.

Benedict's *Patterns of Culture* (1934)[2] is the tour de force of the cultural configuration method (which is best viewed as an extension of Boas' historical particular approach). In that seminal monograph, Benedict affirms that cultures can best be envisioned as holistic and synergistic "patterns" that orient their members to think, feel, and behave in certain, predictable ways. By understanding this overarching cultural pattern or configuration, a wide variety of behaviours can be more effectively predicted and/or explained. The value of this approach to the alcohol counsellor is self evident; it is also significant that these perspectives clearly dovetail with the current counselling literature that emphasizes the impact of culture upon behaviour.

A basic premise of *Patterns of Culture* is that at birth people are very flexible and that they have the potential to develop in innumerable ways. Benedict argues, however, that each culture possesses a particular "configuration" and that members of that culture are socialized to behave and respond in accordance with it. Thus, patterns/structures of personality and response are, in large measure, artifacts of unique patterns or structures of the culture. By understanding the influences of the culture upon its members, the future responses of both the individual and the collective society can be more accurately predicted. Again, this method has an obvious value for alcohol counsellors who seek to understand culturally diverse clients.

In *Patterns of Culture*, Benedict presents sketches of three cultures, the Zuni of New Mexico, the Dobu of Melanesia, and the Kwakiutl of the Western coast of North America, discussing in turn the configurations of each of these different cultural traditions. Benedict goes on to argue that these cultural patterns impact both the personalities of specific people and how they react to the circumstances and pressures that they face. Thus, Benedict viewed the society as a structured response to historical pressures and strategies of adaptation people embrace and how they cope with circumstance. Benedict is very clear about how the culture and the individual are intertwined:

> There is no proper antagonism between the role of society and that of the individual ... Society ... is never an entity separable from the individuals who compose it. (1934, 1959)

Quickly following Benedict's *Patterns of Culture* was Margaret Mead's *Sex and Temperament in Three Primitive Societies* (1935),[3] a book that suggested that aspects of personality that scholars had often been linked to the biological fact of one's sex (such as aggressive behaviour among males verses passive responses among females) are actually learned by children during the socialization process and, therefore, they are based on the structures provided by the culture, not upon an innate propensity to act in a specific manner. Studies such as Mead's (connected, as they are, to the historical particularist perspective) point to the impact of culture upon the human personalities and responses. As a result, they underscore that the structure of human response varies widely in different cultures. These insights regarding the flexibility of mankind (and the fact that people are largely products of historical circumstance) have a clear value to the alcohol abuse counsellor since these ideas focus upon patterned responses by clients that are culturally specific and not universal. Nonetheless, they are often the mainsprings that underlie and drive actual behaviour.

Since many human responses are standardized are not "thought out" in rational and tactical ways that respond to specific circumstances, they constitute structured reactions that are dictated by the underlying patterns of a culture. Investigating these overarching influences can, of course, provide alcohol counsellors with invaluable insights and suggest appropriate strategies of therapy. The work of the historical particularistic anthropologists and culture and personality specialists (such as Benedict and Mead) provide a systematic means of dealing with this phenomena and one that counsellors can use when discussing these tendencies with a wide range of clients.

A CONFIGURATION APPROACH FOR CIRCUMSCRIBED GROUPS

The cultural configuration method is powerful tool. In many circumstances, however, it (like social structuralism) has been used to examine general patterns that typify a large culture, not as a means of modeling the behavior of individuals or circumscribed groups. Thus, in her *And Keep Your Powder Dry,* Margaret Mead used the configuration approach to distill the essence of the national character of the United States, a broad-based cultural entity. This approach, however, it is not inherently well suited to deal with smaller sub-groups (such as specific Native American cultures).

If the cultural configuration model is to be used to effectively deal with members of specific Native American cultures and their members, the focus must be shifted from the homogeneous aspects of a larger cultural identity, to the uniqueness of some of its component parts. As we shall see, it is possible to do so. First, the cultural configuration method was developed in order to analyze small, circumscribed groups. Second, disciplines such as folklore facilitate dealing with cultural enclaves that are simultaneously part of a larger cultural unit. Members of the alcohol counseling profession can use these disciplines to adapt the cultural configuration method to their needs.

The cultural configuration method ultimately developed within the context of small, circumscribed social groups. As was indicated above, Ruth Benedict's *Patterns of Culture* was based on the examination of three circumscribed cultural units the Zuni of New Mexico, the Dobu of Melanesia, and the Kwakiutl of the Western coast of North America. Since our topic is about Native Americans, it is worthwhile to note that two of the three case studies provided by Benedict concern specific Native American cultures. Likewise, Margaret Mead's various monographs routinely examine small circumscribed groups and distill the cultural patterns that are inherent within them. Even Mead's *And Keep Your Powder Dry,* the study of a large industrial mass society, applies micro concepts designed to deal with small-scale societies to the analysis of a large industrial culture.

The cultural configuration approach, therefore, is well suited to deal with circumscribed groups. As a result, alcohol counselors seeking to understand the mainsprings that underlie circumscribed groups, such as specific Native American cultures, will find the configuration method to be well suited to their needs.

The usefulness of the cultural configuration model is enhanced by disciplines, such as folklore, and how they have evolved in recent decades. During a pioneering phase, folklorists sought out hinterland populations where the impact of the modern world was still insignificant. Finding such populations, they recorded their music, arts, crafts, and customs. Eventually, however, people who were "untouched" by the outside world become increasingly scarce and, as a result, research interests and strategies changed. Today, folklorists are well aware that the "folk" they study are profoundly influenced by the outside world. And in most cases, the folk will simultaneously be part of both the macro/mainstream and the micro/circumscribed culture. Many individuals are adept in both worlds. In spite of the influence of the larger culture, however, these circumscribed groups have not died (as was predicted by 19th century folklorists who hurried to vestigial communities to gather local lore before its extinction).

Today's folklorists acknowledge that both the mainstream and the circumscribed cultures tend to have their own configurations and that the one may influence the other. Nonetheless, folklorists continue, both of these cultural units tend to survive as distinctive. In my own research, furthermore, (Walle, 1995) I have argued that people tend to be respond to the circumscribed culture at some periods in their lives, while the mass culture will be more dominant at other phases. Disciplines, such as folklore, often develop strategies for dealing with people who have multiple cultural identities and, therefore, respond to diverse influences.

This situation, of course, closely reflects the situation of many Native American people who possess two separate, although perhaps interlocking, identities (one indigenous, the other "mainstream"). At different times in their lives, the influence of these identities and their relative impact upon the individual may vary. This dual membership, furthermore, can be the cause of tensions and confusions among specific people and their families. These perspectives have a profound value to those who provide alcohol counseling to Native Americans.

CULTURAL CONFIGURATIONS AND COUNSELING

Many Native Americans are simultaneously members of two distinct and somewhat conflicting groups: the mainstream American culture and their more circumscribed cultural identity. This situation can cause stress among Native American clients and confusion among counselors.

The cultural configuration model can be useful in this regard. On the one hand, there may be something like an "overarching" cultural configuration that typifies most Americans and influences them. On the other hand, many people possess multiple identities as members of both the mainstream society and their traditional culture. This dual membership can lead to stress that, in turn, can trigger alcoholic behavior.

The cultural configurations approach, as described here, provides a way of dealing with that reality. Members of ethnic groups (such as Native American cultures) tend to simultaneously be part of at least two cultural entities (1) their indigenous culture and (2) mainstream society. This dual membership can create tensions and conflicts within the individual that can lead to problems in coping with life that may trigger alcoholism. People from different cultures, furthermore, may act in accord with "normal" patterns of response that may appear to be "abnormal" if viewed using the yardsticks of evaluations provided by the mainstream culture. Thus, when dealing with circumscribed groups, such as Native American cultures, counselors face a complex situation and one that demands a perspective that is broader than that provided by the mainstream culture.

In recent years, there have been a growing recognition that people who come from specific cultural traditions must be evaluated and counseled accordingly. This book expands the models available by adjusting the lens of the cultural configuration approach to the needs of the counseling profession.

NOTES

1. For discussions of my views of poststrucutral analysis and how it transcends structural analysis, consult my earlier work (Walle, 2000, 2000a).
2. Benedict (1934), *Patterns of Culture.*
3. Mead (1935).

REFERENCES

Arrendondo, D., & McDavis (1992) Mulitcultural Counseling and Competencies and Standards. *Journal of Counseling and Development,* 79, 477–486.

Benedict, R. (1934). Anthropology and the abnormal. *Journal of General Psychology,* 10, 59–79.

Benedict, R. (1934). *Patterns of culture.* Boston: Houghton Mifflin.

Christopher, Jack (1997) *How to stay sober: Recovery without religion* (New York: Prometheus Books.)

Leighton, A. (1968). Some propositions regarding the relationship of sociocultural integration to mental health. In J. Zubin & F.A. Freyhaw (Eds.), *Social Psychology.* New York: Grunet and Stratton.

McFadden, J. (1988). Cross-cultural counseling: Caribbean perspective. *Journal of Multicultural Counseling and Development,* 16, 24–40.

McIver (1950). *The ramparts we guard.* New York: MacMillian.

Mead, M. (1935). *Sex and temperament in three primitive societies.* New York: Morrow.

Mead, M. (1942). *And Keep Your Powder Dry.*

Merton, R. (1957). *Social theory and social structure.* New York: Free Press

Richardson, T. Q. & Molinaro, K. L. (1996). White counselor self awareness: A prerequisite for developing multicultural competence. *Journal of Counseling and Development,* 74, 238–242.

Opler, M.K. (1967). *Culture and social psychiatry.* New York: Atherthon Press.

Salzman, M.B. (1995). Attributional discrepancies and bias in cross-cultural interactions. *Journal of Multicultural Counseling and Development,* 23, July 181–193.

Salzman, M.B. (2001). Cultural trauma and recovery: Perspectives from terror management theory. *Trauma, Violence, and Abuse,* 2, April 172–191.

Sue, S. (1997). Community health services to minority groups: Some optimism, some pessimism. *American Psychologist,* 32, 616–624.

Sue, D. W., Arredondo, P., & McDavis, R. J. (1992). Multicultural counseling competencies and standards: A call to the profession. *Journal of Counseling and Development,* 70, 477–486.

Vontress, C. (1988). An existential approach to cross-cultural counseling. *Journal of Multicultural Counseling and Development,* 16, 73–83.

Walle, A.H. (1995). George Davis: Beyond the singing miner. *Southern Folklore,* 52, Spring 53–67.

Wrenn, C. G. (1962). The culturally encapsulated counselor. *Harvard Educational Review,* 32, 444–449.

CHAPTER 2

HISTORY OF NATIVE AMERICANS

A Relevant Overview

Although often stereotyped as a homogeneous group in the public imagination (in examples of popular culture such as cowboy movies), there exists profound diversity among various Native American populations. Nonetheless, in spite of cultural differences and long-standing rivalries between various indigenous tribes, bands, and nations, Native Americans, as a collective entity, are beginning to collaborate and cooperate as never before. This trend towards a greater collective identity results from the recognition that parallel influences have led to shared experiences, mutual interests, and similar strategies for coping with the dominant culture. The feelings and attitudes deriving from this increased cooperation and sense of shared identity are impacted and influenced by strategies of activism and political action that are embraced by some members of the Native American community. Nonetheless, the distinctiveness of specific Native cultural traditions remains. In this chapter, a brief overview of Native American cultures provides a point of reference for alcohol abuse counselors who deal with Native clients. This analysis is followed by documenting how the history of various Native Americans peoples is parallel to the experiences of other Native groups such as Native Hawaiians and

The Path of Handsome Lake: A Model of Recovery for Native People, pages 21–37

Maori of New Zealand. These parallels demonstrate possible applications of this book beyond the confines of North America).

NATIVE AMERICANS: A THUMBNAIL SKETCH

When Christopher Columbus "discovered" America in 1492, he met indigenous populations, descendants of the original settlers who, in prehistoric times, traveled across the land bridge that once connected Siberia and Alaska (or arrived via a different route). Eventually, the descendants of these original pioneers settled throughout both North and South America and adapted to local conditions. Thus, before White contact, a wide variety of indigenous cultures existed in the Americas, ranging from complex civilizations, on the one extreme, to small local bands of nomads, on the other.

White contact, of course, has exerted a profound impact upon indigenous populations. Initially, for example, Native Americans possessed little resistance to a number of diseases of European origin. As a result, a significant percentage of the Native American population died of maladies (such as the common cold) that today, are dismissed as mere nuisances by Natives and non-Natives alike. The resulting epidemics were particularly disruptive because, in many cases, a rapid and unexpected decimation left the culture and the economic base in shambles, thereby creating profound pain, suffering, and disorientation. The legacy of those traumas remains to this day in many places and it has been linked to alcoholic tendencies (Napoleon, 1996).

White intruders, furthermore, often fought wars of conquest and went on to enslave the local inhabitants. In addition, they frequently systematically dismantled the cultures they conquered. This process was especially prevalent in Spanish territory. In the regions of North America that were controlled by England and France, in contrast, patterns of trade between the indigenous people and Europeans resulted in some Native groups gaining political, technological, and economic advantages over their neighbors; as a result, White contact often transformed Native Americans life by shifting the balance of power. Even when no direct contact with local populations took place, the Native peoples and their relationships with one another were often profoundly impacted.

Up through the first half of the 19th century, Native populations (while typically displaced in the Eastern United States) were largely allowed a free reign west of the Mississippi River. During this period, furthermore, Russia (which controlled Alaska during that era) viewed its colony primarily as a source of raw materials and did not attempt significant colonization, enslave the local peoples, and/or profoundly disrupt their ways of life (even though some missionary work was conducted by the Russian Orthodox Church).

Even in such areas, however, the impact of the White man loomed heavily. The plains tribes, for example, although not in contact with Whites, did gain horses (that had originally arrived with White settlers and soldiers). The mobility provided by horses profoundly transformed the lives and cultures of the plains peoples. As another example, in Alaska, trappers and whalers exerted a profound impact that often led to local crises as food supplies dwindled.

After the American Civil War (1861–1865), a flood of immigrants came to the United States from the Old World in search of farmland. This demand led to the rapid settling of the Western regions of the United States. Understandably, as this process occurred, conflicts between the Western Indians and the Whites settlers accelerated. Ultimately, the Natives suffered heavy losses and once they surrendered or capitulated, they tended to be concentrated on reservations. This situation, while somewhat tolerable for the more sedentary societies, proved to be a profound economic and emotional hardship for members of the more nomadic cultures.

Although the United States purchased Alaska from Russia in 1867, settlement continued to be insignificant until the discovery of gold around the turn of the 20th century. Eventually, epidemics caused by White contact exerted profound impacts, and stress, alienation, and dysfunctional behaviors (such as alcoholism) emerged as chronic problems.

Surviving great stresses and challenges, many Native American groups continue to function as cultures and as political entities. In recent decades, the plight of many Native entities has somewhat improved although, as minority groups, they and their members continue to be poorer and more rural than most Americans.

Approximately one third of Native Americans live on reservations, while about one half resides in urban areas (that tend to be close to reservations). As with other groups within American society, considerable variation exists among Native Americans (and different Native American nations). Furthermore, on many occasions, one segment of a particular Native culture will embrace conservative attitudes and they struggle to remain distinct from the mainstream of American society while other, more mainstream, members of the same culture, seek to mesh more completely with the larger society and economy.

An analogy of this situation can be seen in Philip Roth's novel *Goodbye Columbus* that portrays how different segments of the Jewish American population respond to life in the United States. Some of the Jews that Roth writes about treasure their religious and ethnic heritages and the close-knit community that they make possible. These people feel a profound sense of loss as members of the younger generation lose their distinctively Jewish attitudes, personas, and characters. Other Jews, in contrast, while perhaps remaining proud of their Judaism and their specific ethnic identity, primarily identify with the mainstream of American culture and they don't want to be held back by a strong Jewish identity that, they feel, will limit their options. The same tension often exists within Native Americans communities: one segment of a particular culture might look inward towards their heritage and traditions while others look outward towards the larger world.

While many Native American groups have long nurtured distinctive cultural heritages that are meaningful to them, the current "pan Indian movement" is transcending these differences by seeking to overcome the rivalries of the past in order for different Native Americans cultures to work together for their common good. Thus, a homogeneous "Native American" identity is coming to supplement (while not replacing) the specific and distinctive affiliations with particular Native American cultures and traditions.

SUBGROUPS AND THEIR SIGNIFICANCE

The overview provided above, although accurate, does not adequately emphasize the fact that diverse Native Americans groups continue to exist and that they exhibit a profound range of cultural variation that are products of their own distinctive histories. In order to demonstrate this diversity, a brief discussion of the major North American "cultural areas" is presented and juxtaposed with one another. Recognized culture areas of North America include the Southwest, the Eastern Woodlands, the Southeast, the Plains, the California-Intermountain region, the Plateau, the Pacific Northwest Coast, the Subarctic, and the Arctic. It is hoped that by looking briefly on these distinct cultural areas, the richness, variation, and complexity of Native American culture will be appreciated.

The Southwestern Cultural Area

The Southwestern culture area is largely associated with the so-called "four corners" region Arizona, Utah, New Mexico, and Colorado, and it extends into the Mexican states of Sonora and Chihuahua. This is the region that gave rise to the awe inspiring "cliff dwellings" that are considered some of the most impressive achievements of the pre-historic populations of what is now the United States.

In prehistoric times, corn (that had already been domesticated in what is now Mexico) was introduced to the Southwest. Although agriculture was, initially, an insignificant source of food, the people eventually became dependent upon farming, adopted a sedentary lifestyle, and settled in towns made of adobe. Various descendants of this cultural tradition (such as Pima and Papago (now Tohono O'Odham) largely preserve this way of life in the southern part of the region.

In the more northern areas, members of the Anasazi tradition lived in towns constructed from stone and adobe. The economic mainstays included maize, beans, and squash. Eventually (after 1275 AD) severe droughts caused many Anasazi regions to be abandoned. Along the Rio Grande, however, irrigation systems allowed habitation and agriculture to continue. Conquered by the Spanish in 1598, these peoples successfully rebelled in 1680 but were re-conquered in 1692. Although constantly under the domination of the Spanish, Mexico, and eventually the United States, the Pueblos have largely preserved their culture and many of these people continue to farm and live in their small adobe towns. Although, their traditional religions and governments were long suppressed, they survived covertly and they continue to function today. Approximately 20 indigenous Pueblo towns continue to exist as "going concerns."

The Navaho, in contrast, are relative new comers, arriving as hunters in the 1400s, having migrated southward along the plains. The Navaho speak an Athabascan language and are directly related to the Athabascan tribes of interior Alaska. After initially raiding the Pueblo towns as a source of livelihood, they eventually learned the essentials of farming and animal husbandry. The Apache, also late-comers to the region, maintained a more nomadic way of life.

The Eastern Woodland Cultural Area

The eastern part of North America (geographically situated south of the subartic and north the Southern regions, such as North Carolina) is home of the Eastern Woodlands cultural area. Originally the region was heavily forested and nomadic hunters/gatherers inhabited the region in prehistoric times. Eventually, the more sedentary populations adopted agriculture. Fishing was also of economic importance. Due to economic specialization, different groups of people (some nomadic, some sedentary) often shared a single geographic area.

The Iroquois are among the best-known Woodland people. They were (and are) well organized and, traditionally, they lived in villages. The Algonquian-speaking peoples, in contrast, were more nomadic. In the 17th century, the Algonquian became embroiled in a battle for power with the Iroquois and the Iroquois emerged victorious. As a result, the Algonquian were largely dispersed and their power declined, although they continue to exist. To this day, the Iroquois is a vital force in New York State and the Province of Ontario.

The Southeast Cultural Area

The Southeast cultural area ranges from the Gulf of Mexico on the south to the Eastern Woodlands region on the north and extends from the Atlantic Ocean to central Texas. The Indians of this region were thriving when Hernando De Soto, the first European to visit the region, made contact. Epidemics brought by the Spanish, however, quickly took a heavy toll. Before the onslaught of disease, however, De Soto witnessed a culture typified by town life, agriculture, and a significant amount of highly organized trade.

Best known today are the Cherokee, the Choctaw, the Chickasaw, the Creek, and the Seminole. After the American Revolution and before the Civil War, these highly civilized Indian nations were crushed by the United States government. Andrew Jackson, for example, forced the removal (in 1838) of the Cherokee from Tennessee and North Carolina to what is now Oklahoma in an infamous migration known as "the trail of tears."

The Natchez were another famous Southeastern people whose complex and sophisticated culture was destroyed by Europeans in the 18th century. Today, the Natchez are considered to be extinct as a culture, although, genetically, some descendants of the Natchez may remain.

The Plains Cultural Area

The North American plains consists of grasslands ranging from central Canada to Mexico and from the Midwest westward to the Rocky Mountains. The Plains Indians relied heavily upon bison for their livelihood and they suffered grievously after the herds were exterminated in the 1880s. Traditionally, the people of the plains lived in small nomadic bands that followed the moving herds. A few towns that practiced agriculture did exist, but they were the exception to the rule.

In many ways, the image of the plains people have come to represent "the American Indian" as envisioned in the popular imagination. They, for example, were the people who originally wore long feather headdress, smoked peace pipes, and lived in tepees.

The plains Natives began to quickly evolve after the arrival of the horse because it increased their speed, range, and their ability to harvest bison. At the same time, as Europeans conquered the East, various refugees from the Eastern Woodlands drifted into the area.

The California Intermountain Cultural Area

The mountainous regions of Utah, Nevada, and California possess pine forests, grasslands, marshes, and valleys. Largely left to themselves, an archaic way of life (typified by hunting, fishing, harvesting pine nuts and other wild grains) emerged as early as 8000 BC and survived with no significant changes until about 1850. Seemingly primitive, the strategies and technologies of harvesting, processing, and storing food were very sophisticated. The artistry of their basket making demonstrates both skill and an artistic eye.

The Paiute, Ute, and Shoshoni are the best-known peoples of the Intermountain cultural area. Northern California tribes include the Klamath, the Modoc, and the Yurok, the Pomo, Maidu, Miwok, Patwin, and Wintun. The Intermountain Cultural area also includes the so-called "mission tribes" (such as the Diegueno that were supposedly named by the Spanish who conquered them.

The Plateau Cultural Area

In parts of Idaho, Oregon, Washington, Montana, and the adjacent Canadian provinces of Alberta and British Columbia, evergreen forests in the mountains are interspersed with grassy valleys. As with the California Intermountain Culture area, the people of the plateau maintained an archaic pattern of life that was enriched by annual runs of salmon and by the various lucrative harvests of various wild plants that grew in the valleys. The people lived in villages in the winter and camped out during the summer. Large quantities of salmon were dried and eaten during the winter.

Perhaps the most famous Plateau people are the Nez Percé, (the name derives from a French description of their pierced noses (Nez Pere means "pierced nose"). The Nez Perce were a prosperous tribe who lived by salmon fishing. They eventually gained horseback riding skills and supplemented their economic life accordingly. Initially, they signed a treaty with the United States government and surrendered the bulk of their territories in return for a reservation. The discovery of gold on the reservation, however, led to their eviction. This event that was the catalyst for the famous rebellion of Chief Joseph who, after fighting a brilliant military campaign, was stalled by a snowstorm and captured in 1877. The Nez Perce ultimately declined in numbers and today only about 4,000 people claim Nez Perce descent.

Other Plateau people include the Wallawalla, Yakima Indians, Umatilla, and the "Flatheads."

The Pacific Northwest Coast Cultural Area

The Pacific west coast of North America (from southern Alaska to northern California) is bordered on the east by mountains, the habitable land of the region is usually a narrow strip lying between the sea and the mountain barriers that separates it from the inland areas. The sea is rich in fish (salmon) and sea mammals. The land offers a bounty of mountain sheep, goats, elk as well as edible plants. These plentiful resources were able to supported a much higher population than is usually possible for a hunting and gathering people. Members of the Pacific Northwest Coast cultural area tended to live in large houses that sheltered an entire extended family and, possibly, the slaves it owned. The most famous people of the Northwest Coast are the Kwakiutl who staged complex and expensive celebrations (Potlatches) that were designed to enhance the social status of the host while redistributing resources to those in need. The Northwest Coast is known for its magnificent wooden carvings, such at totem polls. Tribes of the Northwest Coast include the Tlingit, Tsimshian, Haida, Kwakiutl, Nootka, Chinook Salish, Makah, and Tillamook.

The Subartic Culture Area

The Subarctic region comprises the larger part of Canada and interior Alaska, stretching from the Atlantic to the Pacific oceans. It begins about 200 miles north of the border of the United States and continues to the beginnings of the tundra. Since the eastern half of this region was once covered by glaciers, the soil is poor and Due to the short growing season, agriculture is not possible; as a result, peoples earn a livelihood by hunting moose and caribou and by fishing. The people traditionally lived a nomadic life. As might be expected in such environment, the population was always small.

As was the case with various other Native populations located in the "lower 48," White contact brought disruptions and epidemics that led to profound trauma and social disruption. In many cases, these events took place in living memory and people continue to be impacted by them. In addition, missionaries, gaining power after the epidemics, often sought to undercut the local culture, a situation that also caused significant stress and disruption.

In the east, the Subarctic people were of Algonquian descent and included the Cree and the Chippewa among others. In the west, people speak Athabascan languages, including the Chipewyan. Even today, many Subarctic Indians continue to trap, fish, and hunt commercially, although they live in villages and are no longer nomadic. Nonetheless, many of them practice a subsistence way of life based on fishing and hunting.

The Arctic Cultural Area

The Arctic cultural area rings Alaska and northern Canada and stretches into Asia and Greenland. Agriculture is impossible and people live by fishing and by hunting seal, caribou, and, in some places, whales. The arctic, of course, is also the home of the Eskimont,[1] a group that is distinct from their Athabascan neighbors. Like the Subarctic peoples (such as the Athabascan), but unlike most Natives who live in the "lower 48" of the United States, the people of the Arctic retain much of their ancient way of life due to their remote locations.

As was the case with the Subartic peoples, however, epidemics brought by White contact exerted a profound influence and since these hardships are within the living memory of some Natives, these experiences continue to cause stress (Napoleon, 1996).

AN ERA OF CONVERGENCE

Years ago, I had an opportunity to interview Colonel Tim McCoy, a famous hero in cowboy movies made during the 1930s. At some point in the interview we began discussing his work with Native American actor Chief Dan George. McCoy observed: "Chief Dan George is a great actor ... he can play a Navaho, an Apache, or an Iroquois all equally well." This statement, more than any other, indicates to me that McCoy truly understood Native Americans. He realized that Native Americans are a diverse lot and that they cannot be easily stereotyped. An actor who could portray all three would be skilled, indeed.

The foregoing overview of various Native Americans cultural areas has demonstrated profound differences between various societies, cultures, and populations; the purpose of providing these discussions is to underscore the fact that Native Americans are not a homogeneous group of people that can be described in general terms. Historically, Native American cultures ranged from extremely archaic "holdovers" from a more primitive time, to highly complex societies that made sophisticated use of trade, relied on agriculture, and lived in towns.

In addition, Native Americans groups also exhibit significant biological differences from one another. Just like the blond, blue-eyed Nordics of Scandinavia look very different from Southern Italians, various groups of Native Americans exhibit an equally marked degree of physical variation.

Besides cultural and biological differences, heated rivalries between different Native Americans cultures have long been the norm. Indeed, in colonial days, the Europeans often exploited the hatred and rivalries of one Native group against another in order to further their colonial goals. Indeed, the British were consciously aware of the tensions between various Native populations and they consciously took advantage of that situation. Thus MacLeod in his *The American Indian Frontier* (1928) reports that the British overtly instructed their leaders in the New World to pit one tribe against the other (as they had done in Ireland) in order to achieve their goals while simultaneously weakening the native populations. It has often been observed by historians and anthropologists that if the various Native populations had not been hostile to one other, the Europeans would probably have been unable to dislodge them (at least until the 19th century when the technology of warfare became more mechanized).

Even when the Europeans were not encouraging warfare, the differential advantage created by trade with the Whites often upset the balance of power and various regions were transformed accordingly. The case of the Winnebago in Wisconsin is a classic example.

Before contact with the White fur traders, the Winnebago were a vulnerable sedentary people largely surrounded and harassed by the more nomadic Algonquin who subsisted by hunting and gathering. When the fur traders first came to the area, these intruders sought out the hunting and gathering people (who were adept at capturing beaver), but since the Algonquin were nomadic and traveled from place to place, the fur traders were forced to deal with the Winnebago who, living a sedentary lifestyle, could easily be located. Although the Winnebago were initially rather inept hunters, they were successful enough to begin a trading relationship that ultimately resulting in their access to firearms.

Firearms, in turn, altered the balance of power and, as a result, the Winnebago were able to defeat their Algonquin neighbors and drive them away. This left the fur trade in the hands of the Winnebago who went on to gain the hunting and trapping skills required to exploit this resource (Walle, 1979).

As demonstrated by this example (and the many other that it represents) tensions ran high among various Native communities, and with the intrusion and eventual dominance of the Whites, these tensions often grew. As a result, Native peoples remained in a fragmented state and they were largely unable to cooperate in ways that advanced their collective interests vas a vas the Whites.

In recent years, various members of the Native American community, while still embracing their specific traditions, are increasingly coming to view themselves as part of a multi-faceted group that shares many collective interests, vulnerabilities, and needs. At long last, Native Americans are learning to cooperate for the collective benefit of all. Some of these activities are clearly political while others have more of a cultural orientation (such as Pow Wows attended more then one Native culture or nation); both political and cultural solidarity are beginning to broaden the arena of cooperation between different Native peoples.

To my mind, an analogy between these developments is the growth of romantic nationalism among 19th century Europeans. As the reader may recall, romantic nationalism represents the reasserting of cultural traditions by colonized European peoples in order to temper the impacts of foreign domination and technological change. While specific European cultures were concerned with advancing their own specific heritages, the broader romantic movement linked different groups that were attempting to re-establish their distinctive national heritages. A similar situation is appearing among Native Americans, as various groups seek to advance their own goals and agendas, on the one hand, while acting collectively in order to do so.

INTERNAL RIVALRIES

As indicated, different Native Americans cultures were long at odds with each other. That kind of tension has somewhat subsided. This does not mean that total harmony reigns; today's tensions, however, are more likely to take place internally between members of the same group who jockey for power and hold different opinions regarding what is best for specific Native Americans groups. As indicated above, there are often tensions between "traditionalists" and more "mainstream" people.

Some Natives (on and off the reservation) place a high value on their traditional culture. In addition, they may embrace a traditional religion and adhere to various moral and ethical guidelines that stem from their unique cultural traditions. Other competing groups, in contrast, may be more connected with the mainstream culture and they may seek more close participation within the modern economy and contemporary social life. Thus, one segment of a tribe may oppose gambling and seek to maintain a more traditional lifestyle while rivals seek to open a gambling casino in order to foster economic development. Some Alaskan Natives, likewise, may advocate drilling for oil or natural gas while others oppose it. In addition, some segments of a Native culture may place a high value of maintaining a subsistence way of life while this consideration is not a high priority for others.

WHAT IS A NATIVE AMERICAN?

As used here, the definition of Native Americans does not rely solely upon genetics. Instead, the degree to which a person embraces a Native American culture must also be considered. As with the Natchez (mentioned above) some Native Americans cultures are extinct although genetically/biologically, descendants may live on. It is an established fact that the members of many Native Americans cultures have, biologically, merged with the larger population. Thus, it may be rather hard to find a "biologically pure" member of many Native cultures.

A personal anecdote will demonstrate the degree to which the "gene pool" of Native Americans is broad based and contains genes from other races. I am of Scandinavian and Scotch descent, have blue eyes, a fair complexion, and light brown hair. To my knowledge, I have no Native Americans blood. I do, however, have a reasonable amount of knowledge about the Native Americans.

A few years ago, I attended a Pow Wow on the Mohawk Indian reservation (near Rooseveltown, New York). While there, several tribal members I met wanted to know what my clan affiliation was. In 2002, in Fairbanks, Alaska, I was at another Pow Wow and again I was asked about my Native American affiliation. Although I don't "look like" a Native, my attendance at a Native event overshadowed my appearance. Obviously, cultural identity and genetic pedigree are somewhat distinct.

The opposite situation is equally revealing; various individuals clearly have a genetic heritage that is Native American, while their cultural heritage has largely or completely lapsed. Are these people Natives? Genetically, they can be defined as Native, but culturally few, if any, cultural traditions remain. The legal criterion that is used to establish a Native American identity (however defined), furthermore, largely relies upon cultural, not merely genetic considerations. Thus, the legal hurdles needed to establish a Native identity usually stipulate that the culture must survive as "a going concern" for a Native status to be recognized.

This book is primarily concerned with individuals who maintain a cultural identity as Natives even if they have a simultaneous identity within the larger community. This, of course, is not the only possibly definition of Native American and this book does not necessarily conflict with these alternative views. Nonetheless, this book focuses on cultural, not genetic, heritages (although it is recognized that Native Americans may be especially vulnerable to alcoholism due to their genetic makeup).

HAWAIIANS AND MAORI: PARALLEL EXAMPLES

While this book deals primarily with Native Americans, other Native peoples have been subjected to similar experiences. Two revealing examples are Native Hawaiians and the Maori of New Zealand. By briefly looking at their history (1) the plight of Native Americans can be put in a broader perspective and (2) it can be argued that the findings and recommendations of this book may have applications that extend beyond North America. In order to make these points, both the Hawaiian and Maori experiences will be analyzed from this perspective.

Hawaiians

Before White contact, the Hawaiian Islands had a population that ranged from 200,000 (Stannard, 1989) to 800,000 (Bushnell, 1989). They lived in a pleasant world and the Native culture and its people were well adapted to it. Just like the Native Americans, however, the Hawaiian people had no immunity to various European diseases and, as a result, profoundly disruptive epidemics followed the first contact by Captain Cook. According to Salzman, the Hawaiians "understood [these epidemics] in the same way that the [Alaskan] Yupik understood their great death" (2001) and they tended to blame themselves for the misfortune that came their way.

And just as "experts" predicted the extinction of the Native peoples and their cultural traditions of North America, the total disappearance of the Hawaiian people was long "thought of as inevitable" (Davis, 1968). Disease, cultural change, and outside intervention struck powerful blows. As Salzman synthesizes:

> Old Hawaiian customs previously bonded together by ancient Polynesian beliefs, now fractured by the overthrow of the traditional religion were, collapsing at all levels, As a result of the understandably bewildered Hawaiians plunged to a new low (Salzman, 2001).

Under such circumstances, Christian missionaries took advantage of the situation and converted the Native people who felt their traditional religions had failed them. This is another parallel between Hawaii and the Native Alaskan/Native American experience. (Ultimately, the descendants of the Christian missionaries to Hawaii emerged as rich landlords; a well known adage among native Hawaiians is the "The missionaries came to do good and did very well").

Although reduced in numbers, status, and power the Hawaiian people, nonetheless, have survived and Native cultural traditions are re-emerging as a powerful force. Efforts include strategies for reaffirming the language, lore, and traditions of the Native Hawaiians. This trend also largely parallels the Natives American trends in which indigenous cultures are being reaffirmed. Thus, although North America has its own unique history, the experiences of the Native people in both North American and Hawaii are largely parallel.

The Maori

The Maori of New Zealand are a Native people who (like Native Hawaiians and Native North Americans) faced trauma as a result of White contact. Comparing the Maori experience to that of Native Alaskans, for example, Gilgen observes:

> There are many similarities between [Native Alaskan and Maori] experiences....a disproportionate over-representation in the prisons, abhorrent statistics regarding disease and health issues, dismal failure in the education system, and the highest ratio of unemployed people in the country (1996).

Gilgen does see some differences, primarily with regard to the fact that he feels that Native Alaskans are now in the position that the Maori faced at the turn of the 20th century. Although this may be true of Native Alaskans, the Maori experience may more closely parallel the situation of many Native Americans in the "lower 48." Gilgen continues:

> My ancestors were traumatized by a great death, a period in which Maaori culture was attacked physically, spiritually, and culturally through disease, land confiscation, inter-tribal warfare, and the introduction of alcohol and non-indigenous religions. To deal with the rape of our land and culture, we also used a range of coping mechanisms that included self-blame, alcohol abuse, violence among ourselves, depression, suicide, and denial (1996).

As has often been the case in North America, the Native population of New Zealand was reduced to second class citizenship as an artifact of the White domination that first began in the mid 19th century and continues to this day. And these losses were often accompanied by alcoholic behavior:

> [In the areas most affected, the Maoris] were living in debt and confined to run-down reserves, poorly administered because of the confusion of multiple ownership brought about by land courts. Already, South Island Maaoris had passed though liquor craze in the mid-1960s which left them "squalid, miserable, lifeless" foreshadowing the the fate of the North Island tribes later in the decade....This upturn in drinking assisted in the breakdown in the traditional leadership.(Alcohol Reserach Unit 1984).

According to Barbara Harrison:

> Alcohol ... continues to be a problem today. In 1986, the Maaori admission rate for alcohol dependance or abuse was approximately double the non-Maaori rate, and I know from my experiences in a Maaori community that young people die in alcohol-related accidents and middle aged people die sooner than necessary because of alcohol-related disease (1996).

The examples of Hawaii and New Zealand demonstrate that although the Native people of North America have their own unique histories, their experiences and responses have strong parallels to other Native peoples that have experienced the disruption caused by White contact. As a result, while keeping unique experiences in mind, it is also useful to think in terms or recurring patterns.

ONCE WERE WARRIORS: A CASE STUDY

While professional books typically rely upon scientific research, alternative data is, on occasion, useful. Here, a brief review of *Once Were Warriors*, a powerful and influential feature film from New Zealand, dramatizes the parallels that have been discussed above. Its importance lies in the fact that the film crystallizes the dilemma faced by many Maori living in today's New Zealand and the struggles facing those who seek to cope with the dysfunction it triggers.

Once Were Warriors is a dark film about the Native Maori people of New Zealand and the pressures that an underclass existence has exerted upon them. The plot-line depicts a woman of Maori descent, living in a slum with a violent and wasteful husband who is more concerned with his drinking buddies than with his wife and children.

Jake Heke, the husband, is convincing as a man who has slipped so far into a pointless life of drinking and violence that he is seemingly unable to perceive his own brutality for what it is. And the audience is able to understand how a strong and vital woman, physically weaker than Jake, learns to bend to his wishes. Not completely broken, she occasionally states her mind, but is bloodied and raped as her reward for doing so.

Jake's character and his ultimate fate are revealed towards the end of the film when Beth, the wife, affirms that he is the son of slaves and still a slave himself. He has not been able to find any true identity and, as a result, his responses are pointless and his rage is directed towards his own people. Finally, after settling a score with violence (his usual tactic), he is left alone with the police sirens blaring and the patrol cars closing in.

While Jake represents the traditionless mentality of the slave, Beth shines as an archetype of the re-emergence of a powerful people. Salvation results from embracing the stature and dignity of a heritage that had been discarded along the way. Little by little, triggered by tragedy and abuse, Beth begins to envision the better life that her traditions offer. The power and dignity of the Maori people eventually return to her and, at film's end, Beth breaks with her underclass existence and reaffirm her place within her Maori life.

This transformation, and the possibility of achieving it, is underscored by the subplot of two of Beth's sons. One joins a Maori street gang and becomes adorned with traditional Maori tattoos. The other does not alter his body, but declares that he has internalized the essence of Maori life just as much as those who give outward signs of their identity. Both options are presented as examples of how people can maintain and regain their identity and that doing so is a central component of the healing process.

In essence, Beth's (and her family's) salvation springs from the re-affirming of traditions and the power and strength that comes from doing so. The American novelist Thomas Wolfe wrote "you can't go home again." But he wasn't speaking about the Maori and he didn't write the script for *Once Were Warriors.* Beth represents Native people who, although displaced by the modern Western world, return to wholeness by rembracing their identity.

As discussed above, Native Americans and other Native peoples throughout the world have been subjected to profound and hurtful stress. On the one hand, Natives tend to be poor and/or members of an underclass. This resulting poverty is often disabling. Equally stressful is the fact that Native people tend to face significant discrimination. And, perhaps most of all, the flux and uncertainty to which Natives are exposed causes profound disruptions that result in profound losses.

Sociologists and psychologists emphasize that stress and its artifacts exert significant pressures upon people and that this toll can (and often does) result in counterproductive behavior, such as alcoholism drinking and other dysfunctional behaviors. Although Native Americans, Hawaiians, and Maori are distinct, their histories and responses also have revealing parallels.

ALCOHOL COUNSELING AND IDENTITY

As is widely known, a high incidence of alcoholism exists among Native people. To a large degree this counterproductive behavior may be an artifact of the specific stresses faced by particular cultural enclaves. When Native alcoholics begin to participate in therapy and self-help groups, they often balk at programs such as Alcoholics Anonymous, complaining that these programs do not speak to them or address their needs as Native people.

The classic "knee-jerk" reaction of some therapists who hear such complaints is to assert that the client isn't really serious about recovery and is merely looking for an excuse to withdraw from therapy and/or to shirk their responsibilities. This book, in contrast, takes such complaints at face value.

Increasingly, models of alcohol therapy are multiplying; the current vogue is to tailor programs of therapy and self-help in order to mesh with individuals and/or the cultural groups to which they belong. I applaud this trend. Native people should benefit from such opportunities. It is useful to (1) look at the unique heritage and history of specific Native people while (2) keeping in mind the various parallels that seemingly occur among Native peoples in different parts of the world. By keeping these issues in mind, therapists and counselors can better tailor their services when dealing with their Native alcoholics. Providing advice on how to do so is the goal of this book.

NOTE

1. Many people feel the term "Eskimo" is derogatory or at least overly generic and prefer more traditional names for specific people such as Yup'ik .

REFERENCES

Alcohol Research Unit. (1984). *Alcohol and the Maaori people (pp. 4–5).* Auckland: Alcohol Research Unit.

Bushnell, O. A. (1993). *The gifts of civilization:Germs and genocide in Hawaii.* Honolulu: University of Hawaii Press.

Davis, G. (1968). *A shoal of time: History of the Hawaiian Islands (p. 86).* Honolulu. University of Hawaii Press.

Gilgen, M. (1996). A response to Harold Napoleon.... In H. Napoleon(Ed.), *Yuyaruq: The way of being human (p. 52).* Fairbanks, Alaska: Alaska Native Knowledge Network.

Harrison, B. (1996). Response to Yuuyaraq: The way of being human. In H. Napoleon (Ed.), *Yuyaruq: The Way of Being Human (p. 59).* Fairbanks, Alaska: Alaska Native Knowledge Network.

MacLeod, W.C. (1928). *The American Indian frontier.* New York: Alfred A. Knoph.

Napoleon, H. (1996).*Yuyaruq: The way of being human.* Fairbanks, Alaska: Alaska Native Knowledge Network.

Salzman, M. (2001). Cultural trauma and recovery: Perspectives from theory management theory. *Trauma, Violence, and Abuse,* 2(2), 172–191.

Stannard, D. E. (1989). *Before the horror.* Honolulu: University of Hawaii Press.

Walle, A.H. (1979). The morphology and social dynamics of a North American Indian folktale. *Kentucky Folklore Record.*

CHAPTER 3

ALCOHOLISM AMONG NATIVE AMERICANS

Researchers and counselors who specialize in addictive behavior do not, as yet, fully understand the complexity of alcoholism. On the one hand, there continues to be considerable mystery regarding why specific individuals develop into alcoholics while others, in seemingly identical circumstances, do not. While some professionals seek to understand alcoholism in general, furthermore, others are more concerned with understanding why specific individuals or distinct groups of people (however categorized) are more prone to alcoholism than others.

Those involved with Native Americans have often observed that members of this racial group appear to be particularly prone to alcoholism. No matter what the theoretic bent of specific researchers or counselors and/or what causal factors are believed to be at work, it cannot be denied that Native Americans have been particular hard hit by alcoholism and its impacts.

While the stereotype of the "drunken Indian" may be distasteful and racist, few challenge the observation that a large number of Native Americans do succumb to alcoholism and, as a group, Native Americans seem to have been profoundly devastated by it. Recognition also exists that the percentage of Native Americans who suffer from alcoholism is extremely high, when compared to alcoholism rates within the general population.

The Path of Handsome Lake: A Model of Recovery for Native People, pages 39–47

A number of theories have been advanced to explain why Native Americans tend to be more susceptible to alcoholism than members of some other social/ethnic/biological groups. In general, these diverse premises are based upon either biological or social/cultural theories. Although points of views differ in significant respects, however, they need not be mutually exclusive since it might be possible for both social and biological factors to combine and, thereby, produce the high incidence of alcoholism that exists among Native Americans. As a result of this reality, both biological and social arguments can be discussed in the same breath.

THE BIOLOGICAL ARGUMENT

It has often been suggested that Native Americans are particularly vulnerable to the risk of alcoholism, once they start drinking, and that this vulnerability is biological in nature and inherent within the genetic makeup of the individual. This premise (often dubbed the "firewater myth," of course, is prevalent both as a "folk belief" and as an intuitive conclusion that many professionals, in the medical and helping professions, have drawn from their professional experiences. Thus, a major theory asserts that Native Americans tend to exhibit uncontrolled, heavy drinking (Mail & Johnson, 1993).

Hardly arising in recent years, the belief that Native Americans are inherently vulnerable to alcoholism has long been recognized and discussed. Both Benjamin Franklin and members of the Lewis and Clark expedition observed that Native Americans tended to drink to the point of intoxication and that these episodes were frequently marred by violence (Duncan & Duncan, 1995). This theory was continued in Zane Grey's famous novel *The Vanishing American* (1927) where the hero is biologically a Native who, being adopted by White parents, was raised in the East, away from and not in contact with his own people. Eventually, he grows up to become a charismatic individual and a fine athlete, seemingly modeled after Jim Thorpe. Nonetheless, he quickly falls victim to a particularly devastating form of alcoholism even though he is far removed from the stresses of Native life. With the support of his lover and by embracing a program of complete abstinence, however, our hero conquers his affliction and reasserts himself as a powerful and positive role model. Grey, incidentally, wrote before the founding of Alcoholics Anonymous and his plotline can be viewed as a reflection of the beliefs of his time, not as the result of influences from self-help groups that emerged at a slightly later date. Nonetheless, the model of recovery presented by Grey is almost a blueprint of what, Alcoholics Anonymous proposed a few years later and what has emerged as an almost ubiquitous model of recovery that is advocated today.

Nonetheless, there has been much speculation centered on explaining the vulnerability of Native Americans to alcoholism. One classic evolutionary argument begins by recalling that in many parts of the world (such as Europe), people have been drinking alcoholic beverages for thousands of years. As a result, the logic continues, over many generations, non-alcoholics and people with non-alcoholic parents have a better chance of surviving and reproducing while, in contrast, alcoholics and children of alcoholics have experienced handicaps that could inhibit their survival and reproduction. This leads to the conclusion that in places like Europe (where alcoholic beverages have long been consumed) a simple process of evolution would, over time, "select against" people with genetic tendencies towards alcoholism. Thus, genes that created a vulnerability to alcoholism would be "weeded out" and occur less frequently in future generations, a phenomenon that could lead to at a greater (although, of course, not a complete) resistance to full-blown alcoholism.

This observation is bolstered by the fact that among Old World populations where drinking alcoholic beverages is an age-old custom (Southern Europe/Circum-Mediterranean basin); the vulnerability to alcoholism seems to be lower than in areas where drinking was introduced at a later date (such as Scandinavia). Thus, European populations with a long history of drinking alcohol appear to be more resistant to its negative effects than European groups with a shorter history of exposure to alcoholic beverages.

In the Americas, there was no widespread use of alcoholic beverages until the era of white contact. (The only example of consuming alcoholic beverages of which I am aware is the custom of fermenting the sap of the Sugar Maple tree during the spring in the Northeastern portion of North America. Those practicing this tradition, however, only produced a mildly alcoholic beverage and the custom was only practiced only during a short period of the year, a situation that would prevent the onslaught of full-blown alcoholism).

As a result of the fact that drinking was not a fact of life among the pre-contact Native Americans, the forces of evolution would not have reduced the genetic propensity towards alcoholism in any way. Since evolution would not have systematically reduced the biological tendency towards alcoholism among Native Americans, once alcoholic beverages became readily available to this population, the impact of alcoholism would be more devastating than among people of European ancestry (whose biological evolution had long been subjected to evolutionary pressures that reduced a tendency towards alcoholism).

Analogies, of course, exist; although the common cold is merely a minor annoyance among most White people, it initially ravaged Native American populations as a deadly plague because the Native population, a biological sub-species, had not evolved to combat the cold because it did not exist in America before White contact. There is, of course, no theoretic reason why an analogous explanation could not explain why high rates of Native American alcoholism that have been observed. Nonetheless, adequately and rigorously researching such theories using the scientific method is difficult, if not impossible (Snipp, 1997). And as Garcia-Andrade et al have observed (1997), there is no evidence that demonstrates that Native Americans have a higher psychological or physiological tendency towards alcoholism than any other group of people. Bolstering such observations, Mail and Johnson (1993) note that drinking patterns vary widely among various Native American groups and no stereotyped pattern can be discerned

SOCIAL IMPACTS

Another set of theories seeks to link alcoholic tendencies among Native Americans to a variety of cultural factors. Some researchers have observed that Native Americans have a strong tradition of employing mind altering substances within a ceremonial setting (Abbott, 1996) while others suggest that Native Americans have often searched for transcendental encounters and that mind-altering substances have often been used to facilitate this experience (Kahn, 1986; Mail & McDonald, 1980). Although these writers make some interesting points, I intuitively sense that there is a difference between a person participating in a highly structured sacred ceremony, on the one hand, and passing out drunk in the gutter, on the other. And this kind of argument (that suggests that a precedent for alcoholism lies in the religious heritage of the various Native American peoples) appears to be conflict with one of the major perspectives of alcoholism research that argues that when mind-altering substances are well integrated within the society and/or its religion, people tend to employ them in responsible ways. Thus, researchers often suggest that in situations where the religion of a culture provides a positive role model for the responsible use of mind-altering substances, the incidence of abuse tends to decline.

Suggesting that the sacred use of mind-altering drugs functions as a catalyst that can result in high levels of alcohol abuse conflicts with the well-established theories (mentioned above) that argue that the formal and well organized use of mind-altering substances in a religious setting leads to more responsible use. In general, theories that link religion practice and alcoholism (or other varieties of substance abuse) goes against the grain of a significant research tradition and, therefore, this theory must be approached with profound caution. This book side steps such theories and seeks alternative explanations.

Yet another chain of thought points out that due to stigma, poverty, and socio/economic reversals during the last century, Native Americans have tended to experience a great deal of stress and that these pressures can, under many circumstances, trigger alcohol abuse. There is a vast social theory on this subject, and various disciplines, such as sociology, anthropology, and applied folklore, have embraced these perspectives. The current trends in research involving ethnic groups reinforce such perspectives. Thus, writing from a general framework, Al-Issa (1997) has argued that drinking patterns among various ethnic groups tend to be influenced by:

1. The stress people face when living in an alien environment,
2. Socio-economic stress including being poverty stricken, and
3. The tensions inherent in minority status.

This will be the primary theoretic underpinning of this book, although biological vulnerability will be acknowledged as another possible but unproven influence. Thus, this book makes use of a variety of social theories (largely stemming from the sociological concept of anomie) and they will be discussed as required. I simultaneously acknowledge, however, that other influences may exist and that a complex synergism between a wide range of influences and vulnerabilities probably provides the most robust and appropriate explanation of the high incidence of alcoholism among Native American populations.

SPECIFIC NEEDS OF NATIVE AMERICANS

Empirically, many Native Americans are not well served by existing alcoholism recovery programs that are based on Alcoholics Anonymous and the 12 Step Program. Those in contact with Native Americans within self-help situations often note that Natives are often uncomfortable with Alcoholics Anonymous and its strategy of treatment. Many members of the counseling profession will also confirm that Native Americans often relate poorly to Alcoholics Anonymous/the 12 Step Program. And, on many occasions, Native Americans in recovery overtly complain that Alcoholics Anonymous/the 12 Step Program does not mesh with who they are and what they experience and/or feel. Apparently, Alcoholics Anonymous does not inevitably provide universal solutions that are suitable for all recovering individuals.

The ineffectiveness of Alcoholics Anonymous among Native Americans appears, at least in part, to result from differences between the orientations of the founders of AA and the cultural origins of many Native alcoholics who seek to recover from their malady. These cultural differences become increasingly significant and disruptive when we remember that Native

Americans are, themselves, a heterogeneous group of cultures, not a homogeneous group. As we saw in Chapter 2, profound cultural diversity exists between various Native American nations, tribes, bands, and enclaves. In addition, since some Native people live in a reservation setting while others reside within the larger community, different individuals face a variety of pressures. Thus, since Native Americans are culturally diverse and since different individuals encounter a variety of threats to their sobriety no single strategy (such as that provided by Alcoholics Anonymous) is likely to be universally applicable to them all.

An appropriate method (or metaphor) for promoting recovery among Native Americans is sorely needed. This technique must be able to transcend the differences between a wide range of Native American cultures, on the one hand, while mitigating various socio-economic pressures that Native people face, on the other. Among these pressures are the profound encroachments by the dominant culture, economic hardships that result from them, and the generally reduced social status experienced by Natives living within the mainstream world.

A process that can be described as "cultural genocide", furthermore impacts many Native Americans. All too often Native people have been the victims of efforts (often largely successful) to strip their cultural and heritage from them. The conflict of being caught between worlds, and being forced to endure the relentless undercutting of their cultural traditions has taken a great toll on many Native people. Cultures and traditions are usually the glue that binds people together and provide meaning and significance to life. If culture and society are quickly disrupted and if no alternative is adequately substituted, trauma can easily result. Such stresses have become a common feature of Native life.

In many cases, therapists and clients attempt to meld a program of recovery to aspects of the traditional culture of American Indian alcoholics. As Beauvais has observed:

> Many Indian people believe that the loss of their culture is the primary cause of many of their existing social problems, especially those associated with alcohol. Many of the community-based alcohol treatment programs in Indian communities across the country have strong a cultural or spiritual component that is intended to revitalize traditional beliefs and serve as the primary source of individual strength in maintaining sobriety (1998).

Unfortunately, however, Beauvais correctly complains that such phenomena are not easily measured, quantified, and examined in "scientific ways." As a result, researchers using the standard scientific approach have not been able to provide foolproof advice in this important area. This book, embracing a more humanistic style of social research examines these questions from a broader perspective. The significance of the issues being examined justifies the research strategies that are embraced.

It is important to clearly recognize the degree to which traditional cultures, such as those of various Native American communities, are under attack by multiple social and economic forces. In addition, both therapists and clients need to acknowledge the important role that a viable cultural tradition should play in promoting good mental health (both for the society and the individual). We, as therapists and counselors, should never forget that Native American cultures have been (and will continue to be) under profound attack and that this stress takes an inevitable toll (if these costs can be conveniently documented using quantitative analysis/the scientific method or not).

Although it is important to recognize that all cultures can and should evolve and that individual people need to respond in positive ways to reality and circumstance, counselors and clients should not forget the negative impact that unmitigated social change can exert upon individuals. While clients may need to make some kind of relevant response to circumstance, furthermore, they should also be encouraged to exercise self-determinism. One aspect of self-determinism is to participate in therapy that is meaningful and appropriate. Thus, the therapist should not "stack the cards" so that some alternatives (that seem preferable to the counselor) are strategically presented in a positive or more preferable light than other options.

In recent years, there has been a strong movement to help members of the counseling profession to gain "multicultural counseling competencies" by (1) being aware of their own values and biases (2) being aware of the client's world view, and (3) choosing appropriate strategies of intervention (Arredondo & McDavis, 1992). The basic concern driving this movement is the fact that, on many occasions, clients may not be well served by counselors and by models of intervention that are not sensitive to the cultural background of the client (and which, perhaps, do not adequately address the trauma that clients face). As we shall see in later chapters, models (such as those deriving from Alcoholics Anonymous and the 12 Step Program) may be culture bound to such a degree that they are counterproductive when being used among a variety of Native people (both in therapeutic and self help situations). A major aspect of this book is to provide ways to correct this imbalance.

Both therapists and clients, furthermore, need to recognize that cultures, although evolving, can maintain themselves and continue to function (even when specific individuals simultaneously have a niche in the larger world and the traditional culture). It is equally vital to remember that when individuals have a niche and a stake in two different (and potentially competing) communities, a profound series of conflicts and stresses are likely to develop. From a more encouraging perspective, even though a culture responds to the pressures that it faces and transforms itself as a result, that adaptation does not mean that the culture is "dying" or ceasing to be a vital force in people's lives. By acknowledging that mental health is often profoundly (albeit subtly) intertwined with a strong and vital cultural underpinning, both therapists and clients are reminded of the connection between mental/psychological well being and viable, intact, and functioning cultures and traditions.

CONCLUDING STATEMENT

Alcoholism is a complex and multi-faceted phenomenon. It is also a malady to which Native Americans appear to be particularly vulnerable. On the one hand, biological arguments typically suggest that Native Americans are particularly vulnerable to alcoholism for genetic reasons. This possible genetic cause (although unproven) may be further encouraged by a range of cultural factors and stresses to which Native Americans are subjected. Combined, these distinct, although interrelated, influences can explain why a high incidence of alcoholism exists among Native Americans.

Alcoholism among Native Americans is a profoundly complex phenomenon that needs to be envisioned in distinctive ways. Unfortunately, many therapies and self-help opportunities that are offered to alcoholics were created within White middle class society and therefore they may not be completely appropriate for Native American populations.

One such method that stems from the White experience is Alcoholics Anonymous/the 12 Step Program. On the one hand, Alcoholics Anonymous is geared towards the orientations of the mainstream population. On the other hand, it is geared towards a stable society, not one that is being racked by social disruption. Apparently because of these characteristics, many Native Americans do not relate well to Alcoholics Anonymous, the 12 Step Program, and the strategy of recovery it offers. Thus, its ineffectiveness among Native people may result from (1) being a product of the White mainstream culture and (2) not adequately addressing the cultural stress that is so commonplace among ethnic groups in general, and Native American populations, in specific.

Clearly, alternatives to which Native Americans can more effectively relate are sorely needed.

REFERENCES

Abbot, P. J. (1996). American Indian and Alaska native aboriginal use of alcohol in the United States. *American Indian and Alaska Native Mental Health Research,* 7(2), 1–13.

Al-Issa, I. (1997). Ethnicity, immigration, and psychology. In I. Al-Issa and M. Tousignant, (Eds.). *Ethnicity, immigration, and psychotherapy.* New York: Plenium pp. 3–15.

Arredondo, P., & McDavis, R.J. (1992). Multicultural counseling competencies and standards: A call to the profession. *Journal of Counseling and Development,* 70.

Beauvais, F. (1998). American Indians and alcohol. *Alcohol Health and Research World,* 22(4), 7, 253–260.

Duran, E., & Duran B. (1995). *Native American postcolonial psychology.* Albany, New York: New York State University Press.

Garcia-Andrade, C.,Wall, T. L, & Ehlers, C. L. (1997). The firewater myth and response to alcohol in mission Indians. *American Journal of Psychiarty,* 154, 983–958.

Grey, Z. (1927). *The vanishing American.* New York: Grosset and Dunlap.

Kahn, M. (1986). Psychological disorders of aboriginal people of the United States and Australia. *Journal of Rural Community Psychology,* 7, 45–59.

Mail, P. D., & Johnson, S. (1993). "Boozing, sniffing and toking: An overview of past, present, and future of substance use by American Indians. *American Indian and Alaska Mental Health Research,* 5(1), 1–33.

Mail, P. D., & McDonald, D. R. (1980). *Tulapai to takani: A bibliography of alcohol use and abuse among native Americans of north America.* New Haven, CT.: HRAF Press.

Snipp, M. (1997). Some observations about racial boundaries and the experiences of American Indians. *Ethnic and Racial Studies,* 20, 665–689.

Part II

ALCOHOLISM, STRESS, AND NATIVE AMERICANS

Historically, strategies of combating alcoholism have focused upon the development and application of general principles that were able to serve all people. In recent years, however, a variety of treatment and self help options have arisen that recognize that different people have their own needs and vulnerabilities and that they need to be treated accordingly.

Chapter four begins with a discussion of the current variations in the treatment of alcoholism that are emerging and it nests the discussion of the treatment and self-help of Native alcoholics within this emerging trend. Not only are Native Americans distinctive, they are also subject to profound stresses that are caused by rapid social change and the fact that their cultures tend to be under severe attack. These pressures need to be acknowledged and factored into programs of alcoholism treatment and self help.

In Chapter 5 "Cultural Stress and Dysfunctional Behavior," the basic theoretic overview of the book is provided and related to the problem of Native alcoholism. By combining Philip Cushman's psychological concept of the "empty soul," with sociological theories such as anomie, and various theories of applied anthropology, a robust and workable model of Native alienation and dysfunction is proposed. Modern terror management theory is used as a synthesizing model that combines various perspectives in a robust and elegant manner.

With the viable theoretic perspective provided in Chapter 5, Chapter 6 (1) applies the resulting techniques to an examination of the historic Iroquois and (2) expands terror management theory accordingly. The result is an evenhanded and multidimensional approach to Native alcoholism.

CHAPTER 4

DIVERSITY, NATIVE AMERICANS, AND RECOVERY

INTRODUCTION

Diversity is a fact of life. Increasingly, alcohol abuse counselors have come to accept that fact and its implications. As a result, differences between people (and peoples) are acknowledged as well as the fact that personal and cultural variations typically exert profound impacts upon alcoholism, recovery, and patterns of relapse. While 10 or 15 years ago, dealing with the implications of diversity was not on the forefront of addictions research and practitioner-oriented strategies of treatment, they have now emerged as significant issues that are widely discussed among laymen, practitioners, and researchers.

Alcoholics Anonymous, founded in the 1930s, is generally praised as the organization that first provided the leadership that led to the development of strong self-help organizations for alcoholics as well providing the models of recovery and treatment that have become institutionalized within the alcohol abuse counseling profession. While that legacy remains unchallenged, today there is a trend to view Alcoholics Anonymous as a specific kind of self help program and one that was formed by laymen, not professionals. As a result, the counseling profession increasingly views Alcoholics Anonymous/12 Step Program as a therapeutic strategy that is most effective in certain, circumscribed situations and as a program that is best suited to certain types of people.

The Path of Handsome Lake: A Model of Recovery for Native People, pages 51–65

This perspective also suggests that when the strategies and tactics of Alcoholics Anonymous venture too far from the specific "target market" that they are best poised to serve, the effectiveness of the program declines. Today's researchers and counselors tend to envision a broader mosaic of strategies for recovery and therapy; as a result, Alcoholics Anonymous is less likely to be viewed as a universal program, easily adjustable to all circumstances and able to seamlessly serve all who suffer from alcoholism.

Thus, today's theoretical and therapeutic advances point to a diversity of methods, each of which is poised to serve (1) the specific needs of particular individuals, (2) the personality structures of specific participants, and (3) the cultural traditions from which specific alcoholics derive. As such, the options available to counselors and recovering alcoholics have been expanded to serve diverse groups in a variety of circumstances that, hitherto, were not overtly acknowledged and/or factored into the dilemma of alcoholism and the process of recovery.

In order to deal with this expansion in the theories and methods that are currently used to deal with alcoholics, this chapter begins with a brief overview of Alcoholics Anonymous, proceeds to an analysis of various options that transcend it, and culminates in a discussion regarding how current trends in therapy and recovery acknowledge differences between people in order to create programs of recovery and self-help that are appropriate to specific people and their circumstances. The current emphasis upon adjusting strategies of recovery towards the needs of specific Native American populations can be viewed as a specific example of this important trend of providing tailored treatments of recovery to specific target populations.

THE ALCOHOLICS ANONYMOUS MODEL

In the early days when alcoholism was first viewed as a distinct disease (not as evidence of a generalized weakness of the individual), there was a tendency to embrace universal models that viewed all alcoholics in a homogeneous manner. The disease model affirmed that since alcoholics suffered from a specific illness, they should not be viewed as bad, weak, or immoral simply because they drank too much. As an alternative, alcoholics came to be viewed as unfortunate people who were suffering from a particular and definable disease. In this way, a distinction between alcoholics and the negative or distasteful behavior associated with their disease was emphasized, and victims came to be viewed as good people who needed help, not censure. The rise of this view has had a profoundly positive effect upon the how alcoholics are perceived and it has helped to facilitate a transition in thought that has given hope to alcoholics, patience to those around them, and a rationale for treatment and recovery. Advancing the disease concept is among the most important contributions of Alcoholics Anonymous.

A key tactic of the Alcoholics Anonymous strategy involves downplaying differences in order to concentrate upon similarities. According to such an orientation, the similar problems that all alcoholics supposedly share emerged as a commonality. The philosophy and dogma of Alcoholics Anonymous, for example, link alcoholism to an inevitable spiritual bankruptcy that both results from uncontrolled drinking and goes on to contribute to it.

Having presented this position, Alcoholics Anonymous strongly urges all members of the organization to regain their spiritual groundings by embracing a higher power. The Alcoholics Anonymous literature goes so far as to depict non-belief in God (or a higher power) as an artifact of the egotism that triggers and maintains alcoholic behavior. Although Alcoholics Anonymous seeks to be all inclusive by embracing phraseology such as "God, as we understood him," the particular vision of God/higher power (personal, good, caring, rational, male etc), that is presented in the Alcoholics Anonymous literature, closely reflects the dogma of the Jewish/Christian/Islamic tradition. An adherence to this specific intellectual/religious tradition can easily preempt other visions of the almighty (such as a reverence for an impersonal "nature," an orientation that reflects the beliefs and spiritual focus of many Native American peoples).

The cornerstone of Alcoholics Anonymous, furthermore, is the "12 step program" which begins when afflicted individuals admit that they are powerless over alcohol. This confession is followed by embracing the notion of the aforementioned "higher power" that, although officially expressed in the most general of terms, in the Alcoholics Anonymous literature, closely resembles the Jewish/Christian/Islamic concept of God (male, all powerful, personal good, etc.).

Having enlisted the aid of some sort of higher power, individuals are urged to assess their lives, acknowledge their shortcomings (to themselves, God, and another person), and do penance in appropriate ways that do not hurt others. This entire process is closely linked to what is perceived to a generalized strategy of spiritual growth. Experiencing a better developed sense of self, embracing a spiritual orientation, and having gotten one's affliction in check with the help of a higher power, it is predicted that participants will experience a spiritual rebirth and that members of Alcoholics Anonymous will go on to "practice these principles in all their affairs."

Another specific emphasis of Alcoholics Anonymous/12 Step Program is that therapy and self-help activities focus upon the dangers of dominance and egotism, suggesting that those who seek too much control in their lives are at risk. Alcoholics Anonymous places a great emphasis upon the premise that alcoholics typically possess an inability to admit that they are not all-powerful. As a result, the logic goes, alcoholics tend to refuse to acknowledge that they are unable to dominate the circumstances they face, cannot control the other people in their lives, and are helpless when confronting alcohol. The dogma of Alcoholics Anonymous continues by suggesting that this inability to acknowledge one's limitations, often results in a broadening and deepening of alcoholic behavior. Until individuals can acknowledge their own weaknesses and gain the insight required to perceive their own limitations, recovery is predicted to remain illusive.

Another aspect of Alcoholics Anonymous is the belief that once people develop alcoholic tendencies, they will continue to suffer from the disease for the rest of their lives. Such a view affirms that the only viable strategy is for people to acknowledge that they are "recovering" and not "cured" and that they need to remain alcohol free for the remainder of their lives or risk the consequences of quickly sinking back into full-blown alcoholism. Practicing what it preaches, local Alcoholics Anonymous groups typically help members to structure their lives around an alcohol-free environment. In doing so, local groups of Alcoholics Anonymous and their members routinely provide a rich social life, free of alcohol, for its members. Typical activities include dances, parties, picnics, etc. in addition to meetings, and long hours spent talking in diners or all night restaurants.

The fact that the dogmas of Alcoholics Anonymous tend to be centered around the quirks of strong willed/dominant individuals is probably an artifact of the fact that Bill Wilson (a man who clearly exhibited these traits himself) was the prolific author of much of Alcoholics Anonymous' classic literature and he was a major force in the establishment of the organization. Being a strong-willed individual who linked a dominant and unyielding personality type to his alcoholic behavior, Wilson seems to have assumed that his responses were one example of a universal tendency that was inevitably repeated by all alcoholics. While Wilson generalized the impact of egotism upon alcoholism, however, this kind of universal theory is currently being rethought by a new generation of scholars and practitioners.

As a result of Wilson's leadership and influence, many of the recommended tactics of Alcoholics Anonymous/the 12 step Program (and the rhetoric underlying them) appear to be tailored around this specific type of dominant and/or narcissist personality. Nonetheless, many members of Alcoholics Anonymous (as well as professional alcohol counselors) are coming to recognize that the classic Alcoholics Anonymous approach, focused as it is around a specific personality type, should not be viewed as a universal program that is assumed to be appropriate for all alcoholics. Thus, some members of Alcoholics Anonymous, although valuing the organization, suggest that Wilson mistook his own personal situation for a universal pattern and that his focus upon egotism, while helpful to many people in AA, does not speak to everybody. As a result, focusing upon the triggers of egotism and dominance in isolation can undermine the recovery of some alcoholics by drawing attention away from other influences and vulnerabilities.

In contrast to this broader view, many advocates of the classic Alcoholics Anonymous approach rebut such reasoning by asserting that if alcoholics focus (1) upon their distinctiveness and (2) how they and their circumstances are different from everybody else, the result will be counterproductive and, perhaps, lead to relapse. One of the classic catch-phrases from the jargon of Alcoholics Anonymous, for example, is "terminal uniqueness." This phrase suggests that if people focus on how they are different, they will never be able to benefit from the bounty of aid and advice that Alcoholics Anonymous has to offer. In the worst case, "terminal uniqueness" is used to refer to the commonplace system of denial that many alcoholics use in order to point to ways they are somehow "different" and thereby deny that they are alcoholic and/or suggest that Alcoholics Anonymous/the 12 step method is not appropriate for them. This syndrome, advocates of the classic Alcoholics Anonymous model insist, can derail programs of recovery and they should be avoided for that reason.

Many alcohol abuse counselors, furthermore, are successful veterans of Alcoholics Anonymous/the 12 step Program. As a result, much professional therapy and the structure of many treatment facilities mirror the tenets of the12 Step Program and the tactics of the program are used as the primary paradigm of therapy and recovery. The services offered by innumerable therapists and residential facilities are based Alcoholics Anonymous/12 Step Program. Indeed, a basic goal of many residential treatment centers is to prepare participants to join Alcoholics Anonymous upon their release. Given this situation, recovery and therapy have often been viewed from a universal, "one size fits all" perspective.

BEYOND THE TWELVE STEP METHOD

As time has gone on, however, there has been a recognition by many scholars and practitioners that a wide array of recovery strategies are needed so recovery can be tailored around the unique needs, belief systems, and personalities of the individual. Some of these methods are provided as alternatives to the religious/spiritual nature of Alcoholics Anonymous/the 12 steps. Thus, the Secular Organization for Recovery (SOS) offers a self help program for people who feel they do not need (or, perhaps, are uncomfortable with) the religious and spiritual ethos of Alcoholics Anonymous/the 12 Step Program (Christopher, 1992, 1997). Rational Recovery (Trimpey, 1985) and Self Management and Recovery Training (Hovarth, 1997), likewise, offer alternatives to the spiritual and religious nature of Alcoholics Anonymous; both are based on the rationalistic therapy methods developed by Albert Ellis and they position themselves as non-spiritual and rational alternatives for those seeking to recover from alcoholism.

Other organizations, such as Women for Sobriety (Kirkpatrick, 1978, 1990), tailor themselves towards the needs of women. Arguing that women, as a group, have a series of special needs (revolving around self-esteem and guilt), Women for Sobriety self-consciously embraces tactics that nurture self-esteem while combating alcoholic behavior. Again, the significance of transcending a universal program of recovery (typified by Alcoholics Anonymous/the 12 Step Program) is affirmed.

Cultural differences (and their impact upon alcoholic behavior and recovery) also need to be addressed. Thus, many Hispanic men are said to embrace a "macho" posture and, as a result, they may be unwilling to admit personal powerlessness, while some Native Americans are rather private and reserved and, as a result, they may not be comfortable admitting their past misdeeds (or even their personal achievements) within the context of an open forum (as encouraged by Alcoholics Anonymous).

And since Alcoholics Anonymous/the 12 Step Program is the brainchild of middle class White men, other segments of the population may be under-served by and uncomfortable with the strategies it employs and the message it presents. Thus, a number of Afro-Americans have confided to the author that they can embrace Alcoholics Anonymous only with difficulty and that much of the rhetoric they hear at meetings is not relevant to them. I have heard numerous Native Americans in recovery make similar complaints.

Thus, after a long era in which alcoholism and recovery were viewed in universal ways (that were dominated by the rhetoric of Alcoholics Anonymous/the 12 Step Program), the current era is witnessing a resurgence of interest in diversity. The alcohol/substance abuse counseling profession is responding accordingly and the results are encouraging.

SPECIFIC TYPES OF DIVERSITY

As has been indicated above, diversity is multifaceted. And a wide variety of self help groups have been established that attempt to provide the foundations of recovery for specific groups of people. The strategy is to transcend the classic Alcoholics Anonymous model in order to help specific groups of people more effectively deal with their alcoholism. These programs can be viewed in terms of (1) Rational vs. irrational, (2) Religious vs. agnostic, (3) Sex/sexual orientation, and (4). Cultural. Each will be briefly discussed:

Rational versus Irrational

Some individuals are best able to seek recovery using tactics that rely upon rational thought and attack alcoholic behavior a highly structured and well-thought out manner. These people tend to believe that people are unique because (1) of their power of reason and rational thought and (2) because of the belief that recovery can best be accomplished through rational action and thought.

An alternative position, in contrast, believes that although people possess a degree of rationality, at the core, people are irrational and not profoundly different from other animals. Freud, for example, believed that rational thought is merely "layered over" an animalistic psyche that remained as a powerful force and motivator. People embracing such models of mankind seek strategies of recovery that transcend the rational and they are more geared around dealing with feelings and emotions.

Religious versus Agnostic

Many people are religious and in America, the vast majority believe in a rational, thinking God that, in some form or fashion, created the world and all in it. Such individuals tend to view God as a conscious architect who is the father of mankind, as well as the force that consciously established specific rules that are intended to govern human behavior. For those holding such beliefs, the strategy of life is to seek God's will, embrace it as a guide, and adjust oneself accordingly.

Other people do not believe in a personal God and/or they do not feel the need to act in accord with it or its will. These people tend to believe that human nature has evolved over time and that it was not created by any rational process, conscious action, or guiding hand. These people tend to view mankind as part of nature and they are likely to emphasize the need for people to fit into the natural order of things. This natural order, however, is not viewed as stemming from the mind of a divine architect.

Sexes/Sexual Orientation

Some people feel that there are innate differences between the sexes and/or people with different sexual orientations. Those who believe that this is true are likely to feel that different programs of recovery from alcoholism are needed for each sex and for individuals who have different sexual orientations.

Others feel that our culture has socialized people in specific ways and that the inherent flexibility in humanity creates the possibility for people to develop in divergent ways and that the resulting diversity requires different strategies of recovery for specific segments of the population.

Many social observers, furthermore, believe that due to their sexual orientation gay man and lesbian women face profound obstacles and pressures not only from the outside world, but because they (as members of their culture) have been socialized to view their sexual preferences as wrong or shameful. As a result, many gays and lesbians experience profound feelings of guilt and shame that can create the need to escape via self-medication or alcoholic drinking.

Cultural

Different cultures deal with alcohol in specific ways and some cultures have been shown to be more vulnerable to alcoholic behavior than others. In addition, certain cultures may be under stress and, therefore, their members may be particularly vulnerable to alcoholism.

Alcoholics Anonymous was created by members of mainstream American culture in the 1930s. Once the program was established, efforts were made to generalize it in order to deal with a wider range of people. But in doing so, profound cultural differences were ignored, in spite of sincere and conscious efforts to deal with diversity. Nonetheless, much of structure, orientation, dogma, and literature of Alcoholics Anonymous is culture bound and, increasingly, these limitations are being recognized.

In specific, Alcoholics Anonymous was founded by people whose culture continued to be a "going concern" (even though these alcoholics had become dysfunctional or alienated from their culture due to their drinking). In many parts of the world, in contrast, Native and traditional cultures are under profound attack and the resulting stress can easily trigger alcoholic behavior. Alcoholics Anonymous/the 12 Step Program, however, did not evolve in ways that conveniently deal with this issue.

Today, more than ever before, there is a recognition that alcoholism is a complex disease that impacts different people in complex and multi-faceted ways. By the same token, therapy and recovery are being viewed in equally diverse manners. Transcending a universal program that is based on the Alcoholics Anonymous/12 Steps Program, a wide variety of options are being tailored around the needs of specific people and groups of people. As a result, greater flexibility in helping alcoholics recover is being advocated; as this occurs, people who once "fell through the cracks" are being provided with tools of recovery that are tailored for them. This trend is applauded.

In the final analysis, Native American alcoholics are, collectively, a specific group of people that benefit when specific programs of recovery are tailored around their unique requirements. Such a program, however needs to be phrased in ways that allow diverse groups and cultures to benefit and participate. This is because many different Native American cultures exist and that they are often very different from one another. In addition, to whatever extent all Native people have needs that are parallel, a program is needed that can accommodate and acknowledge diversity as well as similarities. Creating such a program is clearly consistent with current trends of treatment and recovery that are being advocated by the alcohol abuse counseling profession.

PARALLELS IN DIVERSITY

Although it is now generally recognized that Native Americans possess a cultural heritage that is distinct from the mainstream culture, crafting strategies of recovery around their special needs has been difficult. One reason for this difficulty is the fact that there is profound cultural diversity among different Native American groups. Although some specific Native American cultures may have been able to create a program of therapy and recovery that serves its members, broadening these programs in ways that make them universally appropriate for diverse cultures has not been adequately accomplished.

Nonetheless, many Native Americans share a common ground in spite of their cultural differences. Almost all Native American cultures, for example, are experiencing relentless pressures from the outside world. No matter how specific individuals respond to that pressure, its impact still exists. In some cases, these pressures may function as a "background force" that individuals do not overtly notice. Other individuals may be overtly caught between two different worlds. Some Native people may face stress and ambiguity when they do not adequately mesh with one or both of the worlds in which they must live. All too often, furthermore, people loyal to a Native culture face profound pressures and losses as their way of life shrinks and is taken from them.

UNIVERSAL HEALING IN A SPECIFIC CONTEXT

One of the complexities involved in such discussions is the fact that specific alcoholics social need to be relieved of their affliction, but individuals exist in a specific context that needs to be taken into account. As we have seen from the discussions above, the complexity of situations in which people find themselves can lead to difficulties in choosing appropriate strategies of recovery.

In recent years, the whole idea of multicultural counseling and therapy has emerged as a "hot topic" of research and discussion. Some perspectives (Sue, Arrendondo, & McDavis, 1992) provide long lists of skills, competencies, and standards that counselors need to master in order to effectively pursue multicultural counseling. An alternative perspective, and the one embraced here, deals with a limited number of universal factors that need to be deployed in ways that are relevant for specific people and cultures. According to Fischer, Jome, and Atkinson (1998), four universal factors deserving consideration include (1) the existence of a therapeutic relationship, (2) a shared worldview, (3) client expectations, and (4) some kind of recognized and accepted intervention or therapy.

People in a professional therapeutic relationship, as well as those practicing some sort of self-help therapy, need to realize that they are participating within a therapeutic framework. "The therapeutic relationship... represents the positive, trusting, and healing relationship.... Both the Western or integrationist and the transcultural literatures ... unequivocally support the importance of the therapeutic relationship"(Fischer, Jome, & Atkinson, 1998). While such observations were made with reference to the professional helping professionals, they can also be applied to self-help groups. Thus, a person participating within a self-help program of recovery needs to perceive that the therapeutic nature of the relationship contributes to their recovery. This realization is equally important when people receive professional help.

While alcoholics seeking recovery need to know they are receiving therapy (within a professional and/or self-help context), they also need to collaborate with people who share a similar world view and/or those who possess the gift of empathy and can understand others. "A shared worldview provides a common framework from which both client and counselor [and/or the members of a self-help group] think about their work together. The more the counseling [or self-help] participants share an understanding of each other's worlds, the easier it may be to form a therapeutic relationship" (Fischer, Jome, & Atkinson, 1998).

As we saw above, many recovering alcoholics have come to reject the therapy provided by Alcoholics Anonymous and the 12 Steps Program because its worldview does not jive with their perspectives of life. As a result, alternatives to that classic program of recovery are being established in order to provider a wider variety of options that are available to recovering people. As indicated, people whose cultures are under profound stress may need to deal with those who recognize the power of these impacts and the trauma it can cause. And since the pressures facing Native people are often distinct, worldviews that acknowledge these pressures need to be recognized.

Therapy also requires that participants believe that their efforts towards recovery will bear fruit or at least have a chance of being effective. To recover, alcoholics must (1) believe that recovery is possible and (2) be convinced (or at least have an open mind) that a particular program of therapy will work for them. "Counselors and healers raise client expectations and gain credibility through the setting in which they conduct therapy, the training and degrees they possess, working within a shared worldview with the client, and developing a therapeutic relationship with the client" (Fischer, Jome, & Atkinson, 1998). Self-help organizations may gain credibility because of their reputation for being effective. Some cynical people assume that professionals are only "in it for the money" and, therefore, they prefer self-help groups, run by lay-people (who they find to be more trustworthy). Many advocates of self-help groups, furthermore, emphasize that the membership is made up of recovering alcoholics who have "been in the trenches" so their mentors and are not merely staffed by "bookworms" with lots of theories and little practical experience or empathy. And at times, people from specific racial and ethnic groups may seek counselors and/or self-help associates to whom they can identify on a cultural basis.

The last universal component is some kind of ritual or intervention. "Interventions, rituals, or techniques...are believed by both counselor and client [and members of self-help groups] to have healing potential. Thus, an intervention that is relevant and effective for one client may not be as relevant or effective for another client"(Fischer, Jome, & Atkinson, 1998). While different Native cultures are distinct, the pressures of the outside world can be viewed as a recurring force that profoundly impacts Native people and their ways of life. These pressures and the trauma inherent in responding to them can be viewed as a common experience faced by many Native peoples. As we saw in Chapter 2, these tendencies appear to be present in other groups such as Native Hawaiins and among the Maori, as well as among Native Americans.

As a result, although cultures are different, there are parallels and similarities that unite many peoples. Although cultures may be different, some aspects of the therapeutic relationships appear to be universal.

FROM CLOCKWORKS TO CYBERNETICS

Clearly, those involved with alcoholism and recovery (if they are functioning in a professional or self-help capacity) need perspectives that envision (1) how models of recovery have developed and (2) envision appropriate techniques of intervention. In the discussion above, we saw how profound differences in therapy exist, although very general similarities may simultaneously be present. It is useful to discuss how and why these differences develop.

Kenneth Boulding (1956) provides a means of discussing how theories regarding recovery have developed and how they are evolving beyond models that provide universal answers instead of seeking to serve specific targeted populations. Boulding is one of the early popularizers of general systems theory which, beginning as an analytic method during World War ll, has gone onto exert far-reaching impacts. According to Boulding:

> General systems theory is a name which has come into use to describe a level of theoretic model building which lies somewhere between the highly generalized constructions of pure mathematics and the highly specialized theories of the specific disciplines....Each discipline corresponds to certain segments of the empirical world and develops theories which have particular applicability [there].... This approach leads to a system of systems....One advantage of exhibiting a hierarchy of systems in this way is that it gives us some idea of the present gaps in the theoretical and empirical knowledge (Boulding, 1956).

Having stated his definition, Boulding presents an eleven component hierarchy that ranges from mere description to complex and specialized theoretical constructs. Here, we will only be concerned with the first three: "frameworks," "clockworks," and "cybernetic systems."

Frameworks are the first and most elementary level of scientific knowledge. It consists of the description of a static structure. According to Boulding, this description "is the beginning of organized theoretical knowledge" (1956).

Those concerned with substance abuse, however, are interested in ongoing patterns of recurrent behavior, not static descriptions. Isolating these patterns can be viewed at the clockworks level of general systems theory. According to Boulding, "The next level of systematic analysis is that of the simple dynamic system with predetermined motions. This might be called the level of clockworks" (Boulding, 1956). The clockworks model views behavior within some kind of structured context, with movements and responses fixed in such a manner that everybody is expected to respond to their drinking in a similar and predictable manner. Thus, Alcoholics Anonymous/the 12 Steps Program can be viewed as a clockworks model because all alcoholics are assumed to respond in a predetermined way to their drinking. Those who are ready to recover, the folklore goes, will practice the program. Those who are not adequately predisposed will continue to drink until they reach the level of desperation in which they willingly accept the program and the rigors of sobriety. This predictable pattern is assumed to result from the disease of alcoholism and certain patterns of response to it. Thus, Alcoholics Anonymous and the 12 Steps Program envisions alcoholism as a universal malady with predictable outcomes. People who are alcoholics are assumed to respond in a uniform way and, therefore, the disease can be viewed as possessing predetermined motions that can be used to describe the responses of all who are afflicted.

The explanation of behavior provided by clockworks model, however, is incomplete. After all, the wide degree of variation that is commonly observed both in social life, in general, and in alcoholism/recovery, in specific, is not adequately addressed by overly structured models. As Fischer, Jobe, and Atkinson (1998) observe, even though there may exist some universals in therapy, wide variations in behavior exist and they need to be acknowledged. The strict clockworks paradigm breaks down when applied to such complexity.

Moving from general theories of therapy to the fact that Native people often respond in distinctive fashion, the need for a more complex and robust model becomes evident. Boulding's "cybernetic systems" fills the current void. According to Boulding:

> The next level is that of the control mechanism or cybernetic system....this differs from the simple stable system in the fact that the transmission and interpretation of information is an essential part of the system. As a result of this ....[behavior] is not merely determined by the equations of the system (Boulding, 1956).

As knowledge evolves and as we move from universal/clockworks models to more tailored analyses, the cybernetic style of analysis becomes increasingly appropriate. Such a trend is clearly reflected in new theories regarding alcoholism and in methods of therapy that are being developed to deal with them.

At a relatively elementary stage in the analysis of a phenomenon, highly structured and inflexible clockworks models tend to be created. They envision predictable and predetermined motions and they assume a universal pattern of response. While these models are often an Advance over the complete lack of a theoretic perspective, this level of abstraction also possesses gaps and limitations that eventually must be addressed.

By acknowledging that people are not totally predictable and that the world is complicated, it becomes possible to advance theoretic perspectives beyond rigid and overly structured models that don't really reflect reality. This is what cybernetic models seek to accomplish. Instead of focusing on inevitable patterns, this level of theory building assumes that behavior is "not merely determined by the equations of the system" and looks for additional causal variables. Here, we have poised (1) ethnicity and (2) the experience of massive cultural stress as two of those other variables. And by examining them, a more robust model has emerged. And with that more robust model, more effective strategies of intervention can be proposed.

CULTURAL CONFIGURATIONS AND CYBERNETIC SYSTEMS

Earlier in this book (Chapter 1), various theories from the social sciences were introduced in order to facilitate the understanding of specific cultures and why various patterns of dysfunction exist within specific social contexts. One valuable tool was the concept of anomie, which, most basically refers to a sense of alienation that results from a rapidly changing world where people cannot adequately adjust. Facing such pressures, people often respond in dysfunctional ways. Robert Merton points to the "retreatist" response as likely to be associated with alcoholic behavior. In that situation, the individual rejects both the cultural goals and the institutional methods of achieving them. This can leave people in a situation that parallels a ship without a rudder. Dysfunctional behavior is the likely result.

Merton, however, was writing with the mainstream culture in mind, not small cultural enclaves. Nevertheless, his perspectives can be adapted to smaller scale societies once these more micro groups have been adequately identified and described. In chapter 1, we argued that the "cultural configuration" approach developed by anthropologists such as Ruth Benedict is a useful method to use in such circumstances. This approach deals with cultures as complex patterns of interworking parts. The overarching power of culture predisposes individual people to think, feel, and behave in certain predictable ways. By understanding the shadow that the culture casts on its members, the responses of both individuals and society can be more accurately predicted. Thus, due to cultural influences, many responses become "hardwired" and, therefore, predictable.

As indicated throughout this book (1) many Native people exist both within their indigenous culture and the mainstream society and (2) many Native cultures are under a great deal of stress and may be disintegrating. These situations, coupled with feelings of anomie and the configuration of the culture, can trigger dysfunctional behavior, such as alcoholism.

The pressures facing Native Americans (and other Native people) can result in a tendency to "self medicate" (to use a term from the alcoholism literature) in order to reduce or compensate for the pressures created by a world of change and alienation. On many occasions, this self-medication is an artifact of the fact that the traditional culture is so weakened that it provides minimum spiritual and psychological support for the individual. Under these circumstances, people can become vulnerable to patterns of escapism and alcoholic drinking.

Instead of attempting to explain Native responses in terms of some rigid and structured clockworks model, this book assumes that behavior is complex and multifaceted. Thus, it is largely in line with what Kenneth Boulding calls "cybernetic systems" where variations in the responses of specific people are expected. By combining such models with the cultural configurations approach, a powerful analytic model emerges.

This book, in line with such perspectives, provides a means of dealing with those who are confronting a cultural crisis and who fall into the abyss of alcoholism, in part, due to these outside cultural pressures. The book seeks to accomplish this goal by, among other tactics, providing tools that help people embrace their traditional cultures in positive, appropriate, and therapeutic ways.

REFERENCES

Boulding, K. (1956). General systems theroy: Skeleton of science. *General Systems*,11–17.

Christopher, J. (1992). *SOS sobriety: The proven alternatives to twelve step programs.* New York: Prometheus Books.

Christopher, J. 1997. *How to stay sober: Recovery without religion.* New York: Prometheus Books.

Fischer, A., Jome, R., LaRae M., & Atkinson, D.R. (1998).Reconceptualizing multicultural counseling: Universal healing conditions in a culturally specific context. *The Counseling Psychologist,* 26(4), 525–588.

Kirkpatrick, J. (1978). *Turnabout: Help for a new life.* New York: Doubleday.

Kirkpatrick, J. (1990). *Stages of a new life program.* New York: Doubleday.

Sue, D. W., Arredondo, P., & McDavis. (1992). Multicultural counseling competencies and standards: A call to the profession. *Journal of Counseling and Development,* 70, 477–486.

Trimpey, J. (1985). *Rational recovery: The new cure for substance addiction.* New York: Pocket Books.

Trimpey, J. (1989). *Rational recovery for alcoholics: The small book.* New York: Dell.

CHAPTER 5

CULTURAL STRESS AND DYSFUNCTIONAL BEHAVIOR

Although culturally diverse, Native Americans can also be viewed as a distinct group that possesses its own needs and vulnerabilities. Some have suggested that Natives have a genetic makeup that may make them particularly vulnerable to alcoholism. In addition, Native people tend to face discrimination and, typically, economic hardship. And, of course, Native cultures, are often subjected to pressures that create stress, hardship, and alienation. All of these factors need to be considered by alcohol counselors who serve Native clients. And such issues also need to be dealt with by self-help programs. In order to provide a relevant background, this chapter melds a number of theories that deal with social stress (deriving from psychology, sociology, and applied anthropology among other places) in order to model the process by which escapism, via alcohol abuse, becomes an attractive option.

Initially, a discussion of Philip Cushman's concept of the "empty soul" sets the stage and the tone of this discussion. Cushman's work is then augmented and strengthened by the theory of anomie from sociology and the social separation syndrome model that has been developed in applied anthropology. The result is a more robust view of the impacts that trigger counterproductive and dysfunctional behavior, such as alcoholism. Modern terror management theory provides the synthesizing function needed to

The Path of Handsome Lake: A Model of Recovery for Native People, pages 67–82

usefully meld these distinct theories. In later chapters, such perspectives will be applied to the plight faced by Native Americans and their cultures.

THE "EMPTY SELF" AS A MODEL OF SUBSTANCE ABUSE

Philip Cushman's concept of "the empty self" (1990), if properly adjusted to the needs of Native Americans alcoholics and the counselors who serve them, provides a means of dealing with the stresses that are caused by social change and the dysfunctional behavior triggered by it, such as alcoholic drinking. In essence, Cushman showcases what he calls the "empty self" and he links it to a number of characteristics of modern American society (such as individualism). Concerned with general trends, Cushman observes:

> The central point of my argument is that in a world sorely lacking in community and tradition, the most effective healing response would be to address... societal change... Because that avenue is closed to... [most practitioners, they] can only provide guidance and therapy within the therapist-patient dyad.

Using a broad base of analysis, Cushman links a variety of characteristics of modern society to their cultural origins. In some ways, his work can be seen as a rejoinder to (or as a psychological extension of) a number of classic sociological interpretations of American culture such as Reisman's *The Lonely Crowd* (1950) and Slater's *The Pursuit of Loneliness* (1970). Since his primary focus is psychological and not sociological, however, Cushman's work is a specialized theory that may have some blind spots.

Although the empty self-model is more of a metaphor than a formal theory, it has a role in therapy that has been recognized by members of the drug/alcohol therapy community, such as Miller (1998), who observes:

> This theory can be readily applied in addiction counseling by assisting the client in developing a recovery lifestyle that includes a sense of family, community, and tradition, all supportive of the addiction recovery.

By expanding Cushman's theory through (1) linking it with the concept of anomie that stems from sociology and (2) by dealing with the negative impacts of social and cultural change upon people and their ability to cope with their world, the relevance of the empty self concept can be expanded to deal with the problems faced by Native Americans. But first, it is necessary to provide an overview of Cushman's ideas and their implication.

According to Cushman (1990), the current era is one of profound social change; he suggests that we live in an era of increased urbanization, secularization, and industrialization. As these impersonal forces have gained power and influence families, traditions, and the age-old sense of community have begun to lose their strength. These changes can result in what Cushman calls the "empty self" that he describes as an increased distance from significant others and the eclipse of meaningful world-views that could, otherwise, help people to cope with the challenges they face.

In a provocative conclusion to the article that introduced the concept of the empty self, Cushman states:

> Let us hope that in the years ahead we can construct a society that is less in need of suffering and a self that is less...[impacted by] nihilistic economics and politics...But such changes would require developing a distance from the current normative intellectual discourse regarding individualism (1990).

Cushman's inflammatory stance prompted a number of rejoinders, published a year later, by Ellis (1991), Col (1991), and Rostafinski (1991) Various of their critiques deal with the difficulty of defining the self (Ellis, 1991), the pros and cons of adopting a "social constructionist" position (Col, 1991), and the observation that the concept of the empty self model is stated at a high order of abstraction (Rostakinski, 1991).

Assessing these critiques, Cushman responds by observing:

> I think the vast majority of white middle-class Americans is suffering precisely because they are so individualistic they can't cooperate, participate in-group action and sacrifice individual gain for group goals. These are all qualities of self that people must possess in order to be members of a cohesive community (Cushman, 1991).

I personally feel that Cushman's emphasis upon individualism masks the impact of other social forces that can lead to what he calls the empty self. As will be argued below, I also believe that his work is not adequately nested within the rich intellectual traditions of social theory and, as a result, Cushman ignores a number of significant potentials that could strengthen and expand the empty self-model. Nonetheless, the concept of the empty self has made an important impact, is widely cited, and has had an overt influence upon the helping professions, such as drug/alcohol therapy.

Ultimately, the value of the empty self model is the fact that it models how healthy coping mechanisms are often undercut by the impersonal nature of modern society. This, in turn, can trigger alienation and other unhealthy feelings, beliefs, and attitudes. Dysfunctional behavior such as alcoholic drinking, in turn, may be triggered by these feelings. Thus, traumatized individuals may begin began a pattern of alcoholic drinking in order to help them mitigate the feelings of alienation that Cushman links to the empty soul syndrome.

By paring the idea of the empty self to the bone and by eliminating Cushman's rhetoric on individualism, the concept can be usefully portrayed as:

Table 5.1. The Empty Self Model.

Issue	*Examples*	*Discussion*
Primary Causes	Urbanization, secularization industrialization	The world is changing, becoming more impersonal, and the religious underpinnings of life are weakening. These are generally acknowledged artifacts of the modern, industrial world.
Impact	Family, traditions, community lose their power and influence	In our society, people are increasingly mobile. In addition, people in urban areas often find themselves cut off from other people, their traditions, and the larger community.
Empty Self	The concept of the empty self deals with the fact that as family, tradition, and community lose power, the individual is cut off from meaningful relationships.	In this situation, individuals are not in a position to benefit from their legacies of tradition, community, and family. People become distanced from these positive influences and from each other.
Addictive Response	Addictive behavior is one coping mechanism that people employ when meaningful components of life (analyzed by the empty self syndrome) weaken and the ability to cope is reduced.	The decline of family, tradition, and community results in alienation and psychological pain. Substance abuse is one way of dealing with these negative impacts.

It should be noted that although Cushman makes numerous references to society and social influences ranging from Aeschylus to Alfred North Whitehead, he does not deal in any significant detail with social and sociological theories, or the major theorists of these fields. As a result, Cushman's work is tightly focused on psychology, on the one hand, while he strategically ignores parallel findings from other disciplines, such as sociology, on the other. Now that Cushman's insights have been somewhat digested by the helping professions, it is time to meld his psychological theory of the empty self with relevant social theories that overlap it. That is my task here.

ANOMIE: A SISTER CONCEPT FROM SOCIOLOGY

Cushman developed the concept of the empty self from within the intellectual tradition of psychology. As a result, Cushman did not forcefully tap the wealth of sociological theory and/or seek to draw strong and concrete linkages between psychological and social theories.

It is useful, however, to link the psychological concept of the empty self with parallel theories that have been developed in sociology. By doing so, the concept of the empty self, while continuing to deal with the psychological inner-workings of individuals, can be more effectively nested within a greater social and cultural context. As will be argued, this analytic strategy has applications for those who are concerned with Native American alcoholism.

The concept of anomie, analyzed earlier (Chapters 1, 4), describes a sense of "normlessness" that results when people are subjected to profound and unmitigated change.

As we saw above, Robert Merton provides a typology of responses to anomie that includes (1) conformity, (2) innovation, (3) ritualization, (4) retreatism, and (5) rebellion (Merton, 1957).

The concept of anomie continues to be a useful and viable concept in social theory. Representative applications of the concept have been used to explain the formation of teenage gangs (Cloward & Ohlin, 1960; Jankowski, 1991), to explore deviance in seventeenth century Puritan society (Erikson, 1966), and to explain "moral panics" in contemporary Great Britian (Jenkins, 1992).

The concept of anomie is one of the keystone theories of social change and deviant behavior and it tends to be ubiquitous in social research that deals with these phenomena.

Of special interest is Merton's category of retreatism that he presents as one response to anomie. Merton links retreatism to people who embrace both the goals of society and the proscribed methods of achieving them. Nonetheless, these people are unable to succeed in socially accepted ways, on the one hand, while they have not substituted other (deviant) alternatives that can result in personal success and/or fulfillment, on the other. Merton suggests that retreatists include hermits, the mentally ill, *alcoholics, and drug abusers.*

Thus, according to the concept of anomie, as refined by Merton, anomie is related to an inability to succeed in socially acceptable ways. This inability to succeed causes some people to retreat from society. Alcohol abuse can be viewed as one category of this retreatist response. Thus, according to Merton, some alcoholic behavior can be viewed as a response to anomie.

These perspectives tend to coincide with current trends in alcohol therapy that focus upon addiction as an artifact of feelings of helplessness. Thus, Lance Dodes, best known for his *Heart of Addiction* states:

> Virtually every addictive act is preceded by a feeling of helplessness or powerlessness. Addictive behavior functions to repair is underlying feeling of helplessness. (2002)

In presenting this point, Dodes emphasizes that working to eliminate feelings of helplessness is the key to recovery. Stanton Peele (1992), mirroring Dodes, focuses upon examining addiction as it exists and functions within people and their lives. Alcoholics often describe their addiction as "self medication" that helps them to cope with the pressures of life. Peele presents this argument in a more formal context; he (as Dodes) believes that addiction is a way of dealing with situational stress and tension. Thus, viewing these important works within their most basic context, they emerge as independent inventions of issues such as anomie that have long been a part of the social scientific community.

As with the concept of the empty self, anomie provides a model of the impacts wrought by a breakdown of culture, society, and tradition. Both the concepts of the empty self and anomie can be used to focus upon alcoholism as an artifact of unmitigated social change. While the concept of the empty self is primarily a psychological theory, however, anomie focuses upon the societal side of the equation.

Dealing with the concept of anomie in tabular form, we find:

Table 5.2. The Concept of Anomie

Issue	*Examples*	*Discussion*
Primary Causes	Urbanization, secularization industrialization	Sense of community, folk, and an obligation to others is reduced or eliminated. Largely caused by social and economic change.
Impact	People find that the goals provided by society cannot be achieved in socially acceptable ways.	Due to changes in urbanization, technology, etc., socially sanctioned goals and means of achieving them are not efficient strategies for some people.
Anomie	A form of "normlessness" that causes people to rely almost entirely upon themselves.	Social traditions, the cohesiveness of community, and the family begin to break down. People become distanced from these others and their culture.
Retreatism	Retreatism is a method of coping with anomie that is typically embraced by people who cannot achieve the goals supplied by society in socially acceptable ways. One major form of retreatism is alcoholism.	The normlessness of anomie coupled with a lack of legitimate opportunities to achieve socially acceptable goals can lead to increased alcohol abuse.

As can be seen, the concept of anomie is designed to deal with the impacts of social change and the disruptions that it causes in people's lives. The concept of anomie argues that people can become alienated as cultures change and as the ability to achieve socially sanctioned goals in socially acceptable ways declines. One specific response to the pressures of anomie is retreatism (withdrawing from the world). According to Merton, alcohol abuse is often a form of retreatism that can be explained as a response to anomie.

THE EMPTY SOUL MODEL AND ANOMIE: A COMPARISON

Although the concept of the empty self derives from psychology while the concept of anomie is a product of social theory, they both deal with similar, if not identical, phenomena. Both focus upon social change and how social change can lead to deviant behavior. And both explain alcohol abuse as a deviant response that has been triggered by social change.

The concept of the empty self starts by arguing that urbanization, industrialization, and secularization lead to a breakdown of family, tradition, and community. This breakdown, in turn, is a catalyst for the empty self-syndrome that is characterized by a lack of meaningful relationships with others. In a situation where meaningful relationships with others are not functioning properly, the behavior of people who are adversely affected by this situation is likely to become deviant. One form of deviance is alcohol abuse. Thus, people who suffer from the empty-self syndrome are likely to suffer from alcohol abuse.

The concept of anomie, in a parallel manner, begins by arguing that urbanization, industrialization, and secularization create a situation where the norms of society are no longer appropriate and/or effective. This leads to a decaying of the relationships between specific people and their family and/or community and an undercutting of the prevailing moral structure of society. This breakdown, in turn, leads to anomie that is caused by the flux of social change and the lack of social and moral grounding that results from this change. Dysfunctional behavior, such as alcohol abuse, is one artifact of these disruptions of society and the anomie it causes.

In order to demonstrate the similarities between the concept of the empty self and anomie, Table 5.3 outlines some of their parallels.

The concepts of the empty self and anomie derive from different intellectual traditions; the empty self-concept stems from psychology while anomie is a social theory. Nonetheless, both deal with almost identical perspectives and subject matters. By combining these theories in useful ways, more robust and flexible perspectives and methods result. In addition, by combining social and psychological theories, "a lingua Franca" can be established that facilitates people who from different intellectual/cultural traditions to interact with each other in well organized, mutually respectful, and fruitful ways.

In order to demonstrate the ability of this holistic theory to facilitate mutual understanding between diverse professions and disciplines, I will

Table 5.3. Empty Self Model and Anomie Compared

Issue	*Empty Self*	*Anomie*
Primary Causes	Urbanization, secularization industrialization	Sense of community, folk, and obligation to others is reduced or eliminated. Largely caused by social and economic change.
Impact	Family, traditions, community lose their power and influence	Due to changes in urbanization, technology, etc., socially sanctioned goals and means of achieving them are no efficient strategies.
Results	Increased distance from significant others and from meaningful worldviews that could, otherwise, help people cope with the stresses of life	Anomie: "normlessness" that causes people to rely almost entirely upon themselves.
Addictive Behavior	Alienation and concomitant feelings, beliefs, and attitudes that are counterproductive and/or can trigger alcohol abuse	Retreatism: One form of retreatism is alcohol abuse.
Discussion	It is obvious that the concept of the empty self and anomie are closely related. Due to the fact that one is psychological while the other is sociological, however, each has its own special emphasis. By combining these two models a more robust paradigm can be developed and the strategies of therapy resulting from doing so can become broadened in useful ways.	

discuss relevant perspectives from applied anthropology. It is hoped that this brief discussion will demonstrate the value of such a melding of ideas and how they can foster understanding among members of different intellectual traditions.

IMPACTS UPON SOCIETY: APPLIED ANTHROPOLOGY

As suggested above, the psychological model of the empty self has not developed the linkages that are required to facilitate combining psychological and social theories of alienation and the deviant behavior that is often associated with it. As suggested above, by combining the concept of the empty self with that of anomie, useful connections can be forged. The value of these linkages is demonstrated by showing how practitioner-oriented social sciences, such as applied anthropology, have developed sophisticated tactics of intervention that parallel both anomie and the concept of the empty self.

Applied anthropology has evolved, in part, as a means of understanding and mitigating the disruption caused by significant social change. Applied anthropologists, furthermore, have long recognized that counterproductive responses (such as alcohol abuse) often occur during periods of disruption triggered by the social and economic intrusion of a dominant culture into a more subservient region (such as a hinterland region or developing country).

A typical goal of applied anthropologists is to provide their clients (often residents of developing regions) with information regarding the implications of the impacts they face. A primary purpose of this tactic is to counter or cushion the negative repercussions of disruptions and transformations that are triggered by social, technological, and economic change. Applied anthropologists are quick to dismiss the "cult of progress" and the belief in modernism that many "forward looking" people embrace. Although economic development specialists often assert that the old must invariably give way to the new, applied anthropologists debate this truism. Representative of such ideas is David Maybury-Lewis who observes:

> There is no natural or historic law that militates against small societies. There are only political choices (Maybury-Lewis, 1977).

Thus, although the conventional theories of development (that are so attractive to many) often dismiss ethnic and tribal enclaves as vestigial remains that are slated for inevitable oblivion, applied anthropologists realize that this decline is not pre-ordained, even if such a perspective might serve the interests of social planners and/or some segments of society.

Where change is inevitable, applied anthropologists focus upon preserving the dignity and the quality of life of people whose world is being transformed. On many occasions, this can be accomplished by helping to bolster a people's culture and traditions. Thus, G. N. Appell insists that a viable cultural heritage can help to mitigate the impacts of traumatic change. As a result, he places a great emphasis upon encouraging existing traditions:

> A society undergoing change ... has a right to access to its cultural traditions, its language and its social history (Appell, 1977).

Appell senses that protecting this 'cultural ballast' is vital because people who are experiencing change are often victimized by what he calls the "social separation syndrome... [that] involves role conflict and ambiguity, threat to one's self esteem, and an impaired social identity" (Appell, 1977). He continues:

> Social bereavement arising from social change seems to follow a developmental sequence similar to personal bereavement...There is first a period of denial as numbness accompanied by anxiety, fear, and feelings of threat to one's identity. This is succeeded by a phase of frustrated searching for the lost world or individual, hoping for a reversal and then bitter pining and unrelieved sense of pain. Following this is a period of depression and apathy...Finally there is the phase of reorganization when the bereaved begins to build new plans and assumptions about the world (1977).

Note how this model clearly parallels the concept of the empty self. In both, massive changes are seen as creating tensions and alienation. As a result, people are cut off from their traditions and social relationships. In this situation, deviance is a likely result; alcohol abuse is one form of deviance. For deviant behavior (such as alcohol abuse) to be controlled, this cycle of alienation must be broken. And while Cushman laments that changing society and its impacts is beyond the scope of the psychologically oriented helping professions (1990), applied anthropology actively moves in that direction.

In Tabular form, these parallels can be presented as:

Table 5.4. Social Separation Syndrome and The Empty Self: A Comparison

Issue	*Empty Self*	*Social Separation Syndrome*
Value of Tradition	Family, tradition, community are a positive and stabilizing force.	A ballast that prevents anomie and alienation
Undercutting Phenomena	Social and cultural change	Unmitigated social change
Impact of Undercutting	Alienation, distance from others and meaningful world-views.	Alienation, self-identity and esteem impaired.
Results	Coping mechanisms rendered inoperative. Can lead to drug/alcohol abuse.	Frustrating search for lost world, depression, and apathy. Side effect can be drug/alcohol abuse.
Discussion	The concept of the empty self is a practitioner oriented psychological theory. The concept of the social separation syndrome is a practitioner oriented social theory. Both deal with almost identical phenomena and both are well equipped to deal with alcohol abuse issues. *And while Cushman laments that psychologically oriented practitioners are not in a position to change the impacts of society, applied anthropology actively seeks to do so.*	

It is important to note that both the social separation syndrome model and the empty self-concept view social change as potentially painful and damaging to individuals. The social separation model, however, incorporates social theory while the concept of the empty self is derived from psychology. Both, however, were explicitly developed to explore negative impacts upon people who are facing unmitigated social change.

CULTURAL GENOCIDE

For many years the multi-pronged undermining of the traditional cultures from which people derive has been a basic fact of Native American life. These relentless processes of cultural weakening and disintegration have exerted a great toll and served as a catalyst that has triggered many maladies that inflict specific Native American people as well as entire cultures. Increasingly, there is a growing recognition that many of the dysfunctions exhibited by specific people are triggered by rapid and unmitigated changes to their traditional culture as it competes with and/or is transformed by the outside world.

A bleak and shameful chapter exists in American history, a time when an overt policy of the United States government (as well as those of organized religions and other groups that were supposedly acting on behalf of Natives) sought to systemically undermine and destroy their traditional cultures. On the one hand, some misguided well-wishers hoped to more effectively integrate Native people into the fabric of American life by providing them with "mainstream" attitudes, skills, and knowledge that they needed to be "successful." Wrongly believing old cultures had no place in the modern world, great efforts were made to help (or force) Native people to transcend their past. Thus, just as 19th century immigrants were (at least partially) stripped of their cultural heritage when they were phased into American life, this process of socialization overtly and covertly involved a cultural purging intended to give Native people a better chance of personal success.[1] Schools for future Native American leaders, for example, often discounted traditional cultures to the degree that those who practiced traditional customs or spoke traditional languages were punished or shamed for doing so.

While some of these policies were motivated by legitimate and well-intended goals, others seem to have been intended to undermine Native cultures in order to ease the process by which newcomers could settle the land and do business there. Native peoples were often viewed as obstacles or rivals to be overcome, not as partners and neighbors. Since people possessing weak and unorganized societies are easier to manipulate than people whose cultures are strong and vital, destroying traditional ways of life was often a consciously employed tactic.

As America became increasingly industrialized and as native people became increasingly dispersed and weakened, socio-economic forces combined to further undermine traditional cultures. Many of these changes probably "just happened" and were not planned in any kind of calculated way. Nonetheless, they continued a process of cultural undermining and unmitigated social change that put additional stress on Native individuals and societies. Reservation life became hard and jobs were often few. Young people often had to leave home in order to find work. This tendency typically left the culture in a fragmented condition and forced people to abandon their homelands and/or traditions.

This process can be called cultural genocide. Biologically, perhaps, Native people survived, but culturally, their traditions were being stripped from them, in many cases to the point of cultural extinction. This pattern of cultural decay left many Native people in a situation that can be described with reference to the empty self model and the social separation syndrome. This unhealthy situation provided fertile ground for a personal decline.

As we saw in Chapter 4, this situation was usefully modeled with reference to a version of the cultural configuration model that has used in order to augment a form of systems theory that acknowledges that human behavior, although patterned, responds to diverse variables including the degree to which cultural institutions are under attack. This melding of social theory and general systems theory is more robust than models that precisely predict how people will respond, it is particularly appropriate when examining the impact of widespread and unprecedented stress. Nonetheless, a unifying theuretic perspective is needed.

TERROR MANAGEMENT THEORY: A UNIFYING CONCEPT

So far, this chapter has dealt with a wide variety of theories that revolve around the alienation impacting people who are subjected to profound and unmitigated social change. The concept of the empty self, that derives from psychology, documents the hurtful impacts of modern life upon the psyche of many individuals. The sociological theory of anomie focuses upon the social context of such behavior. And applied anthropologists have worked to apply such concepts to small scale societies that face rapid change and acculturation. Due to the fact that each of these research streams deals with similar phenomena in different ways, the collective validity of the observations is strong. Nonetheless, to be most effective, these theories need to be unified in more concrete ways.

Modern terror management theory provides the "umbrella concepts" needed for this synthesis. Largely an embellishment of the theories of Ernest Becker (1971, 1973), a major social/psychological theorist, terror management theory traces much human response to a fear of death.

In its orthodox version, terror management theory proposes that people, being rational, realize that they are going to die. This knowledge triggers fears. Knowing that they will not live forever, people seek ways to identify with some eternal phenomenon in the hope that by doing so they can live on through it, even after their personal death. People's culture and society tend to be that larger, more permanent entity. By embracing the larger culture and unifying with it, people develop a way to mitigate the anxiety of that revolves around the knowledge of their eventual death.

This mechanism of mitigation can work reasonable well in situations where cultures are stable and where people believe that their society will survive into the foreseeable future. In the case of many Native peoples, however, the culture, its institutions, and traditions are under extreme pressure (if not outright attack) by outside forces. Under such circumstances, people will lose faith in the permanence of their culture. When this happens, their heritage will provide no promise of immortality fear the fear of death and the resulting anxiety will not be adequately mitigated. The resulting unrelieved anxiety, in turn, can trigger dysfunctional behavior such as alcoholic drinking.

The application of terror management theory to the analysis of the trauma faced by Native people has been pioneered by Michael Salzman (2001). Combining terror management theory with the work of Alfred Adler and Adler's emphasis upon self-esteem, Salzman argues that self-esteem can serve as an anxiety buffer. To gain self-esteem, however, people must adhere to a certain standard of acceptability. Culture provides that yardstick of evaluation. When cultures break down and/or when people lose faith in them, however, the socially sanctioned measures of self worth are rendered passé. In such situations, we can expect anxiety to increase. And with increased anxiety, we can predict dysfunctional behaviors to rise.

This application of terror management theory provides a way of unifying the diverse psychological, sociological, and anthropological perspectives discussed above. Graphically, this model is presented in Table 5.5.

Terror management theory, especially as adjusted to the analysis of Native people by Salzman (2001), provides a useful and synthesizing model for dealing with the impact of social change upon Native people and the resulting dysfunctional behavior. Due to the elegance, robustness, and applicability of these perspectives, they are valuable tools.

CONCLUDING STATEMENT

As a direct result of historic events, many Native people became alienated from their heritage. In many cases, no set of beliefs and spiritual orienta-

Table 5.5. Terror Management and Native Response

	Description	*Discussion*
Fear	People have fears related to their mortality. These fears give rise to anxieties that need to be relieved. To address their fears, people often identify with something that is bigger and more permanent than they are.	Historically, people have dealt with their culture and/or society as the larger more permanent entity that can be embraced in the quest for some kind of immortality. When societies are stable and ongoing, this strategy tends to be somewhat effective
Lack of Mitigation	Many native cultures are weakened to the point where people do not believe in their permanence. When this occurs, people can no longer relieve their fears and anxieties of death by embracing their culture	According to terror management theory, people need a means of mitigating the fear of death. They usually do so by identifying with their culture. But when the culture is failing, it can no longer serve as a mitigating force.
Response	One possible response to anxieties that are not mitigated is dysfunctional behavior. Alcoholic drinking is one example of this possible response.	When anxiety is profound and unmitigated, some sort of response will result. One response is to embrace a new world view that provides mitigation. Dysfunctional behavior is another possible response.
Discussion	Various theories from psychology, sociology, and applied anthropology all acknowledge that massive social change can be disruptive and that unmitigated change can trigger dysfunctional behavior. Terror management theory provides a way of unifying these theories in an elegant and robust manner. Since the value of this theory has been demonstrated from a cross disciplinary perspective, it can be viewed as particularly valid and useful.	

tion filled the resulting void. People whose cultural underpinnings are shaken can easily become vulnerable to escapist behaviors such as alcohol abuse. Many observers have pointed to a direct link between cultural decay and alcoholism.

Concepts such as the Empty Self, Anomie, and the Social Separation Syndrome all point to the fact that people facing the stress of cultural decay are likely to be vulnerable to a variety of maladies, including alcoholic behavior. Applying these theories to an analysis of the rampant alcoholism among the Native people of North America, a plausible theory regarding these tendencies can be poised.

When everything that people hold dear is being undermined and when cultural traditions no longer provide a safe haven and guidance, the result is often alienation and anomie. These processes can be described using the empty self and the social separation syndrome models. So described, it becomes only too easy to understand how and why so many Native people exhibit escapist behaviors such as alcoholic behavior.

Terror management theory is a particularly useful model since it can be used to synthesize a variety of theories stemming from psychology, sociology, and applied anthropology. As such, it provides a useful orientation of value to those studying dysfunction within Native cultures.

This chapter has argued that, to a large extent, the high incidence of alcoholic behavior among Native Americans is an artifact of rampant and unmitigated social change and the relentless undermining of traditional cultures. This observation suggests that strengthening the Native culture is a general strategy for helping people to cope with their alcoholism. If much dysfunctional behavior stems from anomie, the empty self, and social separation, the antidote is clearly to reverse those trends and by helping people to reintegrate themselves with their heritage. The dysfunction that results when Native cultures fail to serve as a buffer against anxiety can be usefully modeled by terror management theory.

NOTE

1. This, in my opinion and in the opinion of many of my colleagues was misguided and tragic, but nonetheless, pursued with an eye towards bettering the lot of the people affected.

RFERENCES

Appell, G. N. (1977). The plight of indigenous people: Issues and dilemmas. *Survival International Review, p. 14.*

Becker, E. (1971). *The birth and death of meaning.* New York: Free Press.

Becker, E. (1973). *The denial of death.* New York: Free Press.

Cloward, R.A., & Ohlin, L.E. (1960). *Delinquency and Opportunity: A Theory of Delinquent Gangs.* Glencoe, IL.: Free Press.

Col, D.A. (1991). Some comments on the empty self: A reply to Philip Cushman. *Amercian Psychologis,* 46(5), 540–541.

Cushman, P. (1990). Why the self is empty: Towards a historically situated psychology. *American Psychologist,* 45, 599–611.

Cushman, P. (1991). No empty fixes: A rejoinder to Rostafinski, Ellis, and Col. *American Psychologist,* 46(5), 542–543.

Dodes, L. (2002). *The heart of addiction: A new approach for understanding and managing alcoholism and other addictive behaviors.* New York: HarperCollins.

Dressler, D. (1969). *Sociology: The study of human interaction.* New York: Alfred A. Knoph.

Durkhiem, E. (1893, 1951). *Suicide,* translated by George Simpson. New York: The Free Press.

Ellis, A. (1991). How to fix the empty self. *American Psychologist,* 46(5), 539–540.

Erikson, K. T. (1966). *Wayward puritans: A study in the sociology of deviance.* New York: John Wiley and Sons.

Jankowski, M.S. (1991). *Islands in the street: Gangs and American urban society.* Berkeley: University of California Press.

Jenkins. P. (1992). *Intimate enemies: Moral panics in contemporary Great Britain.* New York: Aldine de Gruyter.

MacIver, R.M. (1950). *The ramparts we guard.* New York: Macmillan.

Maybury-Lewis, D. (1977).Societies on the brink. *Harvard Magazine,*1,2, 56–61).

Merton, R. (1957). *Social theory and social structure.* New York: The Free Press.

Peele, S. (1992). *Truth about addiction and recovery.* Fireside.

Reisman, D. (1950). *The lonely crowd: A study of changing American character.* New Haven, CT.: Yale University Press.

Rostafinski, T.J. (1991). Why the self looks empty: Comment on Cushman. *American Psychologist,* 46(5), 341–342.

Salzman, M.B. (2001). Cultural trauma and recovery: Perspectives from terror management theory. *Trauma, Violence, and Abuse,* 2(2), 172–191.

Slater, P.(1970). *The pursuit of loneliness: American culture at the breaking point.* Boston: Beacon.

Whyte, W. (1956). *The organization man.* Garden City: Doubleday.

CHAPTER 6

TERROR MANAGEMENT THEORY, CULTURAL DISRUPTION, AND THE IROQUOIS

The plight of many Native American cultures, including that of the Iroquois, is a legacy of societal decay and the psychological dysfunction that results when the cultural underpinnings of a people's world collapse. In order to deal effectively with the stress faced by many Native people experiencing social disruptions and disintegration, we will consciously evaluate the impacts of the trauma that result of unmitigated social change for which people are unprepared. In doing so, this chapter deals with a well-documented example from the Native American experience and explores what can happen when the heritage of a people (in this case the Iroquois) is profoundly and quickly undercut by outside forces that are beyond its control and range of experience.

The strategy of analysis (here and in later chapters) results from combining of (1) the cultural configuration approach, that deals with cultures as holistic entities with (2) terror management theory as adapted to the analysis of Native cultures by Salzman (2001). The resulting approach is elegant, while robust, and it provides a useful way of modeling cultures under stress and the dysfunctional behavior that results from such anxiety.

The Path of Handsome Lake: A Model of Recovery for Native People, pages 83–97

Initially, I will present a brief account of what happened to the Iroquois as they lost power due to military defeat, the immigration of Whites into territory that had traditionally been controlled by the Iroquois, the onslaught of unprecedented diseases/epidemics, and economic reversals that accompanied these impacts. Having provided a rather straightforward commentary, an interpretation of these events, based on terror management will provide a means of interpreting the impact of these events in ways that can be applied to other Native groups that also face cultural and social stress from outside forces. Terror management theory, furthermore, is a useful model that will be applied in later chapters that discuss the Iroquois, other Native peoples, and strategies for intervention and self-help that can be used to help such people recover from alcoholism.

THE PLIGHT OF THE IROQUOIS: A NON-THEORETICAL ACCOUNT

This brief analysis will document how the Iroquois of the late 18th/early 19th centuries faced disabling reversals and cultural disruptions. The trauma resulting from these events ultimately led to negative and counterproductive patterns of response that was exhibited by many Iroquois individuals and by the floundering of Iroquois culture as a corporate entity. These dysfunctional responses include a rampant epidemic of alcoholism. Although the present discussion focuses upon the Iroquois as a distinct people, the reader is asked to remember that the stresses that the Iroquois faced are typical of the challenges facing other Native people and, therefore, the reactions of the Iroquois are not unique are often mirrored by the responses of other groups. Thus, the response of the Iroquois can be discussed both as an end in itself and from more general/theoretic perspectives that can be applied to other people.

The Iroquois are (and long have been) an impressive people and a powerful and proud nation. Without the aid of "civilized" Europeans, they formed a complex structure of government that possessed great sophistication and flexibility. Some observers have even maintained that documents like the Declaration of Independence and the United States' Constitution are profoundly influenced by the examples provided by the Iroquois. If these speculations are true or false, is immaterial; by all informed accounts, the historic Iroquois were a complicated group of interrelated societies whose complexity rivals the structure of the contemporary United States in terms of structure, complexity, and purpose. The fact that the Iroquois have suffered "hard times" in recent generations does not undermine this observation or lessen the significance of the Iroquois achievement.

From a cultural configurationist point of view, the Iroquois were a specific people who had carved out a lucrative niche for themselves during colonial times. Largely conquering and evicting their neighbors, they were a proud and victorious people who had faith in themselves and their ability to control their destiny. The cultural configuration of the Iroquois had a rather pronounced division of labor. Women were farmers and performed various domestic chores, while legitimate activities for men included hunting and warfare. This division of labor was fairly rigid and farming was considered to be a shameful and unmanly activity for males.

In the colonial era, the British and the French long competed for control of what is now Central Ontario, Canada and the "Upstate"/Western region of New York in the United States. That region was the heartland of Iroquois territory and the strategically minded Iroquois carefully negotiated with the Whites, often playing one side against the other, to advance their own position. Due to the skill of their leaders, politicians, and statesmen, the Iroquois were, for many generations, able to manipulate the tensions that existed between various European factions and use them to their own advantage. Up through and including the French and Indian War, the Iroquois successfully maintained an enviable situation, controlling the balance of power, and enjoying the prosperity and the relative security such tactics created. Under these conditions, the cultural configuration of the Iroquois meshed with the realities of life, and the Iroquois seemingly enjoy excellent mental and psychological health.

In essence, due to their strategic location, the Iroquois found themselves in an enviable position and, as a result, they prospered. Their success was due, in part, to the alliances and trading relationships with the Whites that gave the Iroquois power and access to guns and European trade goods. As a result, the Iroquois dominated their world and were able to drive their opponents into exile, if not into actual oblivion.

Socially and economically, the Iroquois were a sedentary people that practiced a matrilineal kinship system. As mentioned above, women did the farming and they owned the land while men were valued as hunters and protectors. Iroquois warriors were known as fierce and brave fighters willing to risked themselves to protect family and community. The status gained by prowess and bravery was a central underpinning of self-esteem among Iroquois Men. Iroquois Men were also skilled orators, negotiators, and tacticians. In a world where they played the British against the French, ample opportunity to practice these skills existed.

Although agriculture was viewed as unmanly, the primitive methods of agriculture that women practiced allowed the Iroquois to settle in towns or villages and not be forced to live a more transient or nomadic existence.

Although the Iroquois prospered for many generations, good things do not last forever:

> With the victory of the British in the War with France the Iroquois found themselves outflanked, no longer able to play off the British and French against each other and surrounded by a circle of British forts (Wallace, 1978).

In the emerging situation that followed the French and Indian Wars, a situation developed where White military leaders no longer needed the Iroquois as political and military allies. After all, the French had been conquered and forced to leave North America. As a result, the Iroquois lost their strategic importance. Thus, for twenty years before the Revolution, the Iroquois had begun to suffer economic and political reversals.

When the Revolutionary War began, a generation after the end of the French and Indian Wars, however, the Iroquois again became embroiled in a conflict that was larger than their immediate situation. The Iroquois, caught in the middle between rival forces, had to make a decision regarding which side to support. Historically, the Iroquois had been allies of the British. From a more practical perspective, most Iroquois realized that the British wanted access to Iroquois territory (in what is now upstate New York and Ontario) merely as a trading partner and as a source of raw materials while an American victory could open up the land to settlement by White pioneers. As a result, the Iroquois clearly understood that the British had little immediate interest in populating the area and its victory would help protect Iroquois political dominance within their region.

The Iroquois leaders correctly reasoned that if the revolutionary forces won the war many Whites from the various rebelling colonies would want to migrate into what was Iroquois land. As a result of this likely population shift and its potential threat to Iroquois independence, most Iroquois were concerned about the negative implications of a British defeat. Due to this perceived threat, most Iroquois made the calculated decision to side with Britain because doing so was in their own best interest.[1]

Although the decision to side with the British was a rational and logical choice, doing proved to be costly:

> [During the war, the Iroquois homeland] was devastated by the John Sullivan [United State military commander] expedition in 1778, which in a three-pronged offensive managed to burn the houses and the crops in almost every major Iroquois town. Many of the women and children, and the surviving warriors, took refuge at Fort Niagara with the British, who housed them in a refugee camp, inadequately clothed, inadequately fed, inadequately sheltered, and swept by disease. By the end of the war, despite their military successes, the Iroquois population had been cut approximately in half (Wallace, 1978).

The war took a terrible toll upon the Iroquois, from a socio-economic perspective and in terms of in the cost of human life. The Sullivan raid resulted in the burning and many Iroquois towns, the refugee status of many survivors, the death of a large number of able-bodied men, and a plague (caused by refugee conditions) that killed even more Iroquois

After the war the plight of the Iroquois became increasingly grim. The victorious United States, remembering that the Iroquois had been their enemies in the battle for independence, showed the Iroquois few favors. Due to the fact that the newly established government of the United States understandably viewed the Iroquois as a defeated enemy, no partiality was lavished upon them. And, as the Iroquois leaders had predicted, hordes of White settlers (many of whom had first seen upstate New York as soldiers during raids into Iroquois territory by the revolutionary leader, General Sullivan) were lured back to the area by the vision of fertile farmland. By the turn of the late 18th/early19th centuries, the Iroquois were a beaten people who, having been recently defeated in war and decimated by disease, were increasingly besieged by social and economic rivals. They were ill equipped to effectively compete with these competitors in this rapidly changing world. The result of this unenviable social situation was infighting, and personal resignation/retreat among the Iroquois, often accompanied by dysfunctional behavior such as alcoholic drinking.

The situation faced by the Iroquois at the turn of the 19th century is not a happy one and the foreseeable future of this once-proud people was hardly pretty or encouraging. Anthropologist Anthony Wallace, for example, notes many examples of what therapists, social workers, and psychiatrists commonly identify as pathological social behavior and individual response. They include rampant violence, uncontrolled weeping and pining, fear of peers (as evidenced by accusations of witchcraft), general social disunity, and, of course, widespread alcoholism. Psychological depression was commonplace and Wallace observes that when people were sober, they were likely to be suicidal (1970).

These events, although specific to the Iroquois people, are paralleled by the events facing innumerable other Native peoples. Recall Chapter 2 where we discussed how the Native Hawaiians and the Maori of New Zealand endured similar experiences. As documented in Chapters 2 and 4, the changes wrought by White contact (and its negative impacts) upon both Native cultures and individuals are well known.

The case of the Iroquois, however, is particularly well documented and the facts surrounding the Iroquois, their history (before and after the trauma associated by with this contact), and the long-term impacts of reacting to stress are particularly well known. As a result, the saga of the Iroquois provides a textbook case regarding the stress caused by change, contact, and conflict upon a Native population that was unprepared to cope with the events to which it was subjected.

TERROR MANAGEMENT THEORY: AN OVERVIEW

Although the events impacting the Iroquois and their responses to them can stand alone and be understood without an elaborate theoretical frame, specific models can more effectively crystallize the issues that the example illuminates. One such tool/methodology is *terror management theory*. In order to provide a better understanding of some of the impacts of White contact upon the Iroquois, this theoretic construct will be applied to the skeleton retelling of Iroquois history that was provided above. The model will also be applied, as required, in later chapters. As a result of this analytic strategy, it is appropriate to make the reader aware of how I apply this theory and how I adjust it to serve my specific purposes.

Largely deriving from the work of Becker (1971, 1973, 1975) and developed by social psychologists such as Greenberg, Pyszczynski, and Solomon (1986), terror management theory has arisen to explore why people are so attuned to their heritage and why people so closely identify with their cultures and their ways of life. According to the terror management model, as it has evolved, people (unlike other animals) know that they are going to die and this knowledge causes great fear and anxiety.[2] Terror management theory goes on to assume that people typically seek relief from the terrible anxiety that is triggered by the knowledge of their own future death. This leads to a number of responses to mitigate the anxiety, such as people strongly identifying with their cultures.

Terror management theory continues by arguing that although people know they will die, they cling to the hope that a part of them will live on. Since people realize they are not personally immortal, they come to place a great emphasis upon the survival of their way of life, society, and/or culture. According to this model, if anxiety-ridden people, in fear of their own death, believe that their culture and way of life will survive after they are gone, they will be comforted and better able to cope with their own mortality. And if they believe that their culture is ongoing, they will have a reason to believe that they and what they hold dear will be remembered by future generations, giving them a sort of surrogate immortality because they have an opportunity to survive in the minds of others.

As a result of the belief that the collective/corporate culture may have an existence that extends beyond the life of the mortal individual, people are apt to closely identify with their culture/society/group because doing so provides transcendence and immortality that individual mortals lack. Due to this tendency, people invest heavily in their culture and they make decisions based upon it and the mores it provides. In doing so, individuals adhere to, treasure, and identify with the shared beliefs/mores/values/priorities and patterns of behavior that resonate from group solidarity and the identity provided by group membership. So positioning themselves, people can buffer themselves from anxiety. This mechanism provides a means by which anxiety-ridden people can anticipate their own immortality and find comfort in the process. Believing the groups to which they lend their allegiance will survive and make immortality an achievable goal, people typically seek to bolster their culture and to maintain their identity within it.

Put another way, the culture (as an ongoing corporate entity that transcends the individual) can serve as buffer that protects people from the fear and anxiety of their inevitable death. This buffer can function effectively, but only as long as people believe that their culture and society will survive after they are dead and thereby, extend their own existence through it lengthened shadow.[3]

An easily generated companion theory that extends this model postulates that if the culture and society are weakened to the extent that their survival is in serious question, the fears and anxieties experienced by individuals can be expected to multiply because people will have no reason to believe that they will be able to achieve immorality through the continued existence of their culture. To whatever extent this anxiety of death grows as a result of the vulnerability of the culture, we can expect a parallel expansion in the dysfunctional behaviors that are triggered by the resulting fears. Thus, if the culture is perceived to be at risk or under severe attack from forces beyond control, we can expect anxieties related to the recognition of mortality (and dysfunctions related to this dysfunction) to become more pronounced. When the vehicle that permits immortality is, itself, facing a life and death struggle, the individual's confidence in gaining immortality, through membership in it, will, reasonably enough, weaken. Table 6.1 presents the argument in tabular form.

While the terror management model is robust and widely applicable, there are ways in which it can be revised. Terror management theory, as it has developed, focuses upon fears of dying a physical death and the fact that these fears of being mortal can trigger a strong allegiance to a person's culture. This is because in many cases the culture will live on after them, and, thereby, provide an avenue to immortality. Based on the work of Ernest Becker, existentialism, and the tenets of modern social psychology, terror management theory is robust, has great explanatory value, and is enjoying high growth and respect.

Table 6.1. Terror Management Theory and the Degree of Cultural Stability

	Analysis	*Implications*
Anxiety	People are terrified of their own mortality. They are able to squelch this fear by investing themselves in their culture because their culture is bigger than they are and can exist after they die.	Embracing the culture and the society can serve as a coping mechanism that provides people with a degree of peace of mind and comfort since it offers one avenue of reaching immorality.
Stable culture	In cultures that are stable, individuals will believe that their culture will survive into the future. This provides a means of gaining immortality through participating in this stable and ongoing collective entity.	In many parts of the world, people are members of cultures that are relatively stable and survive over great periods of time. These people envision their culture/society as surviving (albeit evolving) into the foreseeable future and this gives them comfort.
Unstable culture	If cultures are not stable, individuals will fear that their culture will not survive into the future. Due to this fear, people do not have a mechanism to by which they can seek immortality. This can lead to anxiety and personal dysfunction.	Many parts of the world are subjected to profound change and even cultural genocide. This is particularly true of Native peoples. Those facing a high degree of cultural stress will not believe their culture will survive after them and face or anxiety stress as a result.
Discussion	While stable cultures provide a degree of comfort and compensation to people facing death, cultural decline and instability removes the buffer that prevents a fear of death. If and when this buffer is significantly undermined, people will face fear without any means of adequately coping. When this happens, we can expect personal anxiety (and a wide variety of dysfunctional behaviors associated with it) to develop.	

EXPANDING TERROR MANAGEMENT THEORY

Nonetheless, by focusing upon fear and how people compensate for the fear of personal death, the classic terror management model covertly implies that these responses are syndromes of the quest for an impossible dream: immortality. In essence, identifying with the culture becomes a way of compensating for what people cannot personally achieve. As a result, terror management lumps a wide range of behaviors into the category of coping with anxiety related to the fear of death and doing so in dysfunctional ways.

But this raises the question: "Is this all that is going on when people embrace their culture?" Isn't it equally possible for a person to support their culture because they feel that doing so is right and proper? Isn't it possible for people to want their culture (or society, or profession, or family, etc) to survive as an end in itself? The leading theorists of terror management theory would agree that this is possible. Thus, in presenting an overview of their approach, they use the qualifying term "largely" in order to acknowledge the fact that other influences may be present (Solomon, Greenwood, Pyszczynski ND 94). Researching within Western society, they find that the need to relieve the anxiety related to mortality is the major force impacting their subject. Perhaps this is an artifact of the fact most people in Western society do not fear that their culture and heritage is dying. But what, in contrast, about Native cultures in developing regions? These people have doubts about the survival of their way of life as a going concern. Is it possible that in these circumstances people will seek to preserve their culture as an end in itself? I certainly think so.

To whatever extent people seek to preserve their culture as an end in itself, we open the door to rival hypotheses. And rival hypotheses demand a broader and more flexible theoretic foundation. It is useful to develop a reformulation of terror management theory that deals with these issues and usefully broadens its perspectives in order to transcend an overemphasis upon the fear of personal death and its impact upon anxiety. This is especially true when studying societies facing massive and unmitigated stress.

Many people, for example, may work to advance their culture, not in order to (overtly or covertly) gain immortality for themselves, but because they love their culture and want to protect and nurture it. By analogy, I love my son and daughter. I wish them well. My feelings of love and my acts of nurturing are not inevitably triggered by any desire on my part to live through my children now or after I am dead.[4] By the same token, I work hard as a scholar and cultural critic. And at some level, of course, it pleases me when other people like (or at least respect) my work and I am delighted when they apply it to the problems they face. But the main reason I do my work is because I value some things and wish to contribute to them. I seek to expand and preserve the system, not myself. It is ascientific to assume that my behavior is inevitably some rather pathetic syndrome that vainly seeks immorality.

I, furthermore, am an applied folklorist/anthropologists who has worked hard to help others preserve their cultures and their heritages, not mine. In this effort, I do not seek personal immortality, but, in contrast, I seek to help other people preserve their traditions. I have many colleagues who follow a similar path. How can classic terror management theory deal with this? One way to do so is to recall that the issues that Otto Rank considered are multifaceted. They often transform themselves in what can best be viewed from a dialectical perspective. When viewing such phenomena from an ad hoc perspective, this complexity needs to be acknowledged.

To overcome these limitations, the existing terror management theory can be revised by generalizing it beyond the universal axiom that people embrace their culture as a means of countering their own morality. On the one hand, some people may accept their own morality and merely seek to support some thing that is bigger than they are because they love it, believe in it, or feel doing so is right and proper. Secondly, the culture of the individual is not the only possible recipient of such attention. Professions, life's work, family, hobbies, etc. can all be that larger entity that people embrace.

Restated in this way, the new formulation appears as:

Table 6.2. Terror Management Theory: A Revision

	Analysis	*Implications*
Anxiety	People are terrified by the possible loss of what they hold dear (which may be their own mortality, their culture, their life's work, etc.). These fears can be controlled by nurturing and protecting what is viewed as important.	The individual's culture and society are often highly valued. Protecting and strengthening them can serve as a coping mechanism that provides people with a degree of peace of mind and comfort by reducing anxiety. Other entities can also serve this role.
Stable culture	In cultures that are stable, people will believe that what they hold dear will survive into the future. This provides comfort to the individual and can foster good mental health. This is true if people seek immorality or if they merely seek to preserve what they hold dear.	In many parts of the world, people are members of cultures that are relatively stable and survive over great periods of time. Under such circumstances, the belief that what they hold dear will survive is comforting and can reduce stress and dysfunctional behavior.
Unstable culture	If cultures are not stable, individuals will fear that what they hold dear will not survive into the future. This can lead to painful trauma and personal dysfunction among people seeking immorality and those who love their culture.	Many parts of the world are subjected to profound change and even cultural genocide. This is particularly true of Native peoples. Those who do not believe their culture and what they hold dear will survive will face stress and be vulnerable prone to dysfunction as a result.
Discussion	Terror management theory can be revised to eliminate a mandatory emphasis upon the fear of personal death. Instead, fear of losing what is highly valued (whatever that might be) can be substituted for the fear of death. In most cases, the culture and the society are highly valued and people will hope (and even strive) for its continued existence. But these sentiments are not inevitably linked to a vain hope for immortality. By rephrasing terror management theory accordingly, the concept is broadened and counterproductive assumptions (regarding an alleged inevitable motive of gaining immorality) can be eliminated. In this way the model is extended and made more flexible, robust, and rigorous.	

This reformulation, incidentally, is clearly in line with the theories and teachings of Otto Rank, one of Ernest Becker's key influences and a major intellectual force that helped create the intellectual foundation upon which terror management theory is built. Rank was concerned with the "will" (Rank's term that largely parallels what Freud called the "ego") and how it adjusts to life. In general, Rank envisioned three different kinds of responses: the "adapted," the "neurotic," and the "productive."

Rank used the "adapted type" as a kind of "catch all" category into which he placed average people who adequately functioned within society but were not notable in any way. Adapted types tend to do what they are told, follow the rules of society and remain relatively passive. Rank seems to have dismissed this type of person (possibly because he gravitated towards the artistic type of individual and, perhaps, because these people manifest few of the dysfunctions that he studied). In terms of the work of Abraham Maslow, these individuals are content to remain at the relatively lower rungs of the "hierarchy of needs" and never seek the higher levels such as "self actualization."

Rank's "neurotic type, in contrast, consists of people with a stronger will than the average "adapted type" and, as a result, they challenge any forces that seek to dominate them. This, however, typically leads to tensions and dysfunctions. Although Rank recognized that these people had their problems, he also felt they existed on a higher plane than the "adapted" people who live a thoughtless and subservient life and respond to the world and its challenges in "knee-jerk" reaction sort of way.

Continuing his typology, Rank tops it off with the "productive type" as the highest evolved and most noble type of individual. Here he places artists, creative people, and the intellectual leaders of society. (And, incidently, they closely resemble Rank and his artistic bent and strivings.) These productive people have become able to affirm who they are and, working within that reality, they become creative and productive. Viewed in this way, Rank's depiction of specific types of people is largely parallel to the model of Abraham Maslow who also sought to explain genius and nest it atop a hierarchy (with lesser individuals and personality types struggling ever upward.)

But there is another way in which we can deal with Rank's hierarchy. It can be represented by the dichotomy between the "neurotic type" and the "productive" type. Thus, terror management theory, as it has evolved, tends to deal almost exclusively with what is parallel to the "neurotic type" of person. It deals with syndromes, not positive responses. Because of this focus, it concentrates on dysfunction. For terror management theory to reach maturity, however, the actions of healthy and productive people need to be smuggled back into the model. Rank clearly understood that both kinds of people and both kinds of responses exist. By acknowledging this truth (that Rank so clearly recognized), terror management theory can be brought more in line with its intellectual roots. And it the process, the theory can emerge as more robust.

Thus, as an alternative to dealing with a fear of personal death and a quest for immorality, terror management theory can be revised to focus upon the healthy individuals' affirmation of what they hold dear and what they want to preserve for future generations. Adjusting the model in this way transcends an overly narrow focus upon the fact that people recognize they are mortal. While not all people fear death, most are concerned with the preservation of what they hold dear: the organizations, professions, cultures, societies, etc that they embrace and nurture in life. The theory, so modified, is able to deal with this reality.

By rephrasing terror management theory in this way, a model that is not inevitably connected with the fear of personal death emerges. This revised formulation can accomplish all that the current "fear of death" version of terror management theory provides, but it does so with none of the covert intellectual baggage that currently limits the model and which channels our thinking in a specific and non-universal direction.

So transformed, terror management theory, provides a more useful method of dealing with how and why individuals facing profound social change are apt to lapse into various forms of dysfunctional behavior. Connecting concepts of self esteem and vulnerability with the dysfunction caused by rapid and unmitigated social change, a means of dealing with the stress facing many Native people can be developed. In order to demonstrate the value of this theory, I will apply the principles of this revision of terror management theory to the empirical observations regarding the historic Iroquois presented above.

The model as expanded is useful since (1) people may gain comfort when what they hold dear is strong and vital and (2) people are apt to feel discomfort and exhibit dysfunctional behavior when what they hold dear is under profound attack and/or its survival is in serious question.

IROQUOIS TRAUMA/ DYSFUNCTION: A TERROR MANAGEMENT PERSPECTIVE

For many generations before the American Revolution, the Iroquois had enjoyed a strategically strong position and they had been able to play various White colonial forces against each other to their own advantage. During this time, the configurations of Iroquois culture meshed with their environment and they were able to function effectively.

This situation led to prosperity, affluence, and the elimination of rivals. During this period, the historic sex roles of Iroquois society were maintained. The woman practiced farming while the men were warriors who protected society and hunters who provided meat to supplement the diet of corn and vegetables that were grown by the women. Under these conditions, Iroquois society was stable and people were able to live according to established mores and roles and legitimize themselves accordingly. As a result, the culture and its people did not face strong and disabling stress.

The first major blow to the Iroquois position came after the end of the French and Indian War. Once the French surrendered, all of Northeast North American came under British control and these victors no longer needed to lavish favors and trade goods on the Iroquois in order to convince them to serve as allies against the French rivals. While the British did not attack the Iroquois after the French and Indian War, the compensation that had historically they had historically given the Iroquois to secure their friendship was severely curtailed. This situation created a period of hardship for the Iroquois. But the worst was yet to come.

During the American Revolution, most Iroquois fought with the British and they paid dearly as villages were burned and as many Iroquois were subjected to an exile status. The death of many men in their prime made conditions even worse.

After the war, the conditions faced by the Iroquois continued to deteriorate. Immigrants flooded into traditional Iroquois territory, and most of these newcomers practiced modern farming methods. The Iroquois style of agriculture could not compete against European farming methods and, as a result, the Iroquois began to fall behind economically. Men, however, did not take up farming because they felt it to be unmanly. While men preferred the life of a warrior coupled with hunting, game became scarce and there were no wars to fight. As a result many of the men became alienated due to changing circumstances and an inability to fit into the new order of things. This led to a variety of dysfunctional behaviors.

If these challenges were not painful enough, from the time of the revolution diseases and epidemics swept through Iroquois territory killing many members of Iroquois society.

The result of this unenviable situation was a rash of dysfunctional behaviors including infighting and personal resignation. Pathological behaviors, and rampant alcoholism also become commonplace.

These behaviors included uncontrolled weeping and pining, fear of peers (as evidenced by accusations of witchcraft), general social disunity. Psychological depression was commonplace and Wallace observes that when people were sober, they were likely to be suicidal (1970).

It is obvious that Iroquois culture was no longer able to provided comfort to people and, as a result, dysfunctional behavior came to the forefront. According to terror management theory (as discussed above), people cling to society because it gives them a feeling of immortality and/

or because they love it. But when the culture, itself faces substantial and seemingly fatal threats, people find it difficult to look at their culture as a means of transcending their physical bodies and/or surviving after death through it. Placed in this unenviable situation, the Iroquois were no longer soothed and reassured by the thought of the permanence of their traditions. They faced bald and un-compromised anxiety and terror as a result.

As indicated, terror management theory, as outlined above, provides a useful and robust means of modeling the types of tension facing Native people who confront massive cultural change. This model will be used in future chapters as we seek a means of exploring the tensions causes by White interventions into Native lands and the dysfunction that results from this impact.

NOTES

1. As a nation, the Iroquois did not have a pro-British policy; instead individual groups were allowed to make their own decision regarding the war. Most, however, sided with the British.
2. Significantly, while Freud focused on instincts or inborn propensities, Becker does not. Instead, Becker merely states that due to intelligence, mankind is able to perceive and anticipate his own death. This knowledge comes from rational thought, not instinct or archetype. Indeed, it is my feeling that one of Becker's primary strengths is that he was a strong advocate of restructuring Freudian analysis away form instinct and towards conscious thought.
3. I believe it was Ralph Waldo Emerson who said a great organization or business enterprise is the "lengthened shadow of one man." Cultures, however, are the lengthened shadow of many. The motivation for nurturing both businesses and cultures, however, can be the same: to create something that transcends the mortal individual and, thereby, creates immorality.
4. Some people may seek to live through or gain "immortality" from their children. But it is ascientific to assume a priori and without proof that all people are operating are behaving in this way and that this is their inevitable motive in loving and nurturing their children.

REFERENCES

Becker, E. (1971). *The birth and death of meaning* (2nd ed.). New York: Free Press.

Becker, E. (1973). *The denial of death.* New York: Free Press.

Becker, E. (1975). *Escape from evil.* New York: Free Press.

Greenberg, J., Porteus, J., Simon, L., Pyszczynski, T., & Solomon, S. (1995). Evidence of a terror management function of cultural icons: The effects of mortality salience on the inappropriate use of cherished cultural symbols. *Personality and Social Psychology Bulletin,* 21, 1221–1228.

Greenberg, J., Pyszczynski, T., & Solomon, S. (1986).The causes and consequences of a need for self-esteem: A terror management theory. In R.F. Baumeister (Ed.*), Public self and private self* (pp. 189–212). New York:.

Greenberg, J., Pyszczynski, T., Solomon, S., Simon, L., & Breus, M. (1994). Role of consciousness and accessibility of death-related thoughts in mortality salience effects. *Journal of Personality and Social Psychology,* 67, 627–637.

Greenberg, J., Pyszczynski, T., Solomon, S., Pinel, E., Simon, L., & Jordan, K. (1993). Effects of self-esteem on vulnerability-denying defensive distortions: Further evidence of an anxiety-buffering function of self-esteem. *Journal of Experimental Social Psychology,* 29, 229–251.

Greenberg, J., Solomon, S., & Pyszczynski, T., (1997).Terror management theory of self-esteem and social behavior: Empirical assessments and conceptual refinements. In M.P. Zanna (Ed.), *Advances in experimental social psychology* (29, 61–139). New York: Academic Press.

Greenberg, J., Solomon, S., Pyszczynski, T., Rosenblatt, A., Burling, J., Lyon, D., Pinel, E., & Simon, L. (1992). Assessing the terror management analysis of self-esteem: Converging evidence of an anxiety-buffering function. *Journal of Personality and Social Psychology,* 63, 913–922.

Harmon-Jones, E., Greenberg, J., Solomon, S., & Simon, L. (1996). The effects of mortality salience on intergroup bias between minimal groups. *European Journal of Social Psychology,* 25, 781.1–781.5.

Harmon-Jones, E., Simon, L., Greenberg, J., Pyszczynski, T., Solomon, S., & McGregor, H. (1997). Terror management theory and self-esteem: Evidence that increased self-esteem reduces mortality salience effects. *Journal of Personality and Social Psychology,* 72, 24–36.

Springer-Verlag, Greenberg, J., Pyszczynski, T., Solomon, S., Rosenblatt, A., Veeder, M., Kirkland, S., & Lyon, D. (1990). Evidence for terror management theory II: The effects of mortality salience reactions to those who threaten or bolster the cultural worldview. *Journal of Personality and Social Psychology,* 58, 308–318.

Wallace, A. F. C. (1970). *The Death and Rebirth of the Seneca (pp. 196–201).*

Part III

HANDSOME LAKE AND THE IROQUOIS AS A KEY TO RECOVERY

Thus far, this book has provided a variety of background materials that are needed in order to deal with the cultural decline and the resulting anxiety faced by many Native people. By doing so, the dysfunctional behavior that results can be more effectively addressed. With this background in place, we are ready to consider a specific example of Native dysfunction, on the one hand, and discuss how the lessons provided there provide clues and suggestions for various Native people seeking recovery from alcoholism.

Instead of stemming from modern social and psychological theories, this example comes directly from the history of a specific Native people that faced severe cultural and psychological attacks and successfully met those challenges. By gaining a perspective of how the late 18th/early 19th century Iroquois remade their collective culture and stemmed their individual dysfunctional, a model for recovery for contemporary Native people is provided.

Chapter 7 documents the social disruption that confronted the Iroquois after they were defeated during the American Revolution and after hordes of White immigrants streamed into their territory in the decades that followed. During this period, the Iroquois, who had historically dominated Western New York, were subjected to profound political, economic, and social reversals that left them weak and demoralized. Those were dark and hard days for the Iroquois and it appeared that they were doomed to imminent extinction as a cultural entity.

Chapter 8 deals with Handsome Lake, an alcoholic Iroquois who in the late 18th century appeared close to death, but recovered from his alcoholism, emerged as a powerful leader, and developed a strategy by which Iroquois society was restored to good health while dysfunctional many individuals were able to recover. This method involved (1) a restructuring of Iroquois culture to better respond to current conditions, (2) a re-embrace of Iroquois culture, and (3) individual Iroquois overcoming their dysfunction through their own efforts and through a cultural revival. Largely as a result of Handsome Lake's efforts, the Iroquois were able to regroup and today they survive as a powerful and respected Native people. The main goal of this book is to update the lessons of Handsome Lake and present them to the modern world in useable format (that I call "The Path of Handsome Lake"). This approach provides an alternative to various mainstream strategies of recovery because it is culturally sensitive and deals with the hurtful impacts of cultural decline and how the resulting anxiety can trigger alcoholic drinking.

While Chapter 8 deals with a method of recovery that stems from the example and teachings of Handsome Lake, Chapter 9 provides a means of implementing that program. In specific, it offers what is called "The Landmarks of the Path." Both chapters, however, emphasize that recovery benefits from dealing with both (1) the vitality of culture and (2) the needs of the individual and (3) that culture provides a buffer against the anxieties that can lead to dysfunction.

While Chapters 8 and 9 provide general and theoretic discussions, Chapters 10 and 11 demonstrate how they can be applied within a variety of contexts. Chapter 10 deals with professional therapy and intervention while Chapter 11 is concerned with self-help activities. Each chapter discusses how to apply the Handsome Lake method in both (1) individual and group therapy and (2) in circumstances where it is the primary method of treatment versus situations where it is applied in a supplemental fashion.

This cluster of chapters provides useful templates that can be used for those seeking to embrace the Handsome Lake method as a tool of recovery.

CHAPTER 7

HANDSOME LAKE, PERSONAL RECOVERY, AND THE MODERN WORLD

Handsome Lake was a 18th /19th Iroquois leader who fell into the abyss of seemingly incurable alcoholism. Rebounding with a remarkable and unexpected recovery, he emerged as a visionary and as a religious leader for his people. Working tirelessly for the last 15 years of his life, Handsome Lake advocated strategies that brought the Iroquois back from the brink of cultural disintegration and extinction. His recipe for stemming the tide of social and personal decay included (1) a cultural rebirth coupled with (2) personal recovery from alcoholism and dysfunctional behaviors, and (3) sincerely seeking atonement for past misdeeds. By championing both a personal and a cultural renaissance and by pointing to profound linkages between the two, Handsome Lake's example and the strategies he advocated were able to stem the tide of cultural decline among the Iroquois and lead to a cultural renaissance. Today, the Iroquois survive as a vital culture, due in no small part to Handsome Lake's influence and efforts.

From a terror management perspective, it can be argued that traumatic changes in the late 18th century rendered the traditional configuration of Iroquois culture passé and counterproductive. As a result, people experienced profound anxiety, which resulted in dysfunctional behavior. Handsome Lake, however, was able to restructure Iroquois life around a new and

---

The Path of Handsome Lake: A Model of Recovery for Native People, pages 101–115

more appropriate configuration. When this happened, people again came to believe in the permanence of their culture and regained their faith in the future of the Iroquois way of life. This transformation provided comfort to people whom, without this reassurance, would have continued to face profound anxiety. Because Handsome Lake stabilized Iroquois culture, he reduced the stress and anxiety people faced and, as a result, he helped reverse the downward spiral that had been triggered by unmitigated anxiety and the dysfunctional behavior associated with it. These events can be modeled by terror management theory.

Although Handsome Lake directed his efforts towards his own people (the Iroquois), the lessons he taught are relevant to other Native societies who seek to mitigate the profound pressures of stress and change that are often associated with the colonial era, White contact and the resulting disruptions that often accompany such events. Due to these parallels, the example of Handsome Lake and his teachings can be used to develop a program by which various Native people can recover from alcoholism through, cultural rebuilding, abstinence, penance, and developing a respect for a traditional heritage. In this chapter, Handsome Lake and his legacy of cultural rebirth and recovery are presented as historical fact and analyzed, as appropriate, via terror management theory and other concepts that were discussed. In addition, parallels are drawn between what Handsome Lake experienced and advocated and the thought of other contemporary Native people who have faced similar obstacles, threats, and exhibited parallel responses. In later chapters, the Handsome Lake approach is operationalized for use by alcohol abuse counselors and within a self-help context.

IROQUOIS DECLINE AND ITS PARALLELS

The story of Handsome Lake is a saga of social disarray accompanied by rampant alcoholism, on the one hand, and a celebration of the return to personal sobriety coupled with cultural rebirth, on the other. By examining these two different aspects of Handsome Lake and the example he provides, it becomes possible to make some useful observations as they relate to alcoholism among Native American people and, perhaps, to others who are cut off from their cultural roots.

The story takes place during the late 18th/early 19th century, a time when Iroquois society had suffered grievously due to defeat, disease, cultural disruption, social change, and economic reversals. Due to the evolving situation of the late 18th century, the Iroquois were exposed to unmitigated sorrow as the configuration of Iroquois society was unable to cope with contemporary events in any meaningful and constructive way. As discussed above, terror management theory argues that people embrace their culture because it offers permanence and stability in a world of stress and anxiety. When the culture is under profound stress, however, it ceases to adequately mitigate individual fears and stresses and, as a result, people find themselves subjected to unbuffered anxieties. The result of this situation among the Iroquois was the usual pattern of counterproductive and dysfunctional behavior associated with profound and unmitigated anxieties. In specific, alcoholism ran rampant.

All of this is familiar to those who have examined the dysfunctional responses that so often occur when Native cultures face rapid and unmitigated changes brought on by powerful outside forces beyond their control. And as Salzman (2001) has demonstrated, terror management theory is useful when analyzing such responses.

As we saw in the last chapter, rapid and unmitigated social change during the late 18th century undercut Iroquois society and created a situation where Iroquois men (as one example) could not be successful if they lived in accordance with their traditional roles of hunter and warrior (that Iroquois culture revered and honored). The failure of the old ways triggered widespread sorrow and alienation, which led, in turn, to dysfunctional "escapist" behavior, typified in many cases by alcoholism and a general breakdown of Iroquois society. These responses, tended to create a vicious circle in which people, already demoralized and dysfunctional, became even more vulnerable because their own actions made the situations faced even more toxic. Under these conditions, the future of the Iroquois looked bleak and their survival, as a cultural entity, was in serious question.

While the history of the Iroquois is well documented and goes back hundreds of years, the responses of these people are not unique. Parallel impacts have been observed upon a wide variety of Native people who have been subjected to unprecedented and unmitigated stress. Salzman (2001), for example, has analyzed the Native Hawaiians and Harrison (1996) and Gilgen (1996) have examined the Maori of New Zealand in terms of cultural stress and its impact upon dysfunctional behavior.

The legacies of these hurtful impacts continue to be widespread. The writing of Harold Napoleon, a contemporary Yup'ik Eskimo who, like Handsome Lake, is a recovering alcoholic, provides a recent and particularly well-respected example of stress and dysfunction triggered by social disruption. And like Handsome Lake, Harold Napoleon clearly links the decline of his people (and the resulting tendencies towards alcoholism) to the impacts of White contact. He observes:

> When the first White men arrived.... the people did not immediately abandon their old ways. It is an historical fact that they resisted Russian efforts to

> colonize them.... They were not impressed by the White men, even though they quickly adopted their technology and goods (Napoleon, 1996).

Like the situation of the Iroquois many years before, after a period of successful competition and cultural stability, White contact lead to a profound cultural crisis with which the Yup'ik were unable to cope. While the stress facing the Iroquois was caused by military defeat and the rapid invasion of outsiders with superior technology, the Yup'ik were inflicted with massive epidemics of diseases associated with White contact:

> The changes were brought about as a result of the introductions of diseases that had been born in the slums of Europe during the dark and middle ages, diseases carried by the traders, the whalers, and the missionaries. To these diseases, the Yup'ik and other Native tribes had no immunity and to these [diseases] they would lose up to 60% of their people. As a result of epidemics, the Yup'ik world would go upside down; it would end (Napoleon, 1996).

These epidemics, which occurred from time to time, culminated in 1900 with a scourge of influenza known as the "Great Death." These epidemics not only killed approximately 60% of the population, they exerted a profound negative impact upon the survivors:

> Out of the suffering, confusion, desperation, heartbreak, and trauma was born a new generation of Yup'ik people. They were born into shock. They woke to a world in shambles, many of their beliefs strewn around them, dead (Napoleon, 1996).

Napoleon, furthermore, describes the plight of these people in ways that closely resembles the empty self, anomie and the social separation syndrome discussed above:

> The world the survivors woke to was without anchor. The *andalkug* [medicine men], their medicines, and their beliefs had all passed away overnight. They woke up to shock, listless, confused, bewildered, heartbroken, and afraid. Like soldiers on an especially gruesome battlefield, they were shell shocked...Famine, starvation and disease resulting from the epedimic continued to plague them through the 1950s and many more perished. These were the people whom the missionaries would call wretched, lazy, even listless. Gone were the people who Nelson so admired. The long night of suffering had begun for the survivors of the Great Death and their descendants (Napoleon, 1996).

Thus, the situation that Handsome Lake faced in the late 18th and early 19th centuries have their clear parallels among other Native peoples, including those from Alaska. Rapid change, profound stress and resulting defeat, caused by White contact exerted an unrelenting negative impact upon Native people. These people and their societies were completely unequipped to deal with the trauma and the rapid change that they faced.

STRESS AND DYSFUNCTION

The Iroquois of the late 18th century had clearly lost their cultural balance and their spiritual grounding. Here were people facing profound challenges, competitors, and obstacles. Under these circumstances, the Iroquois needed thoughtful, reasoned, and sober solutions to the problems they faced. Their behavior, in general, can be viewed as the total opposite. Society broke down and many individuals slipped into a dysfunctional state. This chaotic situation resulted in further cultural decay/decline, a situation that triggered even more dysfunctional behavior among those who remained. These counterproductive responses, building on each other, made their condition even worse.

The hurtful experiences the Iroquois endured triggered widespread alcoholism and sundry other dysfunctions. Thus, profound cultural and personal trauma led to alienation and depression, which, in turn, became the catalyst for escapist behaviors such as alcoholism. Once these dysfunctions took hold, furthermore, they developed a momentum of their own. And this tide of dysfunction further undercut the Iroquois nation/culture as well as individual members of Iroquois society.

The Yup'ik suffered in a similar way, although the Great Death, brought on by diseases associated with White contact, triggered their decline. As in the Iroquois example, the actual event that caused the trauma (the influenza epidemic) proved to be the tip of the iceberg. Unmitigated change, triggered by misfortune, led to a relentless and ongoing undercutting of the remaining cultural traditions of both the Iroquois and the Yup'ik people. As time went on, new laws (regulating hunting and fishing rights, etc.) were passed that further denied the Yup'ik the right to follow their traditional way of life. According to Napoleon, this led to what he calls "an analomy":

> As their physical lives have improved, the quality of their lives has deteriorated ... Since the 1960s there has been a dramatic rise in alcohol abuse, alcoholism, and associated violent behaviors, which have upset family and village life and resulted in physical and psychological injury, death, and imprisonment. Something self-destructive, violent, frustrated, and angry had been set loose from within Alaska Native people. And it is the young that are dying, going to prison, and maiming themselves. Their families, their friends, their villages say they cannot understand why. Every suicide leaves a stunned family and village. Every violent crime and every alcohol related death elicits the

> same reaction. The alcohol-related nightmare has now become an epidemic (Napeleon, 1996).

Not only that, the cause of dysfunction seems to be caused more by anomie, the social separation syndrome, and the empty soul than anything else:

> One thing we do know-the primary cause of the epidemic is not physical depravation. Native people have never had it so good in terms of food, clothing, and shelter (Napoleon, 1996).

These patterns can collectively be analyzed with reference to terror management theory. Massive social change caused cultural disruptions that led to anxiety because people's cultural heritage was being stripped from them.

The basic point to be made is that the Yup'ik, as discussed by Napoleon, experienced a pattern of cultural and spiritual decline that almost completely duplicates the situation experienced by the Iroquois over 200 years ago. Apparently, profound and unmitigated cultural stress leads to a breakdown of society that can leave people vulnerable to a wide range of dysfunctional behaviors, including alcoholism. And, as we have seen, versions of the terror management model that focus upon anxiety caused by cultural stress provide a useful method of analysis.

POSTTRAUMATIC STRESS DISORDER?

While I have, for the most part, employed theories and methods from the social sciences (although the empty soul model stems from psychology) that have been synthesized with terror management theory, Napoleon has developed another means or metaphor of analysis. Writing in an era when many of us have dealt with dysfunctional Vietnam veterans (many of whom suffer from alcoholism), the concept of posttraumatic stress disorder has become well known. People so afflicted have endured past experiences that were so horrific and grievous that the memories of them were repressed and, as a result, these issues were not dealt with in healthy and therapeutic ways. As a result of pushing their pain "under the rug," the tension and pain, once created, is never released or mitigated. As a result, over the years pain and anxiety continues to undermine the individual. The result of this pattern of denial and repression is often dysfunctional behavior. The tendency for such people to self-medicate via alcohol abuse is commonplace.

According to Napoleon, posttraumatic stress disorder is not merely experienced by soldiers who have witnessed terribly traumatic battles; anyone facing an unbearable experience is vulnerable. Thus, the kinds of social and cultural destruction and events such as the Great Death are able to trigger posttraumatic stress disorder even if they are experienced far from any battlefield. Explaining dysfunctional Native responses, such as alcoholism, with reference to posttraumatic stress disorder provides a model of how rampant alcoholism and dysfunctional behavior among Native people can be fueled by horrific events from the past. Not merely is the theory useful when explaining the behavior of the contemporary Yup'ik, Posttraumatic Stress Disorder can be used to examine the dysfunctional behavior (including alcoholism) of the Iroquois during the late 18th and early 19th centuries. Although posttraumatic stress disorder is more focused than other theories employed in this book, most people in our culture are familiar with posttraumatic stress disorder and understand what it means. As a result, it can serve a particularly useful function when dealing with alcoholics and their loved ones. It can be useful both in therapy and within a self-help context.

Terror management theory, however, is a more general perspective that explores how social change can disrupt cultures to the degree that they no longer provide mitigation from the anxieties of life. As such, while I do not challenge Napoleon's analysis and his use of posttraumatic stress disorder as a model of analysis, it is useful to observe that terror management theory provides a broader perspective within which his interpretation can be nested.

HANDSOME LAKE

Returning to the historic record of the Iroquois, after the American Revolution, Iroquois culture continued to decline in a manner that can be described with reference to posttraumatic stress disorder and terror management theory (among other models). Within the environment of defeat and despair that permeated Iroquois life in the late 18th century, Handsome Lake, a once respected member of Iroquois society, had fallen into the abyss of ungoverned alcoholism. Out of control and seriously ill, it appeared that his productive life was over. By the spring of 1799, his drinking and its negative impacts had grown steadily worse:

> Handsome Lake ... was bedridden, reputedly ... as a consequence of prolonged alcoholic access (Wallace, 1978).

In the June of that year:

> Handsome Lake collapsed ... in the presence of his daughter...; he appeared to have died, but actually he was in a trance state and was experiencing the

first of a series of visions in which messengers of the Creator instructed him in his own and his people's religious obligations (Wallace, 1978).

After his recuperation from apparent death, Handsome Lake emerged as physically and spiritually a new man, and as a leader who dedicated himself both to sobriety and to the cultural rebirth of Iroquois society.

Eventually Handsome Lake's visions (and his insights regarding them), were synthesized into an innovative religion that provided (1) a new way of perceiving life and (2) a proactive strategy by which the Iroquois (as a culture and as specific individuals) could stem their decline.

On the one hand, Handsome Lake encouraged his people to embrace their cultural traditions. The events of the late 18th and early 19th century had devastated the Iroquois leaving their culture in a state of complete disarray. In the midst of this chaos, Handsome Lake forcefully championed his culture and its traditions, pointing to their worth and their value to the Iroquois people.

This embrace of Iroquois culture, however, was not merely envisioned as paying homage to the past. Handsome Lake clearly recognized that, if Iroquois society was to be revitalized, it needed to be transformed in order to mesh with the realities of contemporary life. The victories of the United States during the American Revolution had created a new country and one where many settlers wanted to settle in lands that had traditionally been controlled by the Iroquois. As a result, the Iroquois faced competition that they had never previously experienced. And their historic past provides few clues regarding how to proceed. And the skills of the past were of little value in the new world that was emerging. Even worse, the configuration of traditional Iroquois militated against the Iroquois competing successfully; recall, for example, that the established sex roles of the Iroquois were out of sync with the emerging socio-economic realities of the times.

Iroquois men, for example, were not well equipped to meet this challenge since they had long been hunters and warriors, vocations that were rendered passé. And since they viewed farming to be an unmanly profession, men had few productive and socially acceptable opportunities left open to them. As White people migrated to Iroquois territory, furthermore, new methods of farming (that included men performing their share of the work) began to outstrip Iroquois farming methods and, thereby, undercut the Native economy and culture. Under these trying circumstances, Handsome Lake encouraged Iroquois men to take up farming, view it as an appropriate vocation, and to perceive it as a suitable vocation, not a source of shame or embarrassment. Handsome Lake's half brother and collaborator, for example, came to be known as "Corn Planter," a name that underscored that men, as well was women, could legitimately adopt the farming profession.

In his discussions of anomie, Robert Merton has pointed to "innovation" as one possible response to an environment in which people cannot achieve their goals in socially acceptable ways. When the "innovation" stage is observed, socially acceptable goals (such as providing for one's family) are achieved in a socially unacceptable manner (such as men farming). That is, in essence, what Handsome Lake urged. Farming had long been viewed as a shameful and inappropriate activity for men, but as conditions changed, men found they could not fruitfully pursue traditional male professions. Under these conditions, families suffered. Handsome Lake, in response, created an environment where men could innovate by following a lucrative and productive vocations, even though it had long been stigmatized as unmanly and shameful when practiced by men.

It must be noted, however, that Merton's model of innovation was created within a relatively stable culture and, therefore, he tends to depict innovation as an illegitimate means of achieving success (he often equates it with criminal behavior). Among the Iroquois in an era of massive economic and social change, in contrast, mainstream, "respectable" people were asked to follow what had long been an unacceptable path in order to achieve socially acceptable goals. In doing so, embracing this innovation provided respectable individuals (and Iroquois society as a collective entity) with better opportunities for success and survival. In the process, these strategies were able to help preserve Iroquois society and provide individuals with a viable profession and the sense of self worth that derives from it. As a result, dysfunctional behaviors, such as alcoholic drinking, declined.

In the case of Handsome Lake, he took illegitimate behaviors (men farming, as a prime example) and transformed them into legitimate strategies for individuals and for society. As a result of the innovations that Handsome Lake championed, Iroquois society was in a better position to respond to the socio-economic circumstances it faced in the early 19th century. It is easy to see the value of Handsome Lake's solution; instead of allowing his people to continue to decline by pathetically clinging to the old ways, Handsome Lake chose an innovative alternative that led to a positive cultural rebirth and individual success. And when this occurred, dysfunctional behaviors declined.

While Handsome Lake acknowledged the need for change and went on to encourage the Iroquois to adjust themselves, their culture, and sex roles in order to meet the realities of a changing world, he simultaneously sought to strengthen Iroquois culture and society.

He strongly argued for a return to morality and he called for an end to the dysfunctional patterns of behavior that inflicted so many Iroquois. He founded a religion that (while borrowing somewhat from the Christian tradition) bolstered the essence of traditional Iroquois society in positive ways that meshed with the needs of the times. Thus, Handsome Lake promoted changes in Iroquois culture that preserved its essence. Anthropologists acknowledge that the recommendations Handsome Lake championed are largely responsible for the Iroquois' dramatic return to health as a vital cultural entity that survives to this day.

Coupled with the embrace of a traditional underpinning of society (albeit adjusted to circumstance) was Handsome Lake's insistence that people cease, on an individual basis, to pursue activities that were counterproductive, personally, and disruptive, socially. Drinking alcoholic beverages was high on the list of banned behaviors.[1] Being an alcoholic himself, Handsome Lake was quite aware of the dangers of alcohol and he strongly discouraged the use of alcoholic beverages. Although Handsome Lake's position is more extreme than that of Alcoholics Anonymous (since Alcoholics Anonymous sees no reason for successful social drinkers to abstain), this response seems to be closely akin to the American temperance movement that was taking root during his era and which ultimately flowered into the prohibition movement that ultimately succeeded in the ban of alcoholic beverages in the United States. In addition, Mormonism (another highly successful religion that was formed at approximately the same time and in the same general location as that of Handsome Lake)[2] placed a similar ban on alcoholic beverages. Apparently both White and Native American reformers from Western New York in the early 19th century were aware of the devastating impact of alcohol on both individuals and society; as a result, both urged tight controls.

Having embraced and updated the cultural traditions of the Iroquois people and having quit drinking alcoholic beverages (and other counterproductive activities), Handsome Lake insisted that people acknowledge the sins they had committed and the errors of their earlier life. This admission was to be followed by refraining from performing similar misdeeds in the future.

Largely through the personal example and the message of Handsome Lake, the Iroquois people were able to stem a profound cultural decline and to re-emerge as a vital cultural entity. And many Iroquois individuals who had suffered from alcoholic behavior were able to enjoy what, today, is called "recovery" (reclaiming their lives through spiritual growth coupled with abstinence).

This, in a nutshell, is the history of the heritage and legacy of Handsome Lake. His story is recorded in various places[3] and the reader is encouraged to consult both primary and secondary sources for more details about his life, his bout with alcoholism, the accomplishments after his recovery, and the revitalization of Iroquois society.

SIMILAR PRESSURES, SIMILAR SOLUTIONS

As discussed above, although separated by 200 years and thousands of miles, the situations and dysfunctional responses of Handsome Lake's Iroquois and Napoleon's Yup'ik are surprisingly parallel. Not only that, the recommendations poised by Handsome Lake and Harold Napoleon are almost identical, although Napoleon tends to focus upon therapeutic strategies suggested by Posttraumatic Stress Disorder and the tactics of modern social work/psychological counseling that were not available in the early 19th century when Handsome Lake worked.

Like Handsome Lake, Napoleon seeks to rebuild the culture by (1) restoring the intimacy between people and (2) the viability of the culture. Focusing upon Posttraumatic Stress Disorder, Napoleon urges all members of Native society to begin a dialogue that will result in mutual understanding and a sharing of traditions. From a terror management perspective, these activities are exactly what are needed to rebuild the culture in ways that will preserve it for future generations. By doing so, the trauma associated with continued and permanent cultural disintegration will be mitigated and the anxiety that would otherwise exist can be reduced.

Napoleon suggests that many hurtful experiences and been repressed to the degree that they have not been reconciled and, therefore, they continue to covertly impact people in negative ways. He suggests:

> We ... have to spend some time just talking to... [the elders]. We would have them truthfully tell their life stories, leaving nothing out. The very oldest are the most important because they will be able to tell their remembrances of the whole village ... They must tell why they gave everything up, why they discarded the old ways, the old beliefs, whcy thc allowed the culture to die.... They are the ones who felt the full brunt of the fatal wounding of their world (Napoleon, 1996).

Napoleon then emphasizes that this process of the elders relating the history of a tragic era should be followed by later generations baring their souls and assessing the hurts they have had to endure.

Napoleon believes the need for this dialogue results from the fact that people have become alienated from each another. He observes:

> We must do this because we don't know each other anymore; we have become like strangers to each other The old do not know or understand the young, and the young do not know or understand the old. Parents do not know their children, and the children do not know their parents. As a result.... a gulf has grown between those who love and care for each other the most (Napoleon, 1996).

And paralleling Handsome Lake, Napoleon, besides seeking internal harmony among people, also advocates transforming the culture in positive and constructive ways that will allow people to successful meet the challenges of the future. He recommends:

> It is time to bury the old culture, mourn those who died with it, mourn those who survived it. It is time we buried our many dead who have died in this long night of our suffering, then go forward, lost no more. We have been wandering in a daze for the last 100 years, rocked by a succession of traumatic changes and inundations. Now we have to stop, look at ourselves, and....press on....free of the past the haunted and disabled us, free of the ghosts that haunted our hearts, free to become what we were intended to be (Napoleon, 1996).

Note how similar Napoleon's recommendations are to those that were advanced by Handsome Lake 200 years before. In both cases, people who had been battered by circumstance needed to transform their lives in positive ways, on the one hand, and to reconfiguring their traditions, on the other. In both cases, many of the old ways were no longer appropriate and had to be rethought and reconfigured to meet the challenges of the times. At the same time, however, the heritage and traditions of the past needed to be preserved and embraced. Their preservation led to a stability that was able to mitigate the anxiety of living in a rapidly evolving world.

CONCLUSION

Handsome Lake, responding to cultural and economic stress facing his people 200 years ago, forged a sophisticated strategy of cultural renewal by which people could relieve the pain of cultural decline while simultaneously dealing with their own dysfunction in forceful and concrete ways. Largely through Handsome Lake's efforts, the Iroquois people were able to stem their dysfunctional response to the pressures they faced and embark on a powerful cultural renaissance. The three-prong approach that Handsome Lake recommended includes (1) a re-embrace of the people's cultural traditions, (2) an adjustment of the culture so that it could successfully cope with the contemporary situation that people faced, and (3) overcoming dysfunctional patterns of behavior (such as alcoholic drinking) coupled with a penance for past misdeeds.

A variety of theories can be used to analyze the plight of Handsome Lake's Iroquois and the solutions to the crisis that he forged. In specific, the concepts of the empty soul, anomie, social separation syndrome, and posttraumatic stress disorder call all are employed. Viewed as complementary analytic devices, not as theories in competition with one another, these models provide a broad perspective of the challenges facing 19th century

Iroquois and contemporary groups, such as the Yup'ik as discussed by Harold Napoleon. Terror management theory provides an elegant and robust means of synthesizing these various theories.

While Handsome Lake lived 200 years ago and while his recommendations were aimed at aiding only his people (the Iroquois), the strategies he forged can be generalized in order to help other Native people deal with the stress of rampant and disruptive change and the profound assaults that Native cultures so often must endure. The universal nature of the Handsome Lake approach is underscored by the fact that contemporary Native observers, such as Harold Napoleon, have independently poised an almost identical analysis of the challenges facing other Native people facing similar situations and they have proposed almost identical solutions to such challenges.

Using terror management theory as an analytic diverse, the following process (Table 7.1) can be discerned.

Table 7.1. Cultural Revitalization and Terror Management

	Handsome Lake	*Discussion*
Cultural Crisis	Iroquois in disarray due to impacts of White contact. Complete disintegration of Iroquois culture seems inevitable	White contact triggers profound stress
Terror Management	Terror management theory emphasizes that people look to their culture for permanence in order to mitigate anxieties	Cultures under attack and whose survival is in serious question cannot mitigate anxiety
Cultural Response	Handsome Lake responded by restoring Iroquois traditions and restructuring Iroquois culture around the socio/political/economic realities of his era.	Some cultures under stress do not respond in a productive way and decline. When cultures respond in a productive way, they can return to good health.
Terror Mitigation	Once Iroquois culture was brought in line with the circumstances that were faced, it rebounded. This revitalization reduced anxieties by giving people faith that Iroquois culture was permanent and would live on after them.	Restored to good health, the culture can provide comfort by mitigating the anxieties of life.
Synthesis	Native cultures throughout the world have been shattered due to the impact of White contact and increased anxieties because its permanence was in question. When cultures regroup, however, anxiety can be reduced because a sense of permanence returns. Terror management theory models how a growth of anxiety is correlated decline while stable and healthy cultures provide comfort. Since dysfunctional behavior (such as alcoholic drinking) is often correlated with anxiety, restoring the culture can reduce dysfunction.	

Handsome Lake is a program that was profoundly successful and is a historical fact of Native people. This example can be viewed in ways that transcend the Iroquois and provide a means for other Native people to overcome the stresses they face and do so in culturally relevant ways.

The fact that Handsome was, himself, (1) a recovering alcoholic and (2) encouraged people to recover from alcohol abuse while atoning for past misdeeds though (3) advocated practicing a program of cultural renewal, his legacy has much to contribute to other Native people seeking recovery from alcoholism and to alcohol abuse counselors who seek to help clients pursue that quest.

NOTES

1. Others include promiscuous sexual behavior and the practice of witchcraft that was also disruptive to society and (according to Iroquois beliefs) injurious to specific people.
2. Handsome Lake was born in Avon, New York and promoted his anti-drinking position in the early 19th century. He died in 1815 and the Long House religion that is based on his teachings began to flower in its present form around 1830. The Mormon religion first became an organized force in the 1830s (Joseph Smith, founder of the religion, reports he had a vision from God around 1820 and that in 1827 an angel helps him locate some manuscripts that, after he translated them, became sacred Mormon texts. The religion was formally established in April 1830). This preliminary work of Joseph Smith in establishing the Mormon religion took place in and around Palmyra, New York, the general area of (and within easy reach of) Handsome Lake's birthplace.
3. Important primary sources include A. F. C. Wallace (editor) "Holliday Jackson's Journal to the Seneca Indians," Thomas S. Abler (editor) *Chainbreaker: The Revolutionary War Memoirs of Govern Blacksnake*, and Arthur C. Parker (editor) *The Code of Handsome Lake.*

   The most extensive (and respected) secondary work is A. F. C. Wallace's *The Death and Rebirth of the Seneca.* William Fenton and Elisabeth Tooker's "On the Development of the Handsome Lake Religion" is also insightful. It should be noted that there is an extensive research tradition on Handsome Lake and this is only a suggestive sampling. For those in the counseling profession, however, it is probably adequate.

REFERENCES

Gilgen, M. (1996). A response to Harold Napoleon's paper. In H. Napoleon (Ed.), *Yunarag: The way of being human.* Fairbanks, AL: Alaska Native Knowledge Network.

Harrison, B. (1996). Response to "yuyaraq." In H. Napoleon(Ed.), *Yunarag: The way of being human*(pp. 57–61). Fairbanks, AL: Alaska Native Knowledge Network.

Napoleon, H. (1996). *Yunarag: The way of being human* (pp. 9–28). Fairbanks, AL: Alaska Native Knowledge Network.

Salzman, M.B. (2001). Cultural trauma and recovery: Perspectives from terror management theory. *Trauma, Violence, and Abuse*, 2, 172–191.

CHAPTER 8

HANDSOME LAKE AND MODEL OF RECOVERY

As discussed above, Handsome Lake was an 18th/19th century Iroquois leader who fell into an abyss of seemingly incurable alcoholism. After a remarkable and unexpected recovery, he emerged as the visionary who provided the tools by which the Iroquois people were able to reverse their decline and reemerge as a vital people. In doing so, Handsome Lake showcased strategies for fostering a cultural rebirth and a revitalization of Native societies in a way that provides individual people with the means of (1) overcoming dysfunctional behaviors such as alcoholism while (2) atoning for past misdeeds.

The program of recovery demonstrated by Handsome Lake closely reflects the strategies of anxiety reduction that are currently being advocated by contemporary terror management theory. Handsome Lake's proposals also parallel the methods that other Native people who have struggled to revitalize their cultures and overcome the stresses and assaults inflicted by rapid and unexpected contact with the outside world. Thus, the proposals and tactics developed by Handsome Lake effectively jive with modern psychological theories that seek to counter the negative impacts of stress.

By advocating the rebuilding of Native cultures while simultaneously reclaiming the lives of individuals who had sunk into dysfunction, Handsome Lake helped stem the tide of cultural decay among the Iroquois. In

The Path of Handsome Lake: A Model of Recovery for Native People, pages 117–132

doing so, he also facilitated a viable program of recovery for members of Native cultures who suffer from alcoholism and other forms of dysfunctional behavior. As a result of this important role, Handsome Lake and his vision continue to have significance today.

Here, we will distill some of the essential ingredients of Handsome Lake's strategy for recovery and we will codify them into a format that is appropriate for contemporary life. Although Handsome Lake did not actually create the synthesis presented here, this reformulation clearly stems from his vision and example and, therefore, it will be called "The Path of Handsome Lake."

THE PATH OF HANDSOME LAKE

Having already provided an historic overview of the life of Handsome Lake and his contributions, distilling his vision and achievements into a useable set of principles becomes the central concern. In doing so, a strategy that is appropriate for use by alcohol counselors and within a self-help context is presented. Such a task is accomplished by synthesizing Handsome Lake's suggestions and insights into what I will call the "Path of Handsome Lake." Although the words themselves are not precisely those of Handsome Lake, the basic components of his message clearly reflect his vision. Thus, the Path (as discussed here) can be viewed as a suggested program of cultural and individual recovery that stems from the life and work of one of the most revered and influential Native American reformers and visionaries.

This Path consists of 6 components that combine cultural health with individual well-being. It stresses the fact that combining a cultural focus with the needs of the individual best attacks the ravages of alcoholism. Not only were Handsome Lake's methods effective among the 19th century Iroquois, they provide an intuitive and independently invented means of combating the trauma of profound cultural change. As a result, the Path provides a positive and constructive technique for dealing with the negative impacts experienced by Native people who are subjected to the stresses caused by rapid contact with the outside world.

The six components suggested by the "Path of Handsome Lake" that are discussed here, include: *(1) Embrace tradition, (2) Transform your traditions and keep them strong, (3) Stop Alcohol Abuse and Cultural Apathy, (4) Admit to errors made, (5) Do not repeat errors of the past, and (6) Heritage and recovery are linked.*

This course of action (like Alcoholics Anonymous' 12 Step Program) provides a method that constantly reminds people of appropriate strategies they can follow to achieve sobriety. It transcends the 12 Step Program, however, by providing a means of strengthening and embracing the cultural heritage. And like the 12 Step Program, different people can phase in various parts of the program at their own pace and in their own way.

Before discussing the Path in a holistic and synergistic manner, each component will be briefly outlined.

Embrace Tradition

"I possess a culture and a tradition. Embracing them is sacred, meaningful, and joyful."

As indicated above, due to outside contact, social change, and changing environments the cultures of many Native people are under profound and unrelenting attack. In addition, many Native people have been forced to abandon their cultures and their heritage. During the boarding school era in the United States, for example, the educational system serving Native students made strong efforts to strip Native people of their cultural heritage. Alaska Athabascan, Luke Titus, as a typical example, recalls how when he first arrived at boarding school all newcomers were forced to put their handmade Native clothes and artifacts into a pile and watch them being burned (personal communication). It was commonplace for Native children to have their mouths washed out with soap if the spoke their Native tongues. Every effort was made to undercut the Native culture and totally acculturate the Natives to the modern, mainstream, White world.

On other occasions, cultures were profoundly disrupted by the intrusion of hurtful outside influences (such as diseases) into Native territory. And due to a changing socio-economic environment, old ways of life have often been rendered passé. As a result, for a number of reasons (often working in tandem with each other), many Natives cultures suffered grievously as a result of White contact and the process of colonialization.[1]

Due to this history of contact, traditional cultures have often become weakened. In addition, Native people may be uncomfortable with their heritage and not adequately informed about it. Nevertheless, a people's culture is one of their major bulwarks that protects them against anxiety and the dysfunctional behavior that anxiety so often triggers. As a result, where Native cultures are severely weakened and/or where some individuals are alienated from their heritage, Native people may not have adequate access to the cultural tools and orientations that are needed in order to effectively combat their dysfunctional tendencies.

Due to this legacy, Native people need to acknowledge that they possess a positive cultural heritage that has strength, legitimacy, and the power to be meaningful and joyous. But, as we have observed, many Native people have a weak or incomplete grasp of their heritage. And many others have been taught to discount (if not actually despise) it. The process of regaining access to a heritage and a culture begins by recognizing its value and importance. Doing so is the first step in the Path of Handsome Lake.

Transform Your Tradition to Keep it Strong

"All cultural traditions change and all cultural traditions are under attack. I will strive to help my culture evolve and flourish."

As we have seen, Native cultures are often under attack and, over time, the circumstances within which these cultures function can change. As a result, as circumstances evolve, certain parts of a culture may no longer be appropriate or suitable for evolving conditions. In the case of the Iroquois, for example, we found the culture was unable to cope with changing times as long as people continued to act according to the "old ways." By adjusting Iroquois culture so that it meshed with the circumstances faced in the early 19th century, however, Handsome Lake was able to help the Iroquois respond in positive and productive ways. The culture was revitalized in the process; Handsome Lake clearly emphasized how a response to changing times could help Native culture to survive. By consciously forging new and appropriate solutions to the challenges that Iroquois society faced, he helped the Iroquois to rebound from a downward cycle; as a result, the dysfunction among its members decreased.

Native people experiencing massive social and economic contact/disruption need to cope with the challenge of profound, disruptive, and unexpected changes. When such issues are not adequately addressed, the culture can break down and the resulting cultural disintegration can trigger anxieties that play themselves out as dysfunctional behavior.

Cultures are more than the sum of their parts. They are collective solutions that have been forged of many interrelated components. Strong and well-functioning cultures provide comfort to people and provide relief from the anxieties that people face. In order to remain strong and vital, however, cultures often need to be adjusted to changing times and circumstances. All viable cultures go through this process of constant renewal.

Mainstream American culture, for example, has gone through profound transformations in the last hundred years (with the arrival of the automobile, electronic media, computers, urbanization, etc. If mainstream Americans attempted to live the way they did at the turn of the 20th century, life would be traumatic and full of anxiety. But American culture is a "going concern" and it has the ability to adapt. Many of us may lament this, that, or the other change that has occurred and certainly some people are uneasy or alienated by several of the trends that currently exist. Nevertheless, the culture goes on and it serves most people reasonable well. And by remaining vital and functioning (through the process of constantly reinventing itself), American culture has demonstrated an ability to reduce the anxieties people face and help them solve their problems.

Native cultures, likewise, need to adapt. By adjusting in appropriate ways, they, too, can maintain themselves if in the face of great change and pressure. Handsome Lake and the Iroquois demonstrated that Native people could transform their cultures while retaining their identity. Doing so provides a way for Native cultures to survive, adapt, and help their members to cope.

Stop Alcohol Abuse and Cultural Apathy

"I will break the cycle of personal and cultural decay by ceasing to abuse alcohol."

Cultural decay and personal dysfunctions often go hand in hand. Among Native people, recovery can be expected to be a dual process that involves cultural renewal coupled with positive, healthy, and functional personal choices. Handsome Lake clearly recognized this truth. He simultaneously urged people to strengthen their culture as he encouraged them to rebuild their lives by transcending their dysfunctional habits and counterproductive patterns of response.

Struggles towards recovery will often be ineffective when people lack the psychological ballast that a strong and vital culture can provide. As a result, Native people seeking recovery will often benefit from strengthening their cultural heritage and their relationship to it.

Simply possessing a strong cultural heritage, however, is not all that is needed to recover from alcoholism. Even though a strong culture is a basic tool of recovery, personal dedication and effort are also required. Although the culture can provide some of the tools that are needed, recovery is hard work and it must be pursued at a very personal level.

Even in situations where alcoholic drinking is, primarily, a symptom of anxiety and stress that has been triggered by cultural disarray and/or by individuals being out to touch with their society, dysfunctions have a way of becoming powerful forces in their own right. That must be attacked as separate problems regardless of what may have originally caused them.

Nonetheless, personal and cultural decay can be viewed as intertwined problems that need to be resolved in relation to one another. By keeping this fact in mind, the possibility of both cultural and personal renewal is enhanced.

Admit to Errors Made

"I recognize my past errors and I will remember them when choosing a more noble and fulfilling path."

In the process of sinking into dysfunctional behavior, it becomes easy for people to forget (or, perhaps, minimize) the impact of the decisions they personally make and how these decisions triggered dysfunctional behavior. Unfortunately, hurtful patterns of response, if unrecognized, tend to be repeated. There is an old proverb that says (in a paraphrase) that "if people do not know history they are destined to repeat it". What holds true for countries and civilizations can also be applied to individuals. Those who are not aware of the cause of their past failures and misdeeds are likely to make the same mistakes again and again. Such a realization provides a clear parallel with Alcoholics Anonymous and the 12 Step Program. A key strategy of the 12 Steps is for the recovering person to develop a conscious awareness of what triggered their alcoholic drinking and whatever lapses of judgment and morality that accompanied it.

The process of forging a nobler future path involves comparing and juxtaposing a brighter future with the ignoble failures and/or the misdeeds of the past. By centering upon what triggered past troubles, a more insightful personal vision of the future can result. And this vision can be used to help craft a course of action that leads towards a healthy and permanent sobriety.

Do Not Repeat Errors of the Past

"Having chosen a more noble and fulfilling path, I will strive to keep my errors in the past and correct errors and misjudgments as soon as they occur."

Just as the 12 Step Program centers upon living a good life coupled with sobriety, Handsome Lake was equally concerned with living a good and moral life. Because leading a noble existence can reduce anxiety by reducing regrets, doing so serves personal goals because by reducing anxiety, the tendency towards dysfunctional behavior will also decline. Thus, living a good life serves both altruistic and selfish goals.

Heritage and Recovery are Linked

"My heritage and my traditions give me a spirituality. By denying my heritage and my traditions, I am denying my own self and may become vulnerable to relapse. By embracing who I am, I can better succeed in recovery and in life."

This step is a final culmination of the Path. More than any other, it centers upon the linkages between heritage and recovery. Cultures are profoundly complex configurations of beliefs, attitudes, and values that mesh with and reinforce each other. As such, they directly impact personal character, strength, and vulnerability. Collectively, these cultural traits impact the person's spirituality.

This spirituality is key to the person's identity and the way in which people respond to circumstance. When people deny their culture, they ignore themselves. And when people deny who there are (and their needs), they can suffer from anxiety which, in turn, can trigger dysfunctional behavior.

This, in a nutshell, is a narrative description of the Path of Handsome Lake as it is presented here. Presented in graphic form, we find:

Table 8.1. The Path of Handsome Lake

	Step	*Analysis*
1. Embrace Tradition	The cultural tradition is embraced and its significance and value are acknowledged.	Culture provides relief from anxiety. Being connected with the culture, therefore, can reduce dysfunction related to anxiety.
2. Transform Tradition	Cultures often need to be reformed in order to continue to function appropriately. Thus, transforming cultures may be necessary if they are to reduce anxiety.	Due to changing conditions parts of culture can become passé. Adjustments, however, can restore the culture's ability to deal with crises and, thereby, reduce individual anxiety.
3. Stop Abuse/ Apathy	In order to recover from alcoholism, it is necessary to stop alcohol abuse and to quit being apathetic.	Even if triggered by forces beyond their control, abuse and apathy often develop a life of their own and must be dealt on an individual basis.
4. Admit Errors	Even if cultural stress triggers alcoholism, to recover it is important to focus upon past mistakes and admit to them.	Although admitting (and even realizing) errors may be difficult, doing so provides the insights that can help prevent future dysfunction.
5. Don't Repeat Errors	By admitting to past errors, it becomes easier to avoid repeating them. Consciously avoiding future errors is a vital component of recovery.	By becoming aware of past errors and what might have caused them, it becomes possible to avoid repeating them.
6. A Profound Link	The heritage of the culture and the recovery of the individual are often linked.	Due to the fact that the health of the individual is often linked to the strength of the culture, both need to be bolstered within programs of recovery aimed at Native people whose cultures are under attack.
Discussion	For Native people to recover from dysfunctional behavior, they often need to focus both (1) their culture and their relationship to it and (2) their own behavior and responsibility. Such a dual strategy provides a robust strategy of recovery.	

This strategy of recovery attempts to accomplish two separate goals simultaneously. First, it provides a way to deal with overarching issues that concern the culture and the individual's relationship to it. Secondly, this strategy is able he help people focus upon their own contribution to their dysfunction.

Steps One, Two, and Six center largely upon the culture and way individuals relate to the culture (or, in contrast, have difficulty doing so). As was observed above, for a number of historic reasons many Native people have trouble relating to their culture. When this is true, the culture cannot function to help relieve the anxieties that can trigger dysfunction. As a result, focusing on the culture and its role in mitigating anxiety can be of vital importance.

Steps Three, Four, and Five, in contrast, deal with individual people and how they and their actions may have contributed to their dysfunction. These activities have parallels in other strategies of recovery, such as the 12-step program, which focus upon the importance of acknowledging problems and attacking them on a personal level.

Combined, this program provides a multifaceted means of addressing dysfunctional behavior that is nested within the Native culture. Because Native cultures are often weakened and because people are often alienated from them, bolstering and strengthening this cultural heritage is a vital and much needed component of therapy.

THE PATH OF HANDSOME LAKE AND ALCOHOLICS ANONYMOUS

In many ways, the Path of Handsome Lake and the 12 Steps Program of Alcoholics Anonymous are parallel. Indeed, both of these strategies of recovery are in general agreement. Alcoholics Anonymous, however, does not deal, in meaningful ways, with key issues concerning the health of the culture and the ability of people to embrace it in a productive way that leads to a reduction of anxieties. Such issues, however are of profound importance when dealing with Natives seeking recovery. This gap within the Alcoholic Anonymous/12 Step Program seems to be the result of the fact that the Alcoholics Anonymous/12 Step Program was the product of relatively successful middle class White men who were firmly a part of the dominant culture of their era. These individuals, as a group, do not appear to have been victimized by the impact of rampant social/cultural change and disintegration. Thus, people suffering from profound cultural disruptions did not form Alcoholics Anonymous/the 12 Step Program. As a result, the strategies of recovery stemming from them do not dwell upon the specific issues concerning cultural decline and/or the pain faced by individuals who have become alienated from their culture, society, and traditions.

Table 8.2 discusses the Path of Handsome Lake in terms of the methods suggested by Alcoholics Anonymous/the 12 Step Program:

Table 8.2. The Path of Handsome Lake and Alcoholics Anonymous Compared

Path of Handsome Lake	*Discussion*	*Compared with AA/12 Steps*
1. ***Embrace tradition***: "I possess a culture and a tradition. Embracing them is sacred, meaningful, and joyful".	People often need to be reminded that they are members of social and cultural traditions that profoundly affect them.	AA does not overtly think in terms of specific cultural traditions, but does not rule it out.
2. ***Help keep traditions strong***: "All cultural traditions change and are under attack. I will strive to help my culture evolve and flourish".	Helps people to conceptualize that cultures may be under attack and that both individuals and the collective society should work as a team to strengthen cultural ties.	The founders of AA do not think in terms of cultural stress, the fact that cultures evolve, or the impact of this kind of social stress upon alcoholic behavior.
3. ***Stop alcohol/substance abuse***: " I will break the cycle of personal and cultural decay by ceasing to abuse alcohol".	Deal with both the individual and the cultural impacts of alcohol abuse is vital. Alcoholism is an individual disease with cultural causes and implications	AA embraces the disease concept and emphasized total abstinence. The impact of alcoholism upon others is recognized
4. ***Admit to errors made***: "I recognize my past errors and I will remember them when choosing a more noble and fulfilling path"	Under the influence of alcohol, many individuals act in shameful, careless, or hurtful ways. Acknowledge this potential and make amends is vital.	Steps 4 through 9 of the 12 steps of AA specifically deal with recognizing the errors of the past and atoning for them.
5. ***Do not repeat errors of the past:*** "Having chosen a more noble and fulfilling path, I will strive to keep my errors in the past" and correct them as soon as they occur.	Developing a pattern of appropriate and noble behavior is essential for both the health of the culture, the recovering individual, and the people with whom the recovering individual interacts.	Step 10 of the 12 steps of AA recommends that people maintain a vigilant guard against error and to immediately atone for errors when they do occur.
6. ***Heritage and recovery.*** "My heritage and my traditions give me a spirituality. By denying them, I deny my own self and may become vulnerable to relapse. By embracing, them, I can better succeed in recovery and in life.	The concept of anomie suggests that personal alienation and cultural decay can lead to alcoholic behavior. As a result, recovering people will be less prone to relapse if their culture is a powerful force that is able to provide them with support.	The founders of AA did not specifically deal with the impact of the larger culture upon the health of the individual recovering person.
Analysis	The Path of Handsome Lake and the methods of Alcoholics Anonymous dovetail. The Path of Handsome Lake, however, is better able to deal with cultural stress and the need for people to be attuned to their cultural traditions.	

Nonetheless, the program of Alcoholics Anonymous is not inherently alien to or at odds with the path that Handsome Lake. As a result, although Native Americans who are suffering from cultural stress can clearly benefit from Alcoholics Anonymous, they may need to devote supplemental attention to the fact that their cultures might be faced with profound attacks from pressures that are beyond their control.

In all likelihood, many Native people in recovery will participate within Alcoholics Anonymous. It is, after all, the dominant self help group serving alcoholics and many strategies of treatment are directly modeled after Alcoholics Anonymous and the 12 Step Program. As a result, any and all conflict between Alcoholics Anonymous and the Path of Handsome Lake are to be avoided.

Nonetheless, as we have seen, Native alcoholics typically face a number of issues regarding their culture that Alcoholics Anonymous is not poised to resolve. As a result, Native alcoholics often need, at minimum, a supplemental program of recovery that deals with these issues. That attention to cultural concerns is suggested and recommended here.

THE PATH AND TERROR MANAGEMENT

From a terror management perspective, we have seen that when people feel anxiety, they typically embrace their culture as the permanent and eternal entity in their lives that will survive after they are gone. They also tend to gain self-esteem by being members in good standing of their culture. As a result, the culture provides people with comfort and relief from anxieties that, if unmitigated, could trigger dysfunctional behavior.

As argued above, however, Alcoholics Anonymous, the classic strategy for recovery from alcoholism, is not equipped to deal with the struggles of people whose cultures are being subjected to profound stress. Alcoholics Anonymous, in contrast, was designed to help people who, as a result of alcoholic drinking, become alienated from their culture and from their loved ones. As a result, the Alcoholics Anonymous model typically depicts the culture as remaining robust and intact and that those seeking to recover merely need to rejoin it. Thus, the focus Alcoholics Anonymous is to help alcoholics to restructure their lives so they can return to the status of "members in good standing" within a vital culture and society.

Due to this laudable and legitimate focus, Alcoholics Anonymous has not developed ways that forcefully deal with the fact that many Native cultures are breaking down (or have broken down) to the point where Native alcoholics often do not have a stable and comfortable culture within which they can immerse themselves. Natives (in contrast to those identify primarily with the stable, mainstream culture) often face a situation where their culture has become so weakened that it can no longer serve as a stabilizing force that can nurture people and help them to mitigate their losses and anxieties. Indeed, the very weakening of the culture in the first place might have created the anxiety that triggered alcoholic drinking.

Terror management emphasizes that when people feel anxiety, they tend to rely upon their cultures to mitigate these hurtful feelings. If such anxieties are not mitigated, they can be expected to build up and be released in the form of dysfunctional behaviors. In situations where the culture is undermined and/or where people cannot relate to it, the model continues, there is no way for the impact of these hurtful feelings to be dissipated. The expected result of this situation is a rash of dysfunctional behavior. And that is exactly what has occurred among many native peoples.

The obvious solution to such a problem is to bolster the culture (and people's relationship to their culture) so that it can again serve as a powerful force, which has the power to mitigate anxieties. Where such a stabilizing force exists, people have a means of dealing with their fears and anxieties. And where this is the case, we can expect dysfunctional behavior to become less pronounced. Thus, by seeking to (1) simultaneously strengthen the culture while (2) strengthening the bond between people and their culture, and (3) helping individuals to respond from the ravages of alcoholism, the recovering individual can be provided with the relationship to their cultural institutions that they need to mitigate anxiety. In so doing, a basic trigger of dysfunction is eliminated. The Path of Handsome Lake is poised to serve this dual role.

MAINTAINING A PROPER FOCUS

While it is useful to recall that Handsome Lake experienced a remarkable recovery from seemingly incurable alcoholism, it is equally important to remember that his life and his work also had a more circumscribed and controversial component. Eventually, for example, the teachings and vision of Handsome Lake led to the establishment of the "Long House" tradition: a religion that combined long-established Iroquois traditions with more appropriate socio-economic strategies in order to help the Iroquois cope with the specific challenges faced in the early 19th century. As is often the case, furthermore, the innovative strivings of one generation are apt to become the conservative force of stability in the next. Indeed, today, the Long House tradition (the lengthened shadow of Handsome Lake's vision) is clearly embraced by the more traditional or orthodox element of contemporary Iroquois society. Thus, in the contemporary world, Handsome Lake and the Long House religion represent a specific set of circumscribed principles and many opponents within the Iroquois community (the more "liberal" or "progressive" segments of Iroquois society) are often in opposition to them.

Here, of course, I have no interest in entering into any debate regarding the pros and cons of the contemporary Long House religion and its vision for the future of Iroquois society. Ultimately, the Long House religion (as a formal institution) has been established for over 150 years and it has evolved on its own since the death of Handsome Lake. My concern is with the fact that Handsome Lake recognized that his culture was under profound attack. Faced with these attacks, he forged a way to preserve his traditions, on the one hand, while adjusting them to circumstance, on the other. And he clearly saw a link between a healthy society and personal sobriety and vice versa. Faced with rampant alcoholism among his people, he called for tight restrictions on alcohol and he was personally able to live a model life of recovery.

As a heuristic device, the Path culls a six-fold strategy from the teachings of Handsome Lake in order to affirm and demonstrate how it is possible to restore society to strength and vitality while simultaneously helping specific individuals to regain their sobriety and mental health.

HANDSOME LAKE AND NATIVE AMERICAN RECOVERY

This chapter has viewed the example of Handsome Lake as a model for Native Americans who are struggling towards recovery from alcoholism. It has been suggested that because Handsome Lake personally dealt with issues concerning the decay and rebirth of cultural traditions (and their impact upon alcoholism), he provides a strategy of recovery that transcends, while not totally eclipsing, other self help strategies such as Alcoholics and the 12 Step Program (that do not emphasize the issue of cultural stress). By taking cues directly from the life and teachings of Handsome Lake, a method tailored around the needs of alcoholic Native Americans, who are subjected to social disruption and anomie, has been proposed.

Dealing with Handsome Lake and his legacy within a broad context of recovery, however, is complicated by the fact that Handsome Lake continues to be closely identified with a specific, partisan, and somewhat controversial religion that is embraced by a specific segment of Iroquois society. As a result, different members of the Native American community may be prone to respond to this program in ways that reflect their religious, economic, and political perspectives. I hope his example has been presented in a non-partisan way that can be embraced by all Native people.

Due to this fact, it may be important for the therapist, counselor, or self-help group to clearly articulate to the client/group-member that this program is based upon the early experiences of Handsome Lake and not upon the more partisan religious traditions that grew up after his death. Indeed, Handsome Lake was clearly a political animal and it is important to distinguish his vision of recovery from whatever partisan ploys, motivations, and tactics that he may have embraced during his career as an Iroquois leader.[2]

Clearly, Handsome Lake saw a profound connection between the decay of his proud Native American culture and the alcoholism experienced by various members of his society. And in complete agreement with modern theories of sociology (anomie), he recognized the impact of cultural stress upon alcoholic behavior. Recognizing this connection, Handsome Lake understood that the recovery of the individual and the viability of the society go hand in hand. Given this reality, he affirmed that while his culture should embrace its traditions and heritage, it should also adjust them (and itself) in order to thrive under existing circumstances. And by combining sobriety with more viable cultural traditions, Handsome Lake demonstrates that alcoholic individuals can recover. This strategy and example involved a turning away from the decay of Iroquois society and the rampant alcoholism that accompanied it; the result was a more productive and sober lifestyle for Iroquois society (and for a large percentage of the individuals within Iroquois society who were able to experience fruitful lives in sobriety).

Even when clarifying the context in which Handsome Lake is embraced, it may still be important to distinguish at least three specific groups of clients: (1) Members of the Long House tradition, (2) Non-Long house Iroquois, (3) Non-Iroquois.

Issues concerning each group are discussed below.

Members of the Long House Tradition

Iroquois who are members of the Long House tradition will perceive Handsome Lake to be their religious leader and they can be expected to embrace him with the profound respect that devotees normally show towards the founder of their religion. Long House members, furthermore, will, no doubt, will very much aware of Handsome Lake's own bout with alcoholism as well as his ban upon the drinking of alcoholic beverages.

Unless therapists are experts on the Long House religion (or practicing members of that religion), Long House clients will probably know more about Handsome Lake than they will. As a result, therapists need to carefully avoid making "boners" and incorrect or naive statements regarding Handsome Lake and his teachings. Therapists, however, can ask "open ended" questions and encourage clients to discuss Handsome Lake and how his vision can be used within the context of recovery.

Non-Long House Iroquois

Many non-Long House Iroquois are the political, social, religious, and economic rivals to members of the Long House religion that was originally established by Handsome Lake. Long House people, for example, often oppose schemes of economic development (such as those involving gambling casinos). As a result, there can be significant tension between Long House people and others who favor more "worldly" or "mainstream economic" strategies of development.

Due to this tension, some segments of Iroquois society can be expected to resist any method of recovery that is based upon Handsome Lake and his teachings. As long as these people identify Handsome Lake and his strategy of recovery with their political, economic, religious and social rivals we can expect them to resist the program.

As a result, it is important to emphasize that the components of Handsome Lake's vision that have been embraced in "The Path of Handsome Lake" are not partisan, and, therefore, they should not inhibit any Iroquois from benefiting from a program of recovery that is based on them. Nonetheless, therapists and counselors need to recognize the possible resistance to Handsome Lake's vision by those who are rivals to the Long House religion.

Non-Iroquois

Today, while individual Native American Tribes, Bands, and Nations are preserving their own identity, there is a growing pan-Indian movement that seeks to form alliances and linkages where appropriate. As a result, a program of recovery, such as the Path of Handsome Lake, may appeal to a wide cross section of Native American Alcoholics. Where this is true, people with profoundly different, cultural traditions, viewpoints, and levels of knowledge regarding Handsome Lake may participate in the program suggested here (that is based on his life and message). And, of course, some participants may have absolutely no prior knowledge of Handsome Lake. It is significant, therefore, for all those using the Path of Handsome Lake as a program of recovery to recognize the context in which Handsome Lake is embraced as a role model. Essentially Handsome Lake:

1. Recognized the pain and suffering caused by profound and unmitigated social change.
2. Advocated a strategy that preserved traditions, on the one hand, while updating them to they could function effectively, on the other.

3. Linked recovery to individual effort in tandem with cultural strength and support.

These perspectives were interconnected with other priorities that largely duplicate many of the components of Alcoholics Anonymous that urge personal responsibility, penance, and ongoing vigilance.

A BROADER CONTEXT

Handsome Lake was an Iroquois and a Native American. As a result, it can be expected that his message and program of recovery will be of especially value within the context of North American Native people. While this is true, the experiences of the Iroquois in the late eighteenth/early nineteenth centuries are clearly parallel to the fate of many contemporary people worldwide. This book, for example, has emphasized that the histories of many Native people, ranging from Native Hawaiians to the Maori of New Zealand parallel the experience of Native Americans. As a result, the strategies forged by Handsome Lake have potential relevance to other Native peoples whose experiences parallel those of the Iroquois and Native Americans. I hope this book will be read from within this broader context.

CONCLUDING STATEMENT

In the early 19th century, Handsome Lake created a program of recovery from alcoholism that combined cultural renewal with personal revitalization. In doing so, he created a means of combating the impact of cultural decline upon individual dysfunction.

Updated and generalized, Handsome Lake's strategies of recovery provides a useful alternative to existing tactics of recovery (such as Alcoholics Anonymous and the 12 Step Program) because that model does not deal with the impact of cultural decline. While the Path of Handsome Lake and Alcoholics Anonymous are not in direct conflict, The Path focuses upon strengthening the culture and the individual's relationship to it. Doing so is a vital key for recovery among many Native people.

The Path of Handsome Lake, reflects the orientation of modern terror management theory, which emphasizes that people use their culture as a stable force to which they can identify and with which they can immerse themselves. According to terror management, doing so provides a means by which individuals can mitigate their anxieties.

In situations where the culture is weak and/or where people have trouble embracing it, however, people will not be able to use their heritage as a significant buffer against anxiety. The expected result to such a situation is increased anxiety and a growth in dysfunctional behaviors associated with anxiety. According to terror management theory, therefore, in the early 19th century, Handsome Lake devised a mechanism where anxieties could be mitigated though fostering a cultural renaissance. Under such circumstances, terror management theory would expect dysfunctions triggered by anxiety to decline; empirical evidence exists demonstrating that is the case.

Given the importance of this example, the method of Handsome Lake has been generalized and updated so that it can help other Native people combat alcoholism through cultural renewal.

NOTES

1. Many Native American peoples were not, when strictly speaking, subjected to a "colonial experience" because they went straight from being independent societies to being part of the United States. Nonetheless, terms such as "colonial" and "colonialization" are appropriate and are used for that reason.
2. A specific example is the fact that on purely partisan grounds Handsome Lake accused Red Jacket (a much respected Iroquois Leader) of witchcraft. Like Joe McCarthy during the communist "witch-hunts" of the 1950s, Handsome Lake eventually lost prestige due to his unfounded assertions, although (unlike McCarthy) he mended his ways and regained the respect of his people.

CHAPTER 9

LANDMARKS OF THE PATH

INTRODUCTION

In Chapter 8, a tool of recovery, based on the teachings of Handsome Lake, was presented in order to provide alcoholics (and those offering counseling and therapy to alcoholics) with a strategy of recovery that stems from the Native experience. That approach, with its focus upon Native cultures, was developed in ways to make it a distinct and fruitful alternative to commonly used programs of recovery, such as that provided by Alcoholics Anonymous.

As reasoned above, Alcoholics Anonymous focuses, primarily, upon the individual, and as a result, the cultural heritage from which people derive is not directly addressed. Founded by "mainstream people" who, seemingly, did not sense that their traditions and heritage were under profound and disabling stress, coupled with the fact that (aside from their alcoholic behavior) they were not inherently estranged from their culture, the founders of Alcoholics Anonymous centered upon the predicaments of individual people and how to encourage them to get their behavior back in sync with the rest of the world as they simultaneously abandoned their alcoholic behavior. In creating their 12 Step program of recovery, the founders of Alcoholics Anonymous provided a profound service of lasting significance. Nonetheless, as all focused strategies of self-improvement and therapy, the Alcoholics Anonymous model and its 12 Step Program have their gaps.

A primary feature of the Path of Handsome Lake (presented above) is its ability to transcend Alcoholics Anonymous by devoting significant atten-

The Path of Handsome Lake: A Model of Recovery for Native People, pages 133–146

tion to the cultural traditions from which people derive. This focus is important because people are largely products of a specific cultural heritage, and its traditions usually provide stability and comfort to members. When cultures are undermined and/or when individuals become estranged from their cultural background, however, the results are often traumatic and powerful enough to trigger dysfunctional patterns of behavior, such as alcoholic drinking.

The prevailing environment experienced by Native cultures is often in a state of flux and stress due to rampant social, political, and economic changes that have been triggered by contact with the larger, outside world. As a result of these pressures, Native cultures have often been undermined and weakened to a significant degree. In addition, for a variety of reasons, some members of Native cultures have become alienated or distanced from their traditions. Where such patterns of cultural decline exist, the resulting stress, if unmitigated, can trigger alcoholism, among other dysfunctional patterns of behavior. As a result of these commonly occurring patterns, Native alcoholics often need a program of recovery that helps them more fully interact within the context of their Native society and their cultural heritage. The Path of Handsome Lake provides one way of envisioning recovery from alcoholism and other dysfunctional behaviors in terms of strengthening Native cultural traditions and helping people to more completely connect with them.

While a modern codifying of the Path of Handsome Lake (presented above) is useful, programs of recovery need to be embraced in pragmatic and measurable ways. Strategies for combating alcoholism also need to be conceptualized in a systematic manner. By doing so, those who seek to recover from alcoholism can more accurately recognize their achievements, on the one hand, while being pointed towards future accomplishments, on the other. The purpose of this chapter is to provide such a series of yardsticks and goals. Since this activity involves measuring progress in terms of useful milestones of cultural and personal recovery, it will be called Landmarks of the Path.

THE LANDMARKS AND THEIR PURPOSE

While the Path of Handsome Lake provides a basic orientation for recovery through cultural health and the individuals' connectedness with their culture, the Landmarks of the Path, presented here, introduces more concrete goals and specific targets of action. By doing so, the suggestions of the Path are phrased in action-oriented and pragmatic ways. While the Landmarks are not intended to replace the Path, they do introduce a means of following the guidelines that the Path represents.

As with the Path of Handsome Lake, The Landmarks of the Path can be presented as a six-step process. These steps include: (1) *"We recognize who we are," (2) "We acknowledge that our heritage, culture, and traditions are our strength," (3) "We reject the vulnerability that comes from ignoring our roots," (4) "We realize that others may have their own tradition and we respect them," (5) "We understand that strength comes from embracing ourselves, not retreating from challenges," (6) "Handsome Lake's example and advice may be useful to all who face personal disruptions."*

In this manner, the Landmarks provide a systematic way of addressing the needs of Native alcoholics whose drift into alcoholism may be due, in part, to an alienation from their cultural roots. As such, the Landmarks provide a suggested agenda of action, although, of course, different people will approach recovery (an the tools that promote recovery) in their own distinctive manner. While not all people will follow the Landmarks in the order in which they are provided, this discussion does show how they can build upon each other in positive, constructive, and cumulative ways.

Having listed these six landmarks, each will be discussed with specific reference to the needs of Native alcoholics. These discussions will be followed by a concluding statement, linked to terror management theory, that discusses how the Path and the Landmarks can, and should, work hand in hand.

We Recognize Who We Are

In general, progress in life only comes when people recognize who they are and when they act in accordance with that reality. But since people are so complex, the seemingly simple phrase "who they are"possesses multidimensional dimensions, each of which needs to be addressed. In addition, this tangled bundle of beliefs, attitudes, strengths, and vulnerabilities intertwine with each another in elaborate and complicated ways. As a result, people are the product of many traits and influences, each of which needs to be factored into the total equation of personality and character. Here we will consider a representative number of considerations that need to be addressed when people are examining themselves and when they are being evaluated by others. Some of these categories may include negative traits (such as the fact that the person is vulnerable to alcohol). Other categories, such as personal skills and identities) are positive in nature. In order for people to envision who they are, it becomes necessary to combine a wide variety of attributes into a composite that depicts the full person.

In most cases, people only enter treatment or a self-help program to deal with alcohol-related problems because they (or those who have a degree of control over them) recognize their vulnerability to alcohol and its negative effects upon them. And seeking help typically comes after significant dysfunctional behavior, triggered by drinking, has been exhibited.

Besides a vulnerability to alcohol, of course, alcoholics (like everybody else) usually possess a wide variety of shortcomings, limitations, and vulnerabilitites many of which might have emerged as a result of their uncontrolled drinking and the adventures and misadventures it triggered.

Some people may have other very real shortcomings that prevent them from reaching their goals or gaining self-esteem. In some cases, the person may have personality traits that make them hard to live with. Programs such as Alcoholics Anonymous, for example, urge participants to reflect on their shortcomings (whatever they may be) in order for recovering alcoholics to more effectively restructure their lives in a positive and constructive way. I feel no reason to reject that strategy here.

Some "shortcomings" may merely refer to the lack of some trait that is needed in order to achieve sought after goals. Some people, for whatever reason, lack the skills or abilities they need to excel in some aspect of life. Others may be held back by ghosts of the past, such as a criminal record, crippling debt, or the distrust of others that cropped up due to the indiscretions triggered by drinking. In some cases, a lowering of certain abilities may simply reflect the ebb and flow of life. As people age, for example, they may lose some of the prowess that they once possessed. People need to candidly recognize and accept whatever limitations impact their lives and learn to take them into account when recovering from alcoholism and when just living, in general. This observation does not imply that people should not try to transcend limitations where possible, but merely that people need to realistically accept their limitations.

On some occasions, however, people's perceived shortcomings may merely result from their own self-assessment of themselves and nothing more. Consider a man who owns a successful auto repair shop and, over the years, has built up a large and loyal clientele. From outward appearances, the man would appear to be successful; he is providing a valuable public service and he earns good money. But what if this man was pre-occupied with becoming a professional racing car driver. And what if he, at a very personal level, evaluated his success and personal worth in terms of achieving his dream of racing in the Indianapolis 500 on Memorial Day? In his mind, he would be a failure even if it appeared to everybody else that he was doing very well. And if he was depressed enough by an inability to achieve his treasured goal, he might succumb to dysfunctional behavior, such as alcoholic drinking.

Besides shortcomings and limitations, people have strengths, abilities, and assets that provide the means by which they can positively impact their future and the world. People who have had a string of hard times and disappointments due to drinking, however, may have trouble recognizing these resources.

In Alcoholics Anonymous, people are often asked to "take their inventory." And as that program insists, inventories (and other accounting schemes) acknowledge both assets and liabilities. We agree that considering both strengths and weaknesses and the relationships that exists between them is a healthy and reasonable way for recovering people to evaluate themselves and their options.

Another important component regarding how people respond, stems from their cultural heritage and ethnic identity. As indicated in the last chapter, Native people are often strongly influenced by their cultural origins even if they do not overtly or consciously recognize this impact. The power and significance of the Native heritage, however, typically demands that people address this component of their identity and respond to it in forceful and constructive ways. As a result, it is imperative that Native people address the significance of their cultural heritage and respond to it in an appropriate and acknowledging manner.

As people seek recovery, they need to understand who they are. By possessing this vision of their identity, the influences impacting them, and their potentials for the future, people are better able to meet the challenges of life. And overcoming an addiction to alcohol is one of the greatest battles anybody will ever fight.

We Acknowledge That Our Heritage, Culture, and Traditions Are Our Strength

Not only do people need to understand who they are and the fact that their Native heritage is a big part of their identity, they also need to recognize that, to a great degree, their ethnic identity gives them strength, power, and purpose.

As indicated above, in this complicated world, the cultural heritage from which people derive often must compete with various other identities and distractions. As a result, it can easily become discounted and ignored. Nonetheless, a traditional ethnic identity is a powerful asset and ignoring it can trigger profoundly negative impacts. As was argued above, massive cultural change can provide a breeding ground for alienation and anomie, and the psychological impacts stemming from these experiences can trigger alienation, depression, and dysfunctional behaviors (such as alcoholism). As a result, a strong and positive connection with a traditional heritage is a profound strength even though it is often ignored and discounted as people interact within the larger, mainstream world.

As alcoholics come to accept themselves for who they are, they need to pay special attention to their ethnic identity because although possibly covert or ignored, it often has great power and possesses the potential to be source of significant personal strength. Ignored, in contrast, it can lead to tensions, alienation, and the resulting dysfunctional behavior. By tapping this asset, alcoholics can put themselves in a better position to both understand who they are and to forge appropriate solutions to a variety of problems that stem from their identity. By viewing themselves in view of their cultural heritage, people can practice a personal form of self-determinism as they seek to restructure their lives and overcome the malady of alcoholism.

People need to actively envision how they derive from their cultural heritage and how they have become alienated from their traditions or only incompletely understand their culture and its implications. People are products of their heritage. These identities are ignored at their own risk.

These identities and how they impact people should be acknowledged. Where this is the case, Native alcoholics will no longer be "blindsided" by failing to understand their impact.

We Reject The Vulnerability That Comes From Ignoring Our Roots

As Native cultures have been drawn into the more mainstream world, there has been a tendency for their members to ignore their roots. On many occasions, the stripping away of a cultural heritage was a conscious strategy and a systematic policy of both government and religious leaders who invaded Bastians of Native culture. Thus, missionaries working among Natives as well as schools for Native children forcefully de-emphasized Native ways to the point that those who spoke their traditional languages and practiced traditional ways were often ridiculed and punished for doing so.

In various parts of the United States, furthermore, unprecedented epidemics of diseases brought by White contact killed a large percentage of the Native population and, as a result, the untimely and unanticipated deaths of leaders and elders disrupted Native cultures by destroying the linkages between the past and the present. When such unfortunate events occurred, Native people were denied large segments of their cultural heritage and they experienced profound psychological pain as a result. The impacts caused by this trauma often led to dysfunctional behaviors, such as alcoholism.

In spite of being profoundly undercut, the cultural heritage of people often remains profoundly important to mental health and well-being. As a result, where the cultural heritage is weakened or ignored, vulnerabilities can emerge. Such vulnerabilities, however, can be countered if people develop an awareness of their cultural traditions, make them a more conscious part of their lives, and act accordingly. As argued above, Native cultures often exist in a covert sort of way within many of their members. Where this is true, people tend to be unaware of the impact of their heritage even though they are constantly impacted by it. In such situations, people may develop vulnerabilities because they, to a large degree, ignore who they really are.

The entire field of psychoanalysis empahasizes that mental and psychological dysfunction tend to occur when people repress who they really are and ignore the culturally defined needs and drives that underlie their lives and behavior. While Freud theorized that biological and instinctual drives were the repressed mainsprings driving behavior, modern anthropologists tend to talk in terms of needs and influences that are triggered by culture. When these cultural identities, and the needs they trigger, are ignored and/or thwarted, the results can be hurtful. But by acknowledging these cultural identities and by allowing them to flower, a heritage can emerge as a source of profound personal strength.

Native people need to reject the vulnerability that comes from rejecting their roots. By affirming their cultural identity (and by learning more about it as necessary) they will be better able to connect with who they are. By doing so, Native alcoholics can become more attuned with themselves and better able to cope with the pressures of life.

Having recognized the power and importance of culture, the importance of cultural self reflection becomes all the more obvious. By rejecting the vulnerability that comes from ignoring our roots, the stage for personal progress can be set.

We Realize That Others May Have Their Own Traditions and We Respect Them

Cultural traditions are very personal. As a result, those from different cultures are apt to experience disparate feeling, motives, goals, strengths, and weaknesses. Nonetheless, people who band together in search of recovery often form a cross-section of social and cultural identities. This is true in the mainstream world as well in programs of recovery that are geared around the special needs of Natives, since innumerable Native cultures exist. Even specific Native traditions (such as the Athabascan) are made up of many subgroups that are distinct from each other in significant ways.

On the one hand, those closely interacting with different people need to develop an appreciation (and if necessary a tolerance) for other traditions, beliefs, priorities, and ways of life. Overcoming possible prejudice against those who are culturally different (as well as seeking to better understand other people by providing an arena where all can seek sobriety) should have a high priority.

Other programs of recovery have attempted, in their own way, to deal with the fact that people come from different backgrounds and, yet, they need to work together in search of a common goal: freedom from the ravages of alcoholism. In the case of Alcoholics Anonymous and the 12 Step Program, for example, an attempt is made to generalize people, religions, and maladies to the extent that all alcoholics can relate to each other. The program, for example, struggles to present a vision to which all can respond and build a program from that point. In addition, Alcoholics Anonymous meetings often emphasize that "all drunks are the same" and underscore that they are united by a common disability.

Various Alcoholic Anonymous "folk tales" tell of the derelict college professor or sophisticated scientist who learned the basics of recovery from some working class alcoholic who was short of book-learning, but had found a way to stay sober. The moral of such stories is that all alcoholics have the same basic path to walk and that even chauvinistic intellectuals can learn the path to recovery from the unsophisticated as long as these grass-roots teachers and role models have traveled the road to sobriety and succeeded.

As far as they go, such a vision of alcoholics being united by their infliction is useful. Alcoholics Anonymous has had considerable success in generalizing itself to serve alcoholics from all walks of life. Here, however, we take the opposite tact. Instead of generalizing people and cultures to their lowest common denominators, this program recognizes and celebrates cultural differences and urges those seeking recovery to envision and celebrate their distinctiveness.

On the one hand, people are products of their own cultural background. This provides them with a distinct way of being human. Other people, in contrast, have their own traditions, which are meaningful and powerful to them. Learning about, acknowledging, and celebrating this diversity can be very important and empowering. Understanding cultures on their own terms, makes us better able to deal with others and, by virtue of understanding, translate their perspectives in terms of our own lives. And, of course, tolerance and understanding are profoundly important traits that are both noble and empowering, in addition to helping people expand their vision of themselves.

Each of us comes from a specific cultural tradition, and people bring their own heritage with them. An arena for combating alcoholism is needed in which these differences can be acknowledged. By creating this open forum of respect and tolerance, those seeking recovery can band together in search of sobriety; instead of ignoring differences, distinctiveness can be celebrated.

We Understand That Strength Comes from Embracing Ourselves, Not Retreating from Challenges

If people are to put their lives in order, they need to accept themselves for who they are. A part of this identity involves the degree to which they fit into the mainstream culture. While the larger world (and people's place within it) may need to be acknowledged and embraced, this represents only a part of personal identity. Aspects of the mainstream world, however, are often more overtly obvious and, therefore, they may be more easily addressed. Beyond these overt considerations, however, are move covert issues that involve the heritage of the Native culture and its impact upon people.

Earlier we spoke of the process of anomie in which people are cut off from their traditions. When this happens, people often develop dysfunctional patterns of behavior. One form of anomie, known as "retreatism" involves withdrawing. Retreatism typically involves denying the goals of a culture and what are envisioned as legitimate means of achieving them. Having doing so, people find themselves cut adrift and they often sink into dysfunctional attitudes, lifestyles, and syndromes (such as alcoholism). But while retreating from one's heritage is an often followed path when people face stress and disappointment, it is not the only possible course of action. As an alternative, people may choose to embrace who they are and, responding from the resulting position of strength, forge onward instead of retreating backward.

I am reminded of the term "future shock" that was coined by Alvin Toffler many years ago. Toffler noted that modern society is in such a rapid state of flux and change that people, raised in one world must live in another. As a result, people are often alienated even in their own culture. Toffler, of course, was inspired by the anthropological idea of "culture shock" in which people entering an foreign society often face alienation, confusion, and dysfunction by being thrust into a new cultural environment for which they are not prepared. Native people, of course, are often simultaneously impacted by both future shock and culture shock. The world is changing quickly and their cultures are being overpowered by alien ways of life. It should come as little surprise that many Natives exposed to these pressures and anxieties suffer from alcoholism and other dysfunctions.

By re-embracing their traditions (even though this cultural heritage may exist only covertly and might be covered by layers of other traditions) people can gain strength. When people gain the strength provided by their cultures and their traditions, it becomes easier for them to meet the challenges they faced and not to retreat from them. By embracing who they are, people can better envision what challenges need to be overcome and they can better embrace the tools provided by the culture so they can be used to combat challenges in forceful and constructive ways.

Those suffering from alcoholism have often used drinking as a means of retreating from the challenges they face. In the process, tensions can build up because little is being done to resolve the challenges that exist. People often have two separate identities. One stems from the "mainstream culture." The other derives from the Native heritage. On many occasions, the mainstream culture is more overt and, therefore, its impacts will be more obvious at first glance. This can result in the Native culture being discounted or ignored. Buit if this occurs, many important issues stemming from the Native culture will remain unresolved. This potential needs to be avoided.

On many occasions, Native people have faced crises because their cultures are often in a state of disarray and/or because individual Native people are not adequately attuned with their heritage. Where such patterns exist, the antidote lies in people accepting their cultural heritage and not retreating from it.

Handsome Lake's Example May Be Useful to Others Who Face Personal Disruptions

Programs of recovery typically encourage a degree of altruism. When people are given a second chance in life, they often want to share their good fortune with others. While they should do so in a non-forceful sort of manner, helping others to overcome their maladies is helpful to suffering/recovering alcoholics, to Native cultures, and to those who lend a helping hand by providing counsel, understanding and, perhaps, a positive and constructive example.

This program is built upon building a degree of self-awareness regarding the cultural tradition from which people derive. By gaining the resulting insights, those who suffer from alcoholism can better understand who they are, why they respond in the way they do, and how they might overcome their malady.

Handsome Lake challenged people to live a sober and moral life. He also emphasized that this goal could best be achieved by developing an awareness of who they were and by embracing their traditional culture. Native people suffering crises that were triggered by alcohol can benefit from Handsome Lake's example and his advice. And all people can benefit from acknowledging who they are and using that reality as the starting-point of their program of recovery.

Many people can benefit from this program and they are welcomed. Thus, just as the Path of Handsome Lake provides a program of recovery, the Landmarks of the Path provides a means of assessing progress. Combined, they can be used in a variety of contexts to help Native alcoholics grapple with their affliction. By embracing their cultural heritage and by understanding its impact upon them, a variety of issues can be embraced that can provide a route to recovery. Ignoring their traditions, in contrast, can trigger dysfunctional behavior.

Presented in tabular form (Table 9.1) we find:

Table 9.1. Landmarks of the Path

Landmark	*Significance*	*Discussion*
Recognize who we are	People in recovery need to objectively acknowledge their strengths, weaknesses, and cultural identities	Identity is a multifaceted activity. Although AA's 12 Step program focuses on strengths and weaknesses, it does not deal with cultural identities and their power.
Acknowledge power of culture	People often need to acknowledge their ethnic identity and that it impacts them in significant ways, although possibly covertly.	Even though ethnic identities may exist covertly and not be acknowledged, they are significant and need to be acknowledged.
Transcend alienation	People often become alienated and develop dysfunctional habits when their traditional cultures are undercut. By strengthening these traditions, dysfunction can be countered	Native people are often alienated by attacks on their culture. The dysfunctional behavior resulting form alienation can be reversed by strengthening and embracing these weakened traditions.
Respect other traditions	Other people possess their cultures and traditions that are meaningful to them. These heritages deserve the respect of others.	Those in recovery often need to deal with people who derive from different cultures. As a result, understanding and honoring their heritage is important.
Embrace ourselves	Since ethnic identity is such a crucial part of personality and character, people need to become consciously aware of it and its power.	By better understanding their personality and character as well as the impact caused by the eroding of their cultural base, alcoholics can better restructure their lives and recover from their malady
Many can benefit	Because the alienation and anomie caused by ignoring a cultural identity potentially impacts all people, many different people can benefit from following the Path of Handsome Lake.	Some Native people and some societies have been more overtly impacted by the assault upon their culture than others. Nonetheless, manyt people have suffered grievous impacts, if only by what Alvin Toffler has called "future shock".
Discussion	The Landmarks of the Path provides a means of applying the Path of Handsome Lake and it can be used to gauge the degree of progress being made by individuals. It focuses the power and significance of the cultural heritage. It seeks to unite people of different traditions while acknowledging their distinctiveness in positive ways.	

Viewed in this way, the Landmarks of the Path emerges as a specific set of strategies that people can employ to rebuild their heritage, affirm their connection to it, and live a productive and fruitful life in recovery from alcoholism. While the Landmarks are not the Path provided by Handsome, they do provide clues, suggestions, and orientations on how to follow that path. And by doing so, they provide tools of value in both a therapeutic/ counselor situations and in a self-help context.

THE TERROR OF BROKEN CONFIGURATIONS

As this book argues, the cultural configurations model of social anthropology, although a classic model of society, continues to provide a useful way of envisioning how people relate to their cultures. It also suggests the implications of doing (or not doing) so. The cultural configurationists also argue that cultures are made up a multitude of traits and patterns of belief, attitudes, and behavior. Nonetheless, the entire cultural universe (or most of it) tends to revolve around some basic cultural principles that unite it and its members in profound and overarching ways. Human behavior tends to revolve around a cultural essence just like the planets revolve around the sun.

Even though cultures can evolve over time, these configurations tend to change relatively slowly and in times of rapid change, they might not adequately adjust. A key concept from the social sciences is "cultural lag" which draws attention to the fact that technological and economic change often occur quicker than human relationships and other psychological components of culture. Under such circumstances, we can expect the configurations of the culture to get out of balance. When this happens, people can become disoriented, anxious, and dysfunctional. For a variety of reasons, some members of a culture may lose the ability to properly relate to the configurations that unite them with their culture. When this happens, profound stress can be expected.

As a result of this situation, as one part of the culture gets out of kilter with other parts, the entire system is negatively affected, including the mental health of individual members. Thus, if the cultural configuration of a culture becomes broken or undermined, this situation will impact the entire system and makes it less effective. Such a circumstance, of course, can be viewed as a major crisis for the culture. If the changes taking place within a culture are relatively insignificant and/or if the resulting transformations are taking place at a particularly slow rate, the culture may be able to adjust in relatively painless ways. But if the changes are profound and quick, the culture will be hard pressed to forcefully respond in an effective manner. From a psychological perspective, the impacts of such experiences can be devastating.

In the case of many Native people, unexpected and profoundly significant cultural and economic changes came quickly and were thrust upon Native cultures that were totally unprepared for them. As a result, these cultures were undermined and found it more difficult to provide a strong and vital configuration that people could live by.

According to terror management theory, when cultures are not functioning properly, they lose the ability to mitigate the terrors of life. That is exactly what has happened in innumerable Native cultures. When this occurs, we expect anxieties to rise. With rising anxieties, dysfunctional behavior increases in frequency and severity. The historic record has demonstrated, time and again, that this is exactly what has happened.

When the terrors of life are unmitigated, we can expect anxieties and dysfunction to rise. This has clearly been the case among Native people.

RESTORED CONFIGURATIONS AND PEACE

The obvious antidote for such a set of circumstances is to restore the culture to good health so that people will be able to fully benefit from their heritage and traditions. One such series of benefits is the psychological comfort that can occur when people possess a strong and vibrant cultural heritage.

Terror management theory emphasizes that a major function of culture is to relieve anxieties. As has been suggested, above, however, in order to for cultures to relieve anxieties (1) the culture must be strong and (2) people must be able to relate to it. If either of these conditions are not met, the culture will not be able to mitigate the anxieties of all (or some) of its members. Under such circumstances, dysfunction will increase.

Where the culture is not functioning properly and providing relief from anxieties, it will need to be restored to good health so it can perform the function of relieving anxieties. This realization was the major contribution of Handsome Lake. Restoring the culture (as well as encouraging individuals to begin a process of healthy recovery), however, is a complicated process. Nevertheless, The Landmarks of the Path is designed to provide a way of conceptualizing such progress within a program of individual recovery. Configurations can be restored. And when this happens, people can find peace form anxiety and dysfunction.

DISCUSSION AND CONCLUSION

While the Path of Handsome Lake provides a means by which people can restructure their lives in positive ways through an embrace of their cultural heritage, The Landmarks of the Path provides (1) a strategy for following the Path as well as (2) a set of yardsticks with which to evaluate the progress being made.

Being patterned after the life and work of Handsome Lake, a Native leader who helped his people cope with the trauma caused by social, economic, and political change during a period of change that had been triggered by increased White contact, the program suggested here is designed to acknowledge, address, and mitigate the disruptions that undermined Native cultural traditions as well as the dysfunctional behavior it can trigger.

While many strategies of recovery seek to generalize all alcoholics so they can be dealt with in a uniform manner, this program acknowledges differences between people and cultures and encourages people to accept themselves for who they are. Doing so creates a unified way by which diverse people can connect with each other while acknowledging and honoring their distinctive traditions.

CHAPTER 10

STRATEGIES FOR PROFESSIONAL THERAPY/INTERVENTION

MULTICULTURAL STRATEGIES

Natives experiencing problems with alcohol dependency can benefit from strategies of therapy and intervention that are based on the Path of Handsome Lake/Landmarks of the Path method of recovery. By crafting and employing such a program, professional counselors can deal with Native clients in ways that are more attuned to their needs and, thereby, provide more appropriate and effective therapy. In some situations, a Handsome Lake-style of treatment, aimed at Natives, may be employed as the primary vehicle of treatment. In other cases, a Native centered program of therapy might emerge as a supplemental means by which the special needs of particular Native clients can best be addressed. In both cases, acknowledging a Native identity and focusing therapy/intervention around it can be of significant value.

In recent years, providing helping services (such as alcohol abuse counseling) to diverse people has emerged as a high profile goal. This book is both an artifact of and an example of that trend. In modeling ways to serve divergent groups of people, a number of different strategies have been proposed. One model, presented by Sue, Arrodondo, & McDavis (1992) outlines lists of competencies that counselors need to master in order to

The Path of Handsome Lake: A Model of Recovery for Native People, pages 147–166

professionally serve specific ethnic, racial, and social groups. These competencies are nested under three categories: (1) Counselors' awareness of their cultural bias and values, (2) Counselors' awareness of clients' world-view, and (3) Culturally appropriate intervention strategies. This book mirroring these concerns, emphasizes that since counseling takes place within a culturally diverse world, counselors must adjust themselves (and the therapy they provide) accordingly.

While Sue, Arrondondo, & McDavis (1992) provide long lists of competencies, Fischer, Jome, & Atkinson (1998) seek to phrase the issues of multicultural counseling in a more focused manner. Specifically, they look at the process of healing from a truly cross-cultural perspective and they outline four universal characteristics that routinely occur cross-culturally within helping and healing contexts. These characteristics include: (1) a therapeutic relationship exists, (2) those involved in this relationship have some kind of a shared world-view, (3) the person receiving help has certain expectations, and (4) some kind of ritual or intervention occurs.

This model is useful because it provides an analytic framework to use when talking about both alcohol therapy and self-help programs. In this chapter, formal therapy facilitated by professionals will be considered. In the next chapter, self-help efforts and strategies will be discussed. Here, as in the next chapter, the list of commonly occurring features of therapy will begin the analysis. Each is discussed below:

The Therapeutic Relationship

In order for people to truly benefit from treatment, a therapeutic relationship needs to overtly exist. Thus, when professionals are working to improve the psychological health of an individual, this fact needs to be acknowledged as well as the fact that the relationship is centered around healing. According to Fischer, Tobe, and Atkinson, "In sum, the therapeutic relationship factor represents the positive, trusting, and healing relationship between client and counselor. Both the Western or integrationist and the transcultural literatures ... unequivocally support the importance of the therapeutic relationship" (1998).

As indicated above, therapy, such as the Path of Handsome program, needs to be administered from within the context of a therapeutic relationship. And, of course, programs of recovery and healing need to be built upon trust and confidence. As will be discussed below, a greater feeling of trust and a more positive relationship might develop when using the Handsome Lake program precisely because this method of treatment emphasizes Native perspectives and intertwines them with therapy. As a result, treatment is not merely an extension of foreign/Western ideas from which the client may be alienated.

In recent years, by analogy and extension, counselors and psychological caseworkers have increasingly begun to work in collaboration with Native healers. By doing so, clients can better envision therapy from within the context of their own lives and cultural traditions; this building upon and honoring tradition can build trust. In the same way, embracing a strategy that is based upon Native traditions (such as the Handsome Lake program) can help create a positive and more trusting therapeutic relationship. This is especially true in the case of clients who may look at the mainstream culture with a jaundice eye.

As a result of the fact that the Path of Handsome Lake program is based upon Native traditions, it can serve an important role by creating linkages between counselors and clients in a way that can make therapy more effective by establishing a positive and trusting therapeutic relationship between Native clients and their counselors.

A Shared Worldview

A recurring theme among writers who deal with multicultural counseling is that people from different cultures often have their own worldviews; these perspectives may need to be accommodated during therapy. "Thus, both the Western and transcultural approaches ... support the importance of a shared worldview between counselor and client.... The presence of a shared worldview ...[can] set the stage for positive expectations and to allow the healer to offer explanations or rationales for distress that fit with the client's view of the world."(Fischer, Jobe & Atkinson, 1998).

One of the ways by which therapists and counselors can better understand specific people is to juxtapose different cultures using models (such as that provided by Geert Hofstede, who breaks cultures down into various components such as "individualism vs. collectivism" and "large vs. small power distance"). By comparing and categorizing cultures in such a manner, counselors and clients from very different backgrounds can come to better understand each other. And understanding these characteristics can help clients and counselors to better understand each other and facilitate more effective collaboration. Thus, by envisioning other people in terms of certain patterns that can be observed worldwide, counselors can better understand their culturally diverse clients and begin to work with them with reference to worldviews[1] that are presented in somewhat comparable ways.

This book encourages a strategy of recovery that is based on a specific vision of recovery and the establishment of modes of therapy that are embraced by both the counselor and the client. When doing so, cultures are not merely viewed with reference to some "shards and pieces" of cultural identity that have been ripped from their context and compared with other traditions (as the Hofstede model does). The particular shared worldview that is showcased in this book emphasizes that people from Native cultures often need to embrace their culture in order to be well adjusted and to reduce stress and anxiety. If that culture is to continue to be effective, furthermore, it will probably have to constantly adjust itself in order to keep up with changing times. Although the counselor has no right to inaugurate change or orchestrate that process in any way (because people and cultures possess the right of self-determinism), it is possible for the counselor to be alert for changes and adjustments that do or do not occur. By emphasizing the individual's cultural heritage, the strengths and vulnerabilities deriving from it, and the degree that these characteristics may have been ignored or discounted, effective treatments for alcoholism may present themselves.

The resulting worldview emphasizes that the counselor and the client need to (1) understand the cultural configuration from which clients derive, (2) recognize the importance of this heritage, (3) perceive how cultures are always changing, and (4) specifically work these traditions into a program of recovery. By doing so, the counselor and the client will come to share a worldview based on the vision that cultures are fluid and evolving; in this way they can develop a more effective working relationship.

Expectations

In order for therapy to be grounded and for clients to be motivated for the hard work involved in therapy, they need to believe that significant benefits potentially derive from their efforts. "Overall, it appears that ... client expectations or hope for a positive benefit from therapy is a basic element seen across cultures.... Counselors and healers raise client expectations and gain credibility through the setting in which they conduct therapy, the training and degrees they possess, working within a shared worldview with the client, and developing a therapeutic relationship with the client"(Fischer, Jobe, & Atkinson, 1998). As a corollary, expectations can be strengthened if the people strongly believe that the therapy they are receiving will address concrete needs that they consciously recognize. The Path/Landmarks model of therapy focuses upon the fact that (1) the traditional culture may be under attack and (2) many Native people are estranged from it. This model also affirms that individual dysfunction is often directly linked to a weakening and undermining of the culture. Therapy based on this model provides expectations that (1) cultures can be strengthened, (2) that people can connect with this heritage, and (3) that recovery from alcoholism can be based, in part, upon clients embracing the culture and the strength and stability it provides. These are very real and achievable expectations and they can be easily articulated to clients.

Intervention or Ritual

Not only do clients need to possess the expectation that their therapy will be effective and that it can help relieve their dysfunction in some way, there also has to be some action or process that is believed to have positive effects; "Our forth common factor is conceptualized as interventions, rituals, or techniques that are believed by both counselor and client to have healing potential. Thus, an intervention that is relevant and effective for one client may not be as relevant or effective for another client, depending on the degree of relationship, shared worldview, and positive expectations"(Fischer, Jobe, & Atkinson, 1998).

The Handsome Lake program agrees with the premise that models of treatment need to be appropriate for the specific client and that what works for one person may not work for everybody. Indeed, this book has complained that models of recovery that are based on the Alcoholics Anonymous/12 Steps program may not sufficiently address issues concerning cultural stress. As a result, this book has suggested that while the 12 Steps program may be useful in many contexts, it does not deal with all of the issues that many Native people need to address.

In order to address such considerations, special interventions that allow people to more fully embrace their cultural traditions and recognize the impact of their cultural heritage upon both their alcoholism and their recovery are needed. In this way, a specific series of interventions/rituals based on the Handsome Lake method can be provided. These interventions can be designed to help clients achieve a recovery that stems from a greater cultural awareness and/or that resonates from a more complete connection with their cultural heritage.

Thus, the Handsome Lake program of recovery meets the four criteria of therapy provided by Fischer, Jome, & Atkinson. Being flexible, furthermore, this program can be implemented in a variety of ways ranging from a primary strategy of treatment to a supplemental program. Examples of how the program can serve clients are provided below.

A PRIMARY PROGRAM

Professional therapy and intervention that are focused around Native alcoholics can employ the Handsome Lake program as a primary vehicle of therapy. As mentioned above, many Native people are not adequately attuned to their cultural heritage and/or they may ignore (or be unaware of) the impact of their culture upon their personal identity and upon their tendencies toward dysfunctional behavior, such as alcoholic drinking. Nonetheless, on many occasions, a traditional heritage may continue to exist and impact people in a covert sort of way. In such cases, however, people may not be consciously aware of this influence. Where such patterns of obliviousness exist, unmitigated stress, trauma, and anxiety can easily result. Alcoholic drinking and other dysfunctional behaviors are likely results of this state of affairs.

When Alcoholics Anonymous and the 12 Step Program (and other strategies of therapy) were developed, dealing with the weakening of cultural traditions and the alienation that it can trigger were not worked into strategies of therapy and recovery. These programs, in contrast, were primarily designed to help alcoholics, who were "out of step" with a vital and ongoing culture or society. Under such circumstances, these mainstream programs tend to assume that a healthy and robust cultural foundation exists to which recovering alcoholics can return once they get their life in order. Once these assumptions have been made, little further attention tends to be directed towards the culture and its health.

A significant blind spot within these conventional programs of recovery is that they do little to help Native people cope with the fact that their cultures may be under severe attack and/or that specific Native alcoholics may have become alienated from their traditions and sunk into dysfunction as a result. Nonetheless, many Native alcoholics are subjected to such trauma, the hurtful anxieties it triggers, and the dysfunction that results. Unfortunately, traditional programs of alcohol counseling are not designed to mitigate such cultural stress, anxiety, and alienation. The Path of Handsome Lake/Landmarks of the Path, in contrast, has been specifically designed to do so. Such an approach can be adapted for either individual counseling or group therapy.

Structuring the Program/Setting the Stage

Specific Native clients may or may not be aware that cultural decline and/or the individuals' alienation from their culture heritage might be a source of significant anxiety that can lead to a downward spiral of alcoholic drinking. Where this is true, a first step is to make the client aware of the possible negative impacts that can result from (1) attacks and pressures on their culture and (2) personal alienation from the individual's cultural heritage. Some clients will readily recognize this influence; others will not. As a result, encouraging general discussions regarding the importance of cultures and traditions may be useful before getting into any meaningful discussions regarding the trauma faced by specific clients.

One way of doing so is for the counselor to recommend (or discuss in therapy) Harold Napoleon's analysis of cultural decline among the Yup'ik of Alaska and its impact, as discussed in his *Yuuyaraq: The Way of Being Human* (1996).[2] This book has the advantages of being short and being presented in laymen's terms. In his analysis, Napoleon chronicles how cultural decline, triggered by White contact, can lead to alcoholism and other personal and cultural dysfunction. Once the negative potentials of cultural decline and alienation have been discussed and acknowledged, introducing the example of Handsome Lake (which largely parallels Napoleon's chronicle) can be accomplished in a more effective manner.

When presenting the example of Handsome Lake, it is good to start by observing that he was a seemingly incurable alcoholic who recovered his personal life and became an influential Iroquois leader. By focusing on his personal example of recovery, clients can be encouraged to believe that they, too, can succeed in their quest of sobriety.

Having introduced Handsome Lake, as a man who successfully recovered from alcoholism, his strategy of recovery can be presented with a certain amount of credibility. From this position of strength, the Path of Handsome Lake can be explained and its value emphasized. The way in which Handsome Lake combined personal recovery with cultural renewal and his embrace of his culture's traditions should be emphasized. This introduction can be followed by a similar introduction of the Landmarks of the Path, presented in ways that emphasize the possibility of personal recovery.

In general, clients need to be encouraged to view themselves as Native people who may have been injured and traumatized by an environment where their heritage was ignored and devalued and where they may have been denied their heritage. The possibility that such experiences can lead to anxiety should be emphasized. By doing so, the benefits of the Path of Handsome Lake program of recovery can be highlighted.

It might also be good for clients to be reminded that people are not always overtly conscious of their identity and what influences their behavior. As a result, clients may need time to think about who they are. A greater awareness may be built by having clients complete outside assignments (preferably written) in which they consider these issues on their own and come to therapy sessions ready to discuss what they have gained from personal contemplation.

Many Native cultures, furthermore, have complied and published lists of their values. If such lists exists for the particular Native cultures in question, perhaps they can be used as a point of departure for such discussions. If not, the lists of values of various Native peoples are readily available and they might be able to help the client trigger some sort of response. Perhaps clients can speak with elders or with other culturally-aware individuals who might be able to provide insights regarding the Native cultures and traditions.

As has been emphasized throughout this book, if a program of recovery does not deal with cultural stress and alienation, it is not equipped to deal with a major source of Native alcoholism. As a result, Native alcoholics often need programs and therapies that provide a strong cultural foundation and orientation.

In situations where the Handsome Lake program is practiced, a vibrant and robust Native community may exist. Where this is true, the counselor may have access to important elders and other carriers of tradition. When this is true, it may be possible to enlist the aid of these cultural leaders in order to facilitate recovery. The idea of combining recovery with an embrace of tradition is a long practiced tradition among Native people. The distinctiveness of the Handsome Lake program is that it provides these preexisting programs with a way of focusing on the cultural tradition.

Currently many Native people are well aware of the importance of the traditional culture and that it has the ability to help people deal with the tensions in their lives. Many indigenous programs of recovery overtly seek to connect with traditions and help people to use their traditions while they seek recovery. This book recognizes and applauds these fine efforts. The goal of this book is to provide a structure by which some Native people are able to more effectively employ such strategies of recovery.

In any event, the program needs to be structured in ways that draw attention towards the Native cultural heritage. Doing so provides a way to appropriately showcase the conflicts between the Native and mainstream cultures. Such activities can help clients can to see what has been lost when Native cultures are weakened or as individuals lose touch with their traditions.

Primary Individual Counseling

Individual counseling, by nature, is a "one on one" activity involving a therapist/counselor dyad working together, largely in isolation. Although some group sessions with family members, associates, and friends may take place, individual therapy is largely and typically self-contained and involves a strong relationship between the counselor and the client. This arrangement possesses both strengths and weaknesses that stem from the somewhat isolated character of the therapy. Thus, individual counseling is closely attuned to the needs of the particular client, on the one hand, but the therapy does not benefit from the power of synergism (a major strength of much group therapy), or develop a life of its own that helps facilitate the recovery of the group as a larger entity. In individual counseling, furthermore, the client is protected from the possible shame and humiliation that can be triggered by admitting to past misdeeds within a group context.

Another difference is that in group therapy newcomers may be able to "pick up" the essentials of whatever program is being practiced by watching/listening to other participants and by being coached by them. In individual therapy, in contrast, clients and counselors may be required to exert, considerable time and effort discussing the basics of the program. Getting over the hurdle of these preliminaries can make progress painfully slow at first. A useful alternative is for the client to simultaneously be involved in some kind of group counseling or self-help activities that are centered around the Handsome Lake method as a supplement to "one on one" therapy sessions. In this way, individual therapy sessions need not dwell upon basic information about the nature of the Handsome Lake program and more time can be spent discussing the client's specific circumstances and needs.

In any event, clients need to be consciously aware of the Path and the Landmarks (they should be given copies of both) in order for them to most effectively come to grips with what triggers their dysfunctional behavior and how it might be linked to cultural stress and/or alienation from one's cultural traditions. On many occasions, a particular client may have been previously involved in therapy and counseling for alcoholism and, thereby, have prior experience with a mainstream method of treatment (such as the 12 Step Program). As a result, these clients may harbor preconceptions regarding what to expect in therapy and/or conclude that the program will probably not be relevant to them or an effective method of treatment. Where this is true, the differences between the Path of Handsome Lake and other alternatives need to be emphasized. A good initial move may be to ask the client about earlier therapy, what models were used, and the client's opinion of them.

As has been emphasized throughout this book, the Path of Handsome Lake is deeply concerned with the individuals' cultural heritage. It encourages participants to embrace their traditions and keep them strong while pointing to cultural renewal as a key to recovery. Emphasizing that recovery is linked to a strong and vibrant cultural heritage, the Path of Handsome Lake emphasizes that people often benefit from connecting with their cultural heritage in intimate ways. This whole process of cultural renewal overlays, while not hiding, the personal work of admitting past errors and guarding against future indiscretions.

Discussed in tabular form (Table 10.1), we find:

Table 10.1. Primary/Individual Therapy

	Overview	*Analysis*
Relationship	A strong counselor/client relationship exists that seeks to explore the cultural heritage of the client in order to combat tendencies towards alcoholism.	In individual therapy, the counselor and the client focus upon issues that concern the individual and the Native culture. The cloistered nature of the relationship prevents public shaming and humiliation.
Worldview	The shared worldview emphasizes that significant cultural stress can trigger individual dysfunction. Strengthening the cultural heritage and building the client's cultural awareness and comfort with Native culture can be therapeutic.	The Handsome Lake model of recovery is different from other programs of recovery because it deals with the Native culture as typically under stress. Accepting this worldview, the program centers upon individual vulnerability that is triggered by assaults on culture and/or the client's alienation from the cultural heritage.
Expectation	Working primarily as a dyad, the client and counselor expect to explore the cultural traditions of the client in order to overcome triggers that can lead to dysfunction.	The counselor and client expect to explore aspects of the cultural and heritage in ways that enhance the ability to combat dysfunction. There is an expectation that recovery can result from greater cultural awareness.
Intervention	The Path of Handsome Lake and the Landmarks of the Path are employed in order to make people more in touch with their heritage and less vulnerable to dysfunction resulting from anxiety related to cultural stress.	The intervention consists of practicing the Path of Handsome Lake and the Landmarks of the Path. These interventions build confidence in the ability to achieve sobriety while introducing the elements of the cultural heritage that are useful in recovery.
Discussion	The client and the counselor are involved in a program of therapy that is primarily based upon the Path of Handsome Lake/Landmarks of the Path. Although other programs (such as the 12 Steps program) may be discussed, doing so will only be accomplished in order to more effectively communicate the workings and benefits of the Handsome Lake strategy of recovery. The focus is upon the client's Native culture and the client's relationship to it.	

As argued above, a properly functioning cultural heritage can serve as a profound source of comfort and strength for many people. It can also serve as a buffer against stress and anxiety. In these ways, the cultural heritage can serve as a powerful means of mitigating the tensions that can lead to dysfunctional behavior, such as alcoholic drinking. When cultures are weakened and/or when people no longer identify with their heritage, however, this cultural buffer can cease to operate properly and, as a result, people can be subjected to unmitigated pressures that can trigger dysfunction.

Given this reality, by strengthening cultures and by helping individuals to relate more effectively to their heritage, the stress and anxiety that triggers dysfunction can be lessened and brought under control. In this way, tendencies towards alcoholic drinking can be reduced.

Individual therapy can most effectively explore how and why particular people began their alcoholic drinking and keep an open eye regarding the impact of a weakened culture and/or alienation from a cultural heritage (that might serve as the catalysts that led to dysfunction). In individual therapy, the specific client is able to deal with personal issues and do so in a private context that is often very important as people come to grips with their past behaviors.

Thus, individual one-on-one counseling and therapy employing the usual counselor/client dyad is a viable option when applying the Handsome Lake model of treatment. This, however, is not the only available program of recovery. For various reasons (both practical and as a matter of preference), group therapy may emerge as the most appropriate vehicle of therapy. It will be discussed below.

Primary Group Therapy

As indicated above, individual "one on one" counseling has the advantage of focusing upon the needs of the specific client, but this kind of therapy inevitably takes place in relative isolation. Group therapy, in contrast, being made up of several members, it is able to provide multiple perspectives. In addition, groups often develop an identity that has an elan and therapeutic value of its own. As a result of the interpersonal dynamics that often emerges when people interact, furthermore, group therapy is often more powerful and effective than individual counseling. This book does not show a preference for either type of therapy, but it does emphasize that both individual and group therapies have their own distinctive roles, strengths, and weaknesses. And, as indicated above, group and individual therapy can often work in tandem with each another in positive ways that resonate from the other.

Some therapy groups are ongoing, although specific group members may come and go over time. Where this is true, a knowledge of the Path of Handsome Lake/Landmarks of the Path will emerge and become a permanent feature of that group. As indicated above, where the group is permanent and ongoing, existing members can orient newcomers and make them aware of the basics of the program. This can save time and effort on the part of the counselor. Some ad hoc groups, in contrast, may have been created for a special purpose, have a limited life, and cease to exist on a particular schedule. When a new group is begun (be it a temporary ad hoc group or the beginning of on ongoing group activity), the facilitator will need to outline the basics of the Handsome Lake program and how it differs from other strategies of recovery.

In specific, everyone in the group needs to clearly understand how the Path of Handsome Lake works, why it is structured the way it is, and what it seeks to accomplish. As emphasized above, cultural stress and/or decline coupled with the possible alienation of individuals from their heritage can lead to pressures and anxieties that can trigger dysfunctional behavior. By rebuilding cultural strength and the clients' awareness of and respect for their heritage, valuable perspectives needed for recovery can be established. As a result, clients can become better equipped to lead a sober and fruitful life.

A part of this process can involve a more complete and positive introduction (or re-introduction) to the Native culture. The whole focus is to help individuals within a group setting to connect (or reconnect) with their heritage in positive ways. A particular therapy group, however, will probably be composed of members of various Native cultures; as a result, therapy cannot merely focus upon a specific set of traditions that are linked to one homogeneous group or a unique Native culture.[3] Instead, the program needs to help all members of the group to recognize the power of their own particular cultural heritage. By doing so, each member can better understand how cultural decline and personal alienation from a cultural heritage might trigger alcoholism

Presented in tabular form(Table 10.2), we find:

Table 10.2. Primary Group Therapy

	Overview	*Analysis*
Relationship	A group of people, monitored and led by a facilitator creates a forum where people can explore their cultural heritages in order to combat tendencies towards alcoholism	In group therapy, the facilitator focuses the group's attention around issues concerned with Native cultures. The nature of the group facilitates a freewheeling approach that can provide a rich and varied therapy.
Worldview	The shared worldview emphasizes how cultural stress can trigger individual dysfunction. Strengthening the cultural heritage and building the group's cultural awareness of and developing a comfort for the Native culture can be therapeutic to the group, in general, and to individuals, in specific.	The Handsome Lake model of recovery is different from other programs of recovery because it acknowledges that Native cultures are often under stress. Accepting this worldview, the program centers upon how group members may be vulnerable to assaults upon the culture and personal alienation from their cultural heritage.
Expectation	Working in a group setting, members expect to explore each other's cultural traditions in order to overcome vulnerabilities that can lead to dysfunction. Positive confrontation and criticism is often a positive activity.	The facilitator and the group expect to explore aspects of the cultures and heritages of the members in ways that help all to overcome dysfunction. There is an expectation that recovery can result from greater cultural awareness and becoming comfortable with one's traditions.
Intervention	The group employs the Path of Handsome Lake and the Landmarks of the Path so each person can get more in touch with their heritage and become less vulnerable to dysfunction resulting from anxiety related to cultural stress and/or alienation from a cultural heritage.	In group therapy, the Path of Handsome Lake and the Landmarks of the Path are practiced in order to provide a collective insight to both personal and group problems. These interventions build confidence in the ability to achieve sobriety by strengthening the culture and the individual's relationship to it.
Discussion	The group and its facilitator are involved in a program of therapy that is primarily based upon the Path of Handsome Lake/Landmarks of the Path model. Although other programs (such as the 12 Steps program) may be discussed, they will be discussed in order to more effectively communicate the workings and benefits of the Handsome Lake strategy of recovery. The focus is upon Native cultures and the group members relationship to them.	

In group therapy that is primarily based on the Handsome Lake model, this method, of course, dominates. There are advantages to this arrangement because doing so can more forcefully center therapy upon the Native culture and its role in recovery.

On other occasions, however, the Handsome Lake method may be used in conjunction with other methods or programs of recovery. In an era when other programs are more firmly established, it is inevitable that such an arrangement will be commonplace. As a result, dealing with situations where the Path of Handsome Lake shares the stage (and often serves in a subordinate role) need to be discussed

A SUPPLEMENTAL PROGRAM

In reality, of course, other methods of recovery tend to dominate alcoholism treatment strategies. And the most prevalent method is the 12 Steps Program developed by Alcoholics Anonymous. Without question, these mainstream programs dominate alcoholism therapy and, as a result, many individuals will primarily be served by such agendas. Nevertheless, as discussed above, the limitations of applying mainstream solutions to Native problems may be profound. The 12 Steps Program, for example, does not focus upon cultural stress and the potential decline of Native cultures nor does it seek to counter the alienation that many Native people might feel towards their traditions (not to mention the fact that many Native people may be largely ignorant of their heritage). Thus, although the 12 Steps Program is not inherently antagonistic to the Path of Handsome Lake (and other culturally-centered programs), it does not deal with the entire array of pressures and challenges that many Native people tend to face. Due to this void, the Handsome Lake program can provide a valuable service for Native people seeking recovery.

In such situations, the Path of Handsome Lake can emerge as an invaluable supplement to mainstream programs of recovery. While not conflicting with recovery strategies such as the 12 Step Program, it can provide the specific cultural attention (and opportunities for healing) that Native clients may need.

In the case of the 12 Step Program, for example, the focus is typically upon individuals who are characterized as having lost step with their culture. That culture, however, is depicted as vibrant, permanent, and ongoing. Conceiving the problem in this manner, it logically follows that those seeking to recover can re-embrace their culture as they seek relief from their dysfunction. Under such circumstances, the strength and security of the culture continue to exist and, upon regaining sobriety, the recovering person can reclaim them. Because mainstream programs tend to be structured in this way, the health of the culture is not addressed as a significant issue. Among many Native peoples, however, the culture has been significantly undermined and/or people have become distanced from it, even though mainstream programs do nothing to relieve these triggers of anxiety and dysfunction.

By positioning the Path of Handsome Lake as a useful addendum of treatment that fills in the gaps left by mainstream programs, it can be simultaneously practiced along with other more conventional models of treatment.

When the Handsome Lake program is being used in conjunction with some other program of recovery, clients need to be kept conscious of (1) the similarities and (2) the differences in each program and how each can usefully supplement the other. The lack of conflict between these programs needs to be emphasized. Acting in such a spirit, each program should be dealt with as equally valid (but different) components of recovery. A good point of entry for such issues might be the observation that people can simultaneously be a part of their traditional Native culture and the mainstream world.

Discussions can seek to establish areas where clients feel they are members of the mainstream world and, in contrast, where they believe they are strongly influenced by their traditional culture. It is important to emphasize that these two worlds may be in significant conflict and, therefore, they can trigger tensions, stress, anxiety, and dysfunction. Such discussions can be valuable when focusing upon conflicts that exist and how the resulting anxiety can be mitigated. Such discussions may reveal conflicts that can lead to anxiety, stress, and dysfunctional behavior.

Individual Supplemental Counseling

Individual supplemental counseling has same strengths and weaknesses as primary individual counseling (see discussion above). In summary, it is centered around the needs of one person, but it doesn't benefit from the positive synergism of group participation.

In individual supplemental counseling, it is vital to determine how the client's needs can be addressed via conventional therapy versus the use of more culturally sensitive strategies, such as the Handsome Lake method. As indicated above, mainstream programs (such as the 12 Step Program) are neither strongly attuned to cultural stress/cultural decline nor do they deal with the possibility that people have become alienated from their traditional culture. Probing the client to determine the role that each program should play provides a way to better understand how therapy should proceed. If possible, written assignments prepared outside of the therapy session as "homework" can help clients think about these issues.

A goal should be to determine how the Handsome Lake method can best be applied and how it can be most effectively integrated with other programs of recovery. What benefits will the particular client get from each? How can these benefits be positively blended with each other? Having done so, the program needs to be implemented with reference to the usual tactics of individual therapy. An overview of the program presented in tabular form (Table 10.3) is as follows:

Table 10.3. Supplemental Individual Therapy

	Overview	*Analysis*
Relationship	A strong counselor/client relationship seeks to employ the Handsome Lake model along with other methods in the most effective way. The client and counselor work together to devise the proper structure of their unique program	Where other programs are being employed along with the Handsome Lake model, the client and counselor need to determine the appropriate role of each program. There is no universally "right" or "wrong" strategy because different clients have their own needs and vulnerabilities.
Worldview	The Handsome Lake method and conventional treatments each have strengths and weaknesses. The counselor and client need to determine how each method will be employed. The resulting decision will lead to a worldview regrading the client's needs.	Although the therapeutic relationship may employ two different methods or strategies, they need not conflict. Each method can serve special roles. After determining the client's needs, the role of each method can be determined in a manner that best serves the client.
Expectation	Interacting as a dyad, the client and counselor work towards recovery in a mutually agreeable way. They will expect results to reflect the collective orientations of the client and the counselor.	Because expectations will, to a large extent, be a function of shared worldview of the counselor and client, they will evolve a unique therapeutic relationship. Formally establishing a list of expectations and putting them in writing is a good strategy.
Intervention	An appropriate intervention will be based upon the worldview and expectations of the client and counselor. Components of both the Handsome Lake method and the conventional therapy will be present. The final formula will be based on client needs.	Intervention consists of practicing the Handsome Lake and conventional program in a way that suits the unique client. To whatever degree the client is impacted by cultural decline and alienation from their heritage, the Handsome Lake model will be important. Nonetheless, there is no inherent conflict between different methods employed.
Discussion	The client and the counselor use the Handsome Lake model as a supplemental method. In such situations, the role of different strategies of recovery needs to be determined. Both the client and counselor need to be aware that the Handsome Lake model and other strategies of recovery are not in conflict, but are merely different tools to be used as required. Since each client will typically have unique needs and expectations, it is a good idea create a written list of expectations and a formal plan regarding the use of various methods.	

The Path of Handsome Lake should be presented as a special program that has the potential to provide useful reflection and growth for some people. The program's ability to deal with issues of stress and alienation from a cultural heritage needs to be actively considered. In the process, it may be useful to explain that Alcoholics Anonymous/the 12 Step Program is not equipped to deal cultural stress and decline and with the stress of cultural alienation. Pointing out the strengths and limitations of each program, discussions with the client can be used to determine the degree to which each program should be incorporated in the therapeutic process.

When using the Handsome Lake model within a supplemental capacity, the array of options becomes increasingly complex because no exact and pre-defined template exists upon which to base therapy. Instead, the counselor and the client need to consider the client's particular needs and how they can best be addressed. Although creating an appropriate mix of elements can be difficult, doing so provides a tailored program uniquely suitable to a particular individual. Nonetheless, striking a proper balance can be difficult and cannot be accomplished using rote tactics.

Supplemental Group Therapy

In group therapy, as indicated above, the group has an existence that transcends the individual and the resulting ambience often serves both the individual and the group.

In a supplemental capacity, the Path of Handsome Lake is used in conjunction with some other program. In most cases, this other program will be a conventional strategy of recovery such as the 12 Step Program. As we saw above, however, conventional programs typically do not deal in any meaningful way with cultural stress and alienation. We also saw that in many cases the members comprising the group will come from various backgrounds and derive from a wide variety of cultures. Situations where all group members are from exactly the same culture will be an exception to the rule. As a result, group therapy can be very complex.

On one level, two specific programs are being dealt with simultaneously; this fact adds complexity to group interactions. Secondly, multiple cultures will be represented. These cultural differences are layered over the differences that exist between the personal styles of various members and the persona/professional style of the facilitator.

During sessions, all the group members share various aspects of their cultural heritage and the pressures and stresses that their culture faces/has faced as well as the anxieties triggered by cultural stress and/or individual alienation from a cultural heritage. When specific examples of cultural stress, conflict, and anxiety are analyzed, they can be discussed in general terms so all group members can relate to them. Nevertheless, the specifics of particular cases need to be recognized.

Presented in tabular form (Table 10.4), we find:

Table 10.4. Supplemental Group Therapy

	Overview	*Analysis*
Relationship	The group seeks to explore the advantages of the Handsome Lake and other models of recovery. The group and facilitator understand that different clients have different needs and that each member will practice a unique program of recovery.	Where other programs are being employed along with the Handsome Lake model, the group needs to understand that different members will have their own unique needs. Members must respect the programs of recovery practiced by others and understand that there is no inherently "right" strategy, because different members have their own needs and vulnerabilities.
Worldview	Both the Handsome Lake method and the conventional strategy of treatment have their strengths and weaknesses. The group and the facilitator need to underscore that each program is valuable, but different people will need to implement them in their own ways.	Although the therapeutic relationship may employ two or more different methods or strategies, this does not mean that they are in conflict. Instead, each is able to serve various group members in a unique manner. By allowing all group members to structure their strategy of recovery, they will benefit from self-determinism and the strength provided by group solidarity.
Expectation	The group and facilitator will work towards recovery in the manner agreed upon by the group. Nonetheless, the structure will allow for individual differences and all members will expect this.	Because various strategies are combined, the shared worldview of the group will acknowledge individual variations. As a result, the expectations of each member will be somewhat unique. Formally establishing a list of expectations is a good strategy.
Intervention	An appropriate intervention will be based upon the worldview and expectations of the group and the needs of individual members. Components of both the Handsome Lake method and the conventional therapy will fit into the final formula chosen by individual members.	The intervention consists of practicing the Handsome Lake and conventional methods in a way that conforms to the group consensus and meets the needs of individuals. To whatever degree group members have been impacted by cultural decline and/or be alienation from their heritage, the Handsome Lake model is useful. Nonetheless, there is no inherent conflict between that method and any other.
Discussion	The group and the facilitator are involved in a program where the Handsome Lake model is used in a supplemental fashion as needed to serve the group and its individual clients. It is vital to emphasize that the Handsome Lake model and other strategies of recovery are not in conflict, but are merely different tools to be used as required. Since each member will typically have a unique set of needs and expectations, it is a good idea for each member to create a written list of expectations and perceived needs.	

It is important to emphasize that the Handsome Lake method is not in conflict or in competition with any other strategy of recovery. In addition, the distinctiveness of different cultures needs to be emphasized, although the possibility of diverse cultures may be subjected to similar pressures might emerge as a thread that ties different stories and experiences together.

Thus, on many occasions, the Handsome Lake method will be used in a supplemental manner. Since there is no inherent conflict between the Handsome Lake program and other strategies of therapy, it can be employed in a wide number of ways.

CONCLUSION

According to Fischer, Jobe, & Atkinson (1998), multicultural therapy consists of at least the following components: (1) a therapeutic relationship exists, (2) those involved in this relationship have some kind of a shared world-view, (3) The person receiving help has certain expectations, and (4) some kind of ritual or intervention occurs. In this chapter, the Path of Handsome Lake/Landmarks of the Path method were analyzed according to these criteria. So viewed, it clearly met the criteria of therapy.

While the Handsome Lake model provides a specific means of therapy, it can be used in a variety of ways. On some occasions the method may emerge as the primary vehicle of therapy while, on other occasions, it may serve in a supplemental program. As a result, the Handsome Lake program can be applied in four distinct ways, (1) individual primary therapy, (2) individual supplemental therapy, (3) group primary therapy, and (4) group supplemental therapy. By providing guidelines for each use, the flexibility of the program is demonstrated.

NOTES

1. Hofstede, of course, is primarily a business scholar concerned with cross-cultural management. Nonetheless, the helping professions typically treat people in ways that require the same skills as those who supervise others in the workforce.
2. Those seeking copies of Napoleon's book can acquire them by contacting the Alaska Native Knowledge Network University of Alaska at Fairbanks, Fairbanks, Alaska 99775. The price is reasonable.
3. Even among members of the same Native culture there are often many groups that are unique in their own distinctive ways. Among the Athabascan people of Alaska, for example, the culture is made up of many subsets each having their own traditions and distinctions. As a result, finding a group of Native people who are "identical" is almost impossible.

REFERENCES

Fischer, A.R., Jome, L.R.M., & Atkinson, D.R. (1998). Reconceptualizing multicultural counseling: Universal healing conditions in a culturally specific context. *The Counseling Psychologist,* 26(4), 525–588.

Napoleon, H. (1996). *Yuuyaraq: The way of being human.* Fairbanks, AL.: Alaska Native Knowledge Network.

Sue, D. W., Arrodondo, P., & McDavis R. J. (1992). Multicultural counseling competencies and standards: A call to the profession. *Journal of Counseling and Development, 70*(4), 477–486.

CHAPTER 11

STRATEGIES FOR SELF-HELP

Just as Native alcoholics can benefit from professional interventions that are culturally sensitive, they are also well served by self-help programs that (1) acknowledge the pressures faced by Native people and (2) work to rebuild a connectedness with indigenous traditions. A program of self-help that is based upon the Path of Handsome Lake/Landmarks of the Path model is one example of techniques that can encourage cultural-awareness while simultaneously combating the maladies of uncontrolled drinking.

This chapter discusses how self-help activities that are based on the legacy of Handsome Lake can be used to combat Native alcoholism. In many ways, these dialogues mirror the structure of Chapter 10, although earlier discussions dealt with professional interventions while the topic here is self-help. Although parts of this chapter could have been truncated because they somewhat repeat what appeared earlier, a degree of redundancy has been employed so both chapters can be freestanding and read independently of the other.

As was the case with professional interventions, Native-centered programs of self-help may emerge as a primary vehicle of recovery. Perhaps in most cases, however, those in recovery will also be involved with mainstream programs, such as Alcoholics Anonymous. After all, recovering alcoholics tend to gravitate towards nationally known programs and those that are within easy reach. Although these "genuine" programs may not be tailored to the needs of some participants (such as various Native people

The Path of Handsome Lake: A Model of Recovery for Native People, pages 167–184

seeking recovery), they tend to be the available options. As a result, these tools of recovery are most often relied upon.

Due to this state of affairs, many Native alcoholics seeking recovery will probably be involved in generic programs of recovery, even though they are likely to ignore the uniqueness of Native people and their cultures. This situation can create a need for alternatives that more substantially address cultural issues. As argued throughout this book, by acknowledging and responding to a Native identity, key issues that are skirted by mainstream strategies of therapy can be usefully addressed.

This chapter focuses upon the value of using the Handsome Lake method in a variety of self-help contexts. By doing so, Natives seeking recovery will find it easier to (1) more effectively cope with their cultural heritage and its influences while, (2) addressing the impact of social change upon Native peoples and their cultures. Both of these activities provide culturally sensitive ways for Native people to combat the ravages of alcoholism.

As in Chapter 10, the model used to demonstrate the applicability of the Handsome Lake strategy is derived from the work of Fischer, Jome, & Atkinson (1998). Their model requires a certain amount of adjustment, however, since they are primarily concerned with professional interventions. This chapter, in contrast, deals with self-help avenues to recovery. Nonetheless, as we shall see, their model can easily be adapted for analyzing self-help activities.

Specifically, Fischer, Jome, and Atkinson outline four universal characteristics that need to exist within helping and healing contexts. These characteristics include: (1) a therapeutic relationship is present (2) those involved in the healing relationship embrace some kind of a shared worldview, (3) those receiving help have certain expectations, and (4) rituals and/or interventions occur. So phrased, there is no reason why such a model cannot be applied to self-help activities.

Fischer, Jobe, & Atkinson's model is especially useful because it provides an analytic framework that can be used when self-help programs are being analyzed. Using this model, each characteristic is discussed with reference to self-help groups and the Handsome Lake method.

THE THERAPEUTIC RELATIONSHIP

In order for people to truly benefit from self-help activities, a therapeutic relationship needs to be established. Thus, when people band together for their mutual benefit, it is important that a therapeutic goal is acknowledged. Thus, in any number of self-help groups (such as Alcoholics Anonymous) participants clearly envision the nature of the relationship as therapeutic. Members of Alcoholics Anonymous, for example, often acknowledge that they might not personally like certain fellow members of the meetings they attend, but go on to say that those annoying individuals can still have a positive role in their quest for sobriety.

Self-help groups are convened in order for people to help each other achieve a common goal: sobriety. In many cases, the membership is a cross sample of the general population and particular members who would never associate with each other on a social level are united by their search for recovery. Various catchphrases heard at Alcoholics Anonymous meetings, for example, define meetings as medicine: free medicine that provides relief from alcoholism.

According to Fischer, Tobe, & Atkinson, "In sum, the therapeutic relationship factor represents the positive, trusting, and healing relationship between.... [participants]. Both the Western or integrationist and the transcultural literatures ... unequivocally support the importance of the therapeutic relationship" (1998).

Just like other self-help programs (such as Alcoholics Anonymous), The Handsome Lake method should be applied from within the context of therapy. People need to view the program and the relationships that derive from it as a part of the process of recovery. Even if the relationships established through the program grow to be pleasant ends in themselves and/or if various friendships come to extend beyond the arena of self-help, the therapeutic value of the program needs to be emphasized.

As will be discussed below, Native people seeking recovery may develop greater rapport and trust when using the Handsome Lake system because it is squarely centered upon Native perspectives. As a result, this self-help program is not merely an extension of foreign/Western ideas from which the client may be alienated. In recent years, by analogy, many Native people and strategies of recovery have come to emphasize cultural traditions and, possibly, the advice and teachings of Native elders and cultural leaders. This precedence opens the door to programs such as the Handsome Lake method because it also focuses upon a Native identity. The Handsome Lake approach may be especially useful for Native people who do not trust, are alienated from, and/or are angry at the dominant culture.

As a result of the fact that the Handsome Lake method is based upon Native traditions, it can help create linkages between Natives seeking recovery, their heritage, and a program of therapy. Self-help activities can, thereby, be enhanced and, in the process, participants can more effectively deal with the anxieties of cultural stress and the anxiety that is triggered by becoming alienated from a cultural heritage.

A SHARED WORLDVIEW

Those involved in a therapeutic relationship need a shared worldview regarding their needs and the therapy they are receiving. "Thus, both the Western and transcultural approaches ... support the importance of a shared worldview between [participants].... The presence of a shared worldview ... [can] set the stage for positive expectations and to allow the healer to offer explanations or rationales for distress that fit with the client's view of the world" (Fischer, Jobe, & Atkinson, 1998).

Those involved in Alcoholics Anonymous, for example, tend to share a worldview that assumes that some kind of a higher power exists and that recovery derives from following the dictates of this higher power. This worldview continues by observing that many people are vain, over-prideful, and dominant and that they insist upon doing things their own way. The worldview of Alcoholics Anonymous also emphasizes that alcoholism is an incurable illness, but that recovery can be possible as long as the afflicted person refrains from drinking.

As indicated above, however, this shared worldview does not address the special issues and vulnerabilities faced by Native people as their cultures are placed under stress and/or as individuals become alienated from their traditions. As a result, a self-help group that responds to the special needs of the cultural of this particular population will need to establish and articulate its own special worldview.

One of the ways by which self-help groups can more effectively focus upon a Native worldview is to emphasize that people from Native cultures often need to embrace their heritage in order to reduce stress and anxiety. Shaded and protected by their traditions, recovery can become more easily achieved. The Handsome Lake method is one example of a self-help program that specifically seeks to follow this path. Not only does the Handsome Lake program serve specific individuals seeking recovery, it also emphasizes that cultures often must transform themselves if they are to cope with changing times and evolving conditions. Handsome Lake provides a self-help experience that acknowledges the participants' cultural heritages, the strengths and vulnerabilities deriving from them, and the fact that people may have ignored these traditions. Transcending this situation by embracing the culture and acknowledging its power becomes the shared worldview that typifies the program.

This worldview emphasizes that Natives in recovery typically need to (1) understand their cultural heritage, (2) recognize its power and importance, (3) perceive how cultures are always changing, and (4) specifically work these traditions into a program of recovery. Adopting such a framework, self-help activities will come to embrace a worldview that acknowledges that cultures are fluid and evolving and that people can be vulnerable to unmitigated social and cultural change that, to a greater or lesser degree, is always taking place.

EXPECTATION

In order for self-help groups to be effective, their members need to believe that significant benefits potentially derive from their efforts. "Overall, it appears that ...expectations or hope for a positive benefit from therapy is a basic element seen across cultures....[therapeutic relationships] raise.... expectations and gain credibility through the setting in which they conduct therapy"(Fischer, Jobe, & Atkinson, 1998). As a corollary, expectations can be strengthened if people strongly believe that the therapy they are receiving will address concrete needs that they consciously recognize.

Self-help groups routinely provide positive expectations. Alcoholics Anonymous, for example, predicts that individuals who attend meetings and sincerely "work the program" will experience a spiritual rebirth and that this reawakening will provide the strength and insight they need to successfully combat their affliction. Each component of the 12 Steps Program, furthermore, provides opportunities for personal growth and the ability to transcend dysfunction. The Alcoholics Anonymous program also provides the expectation that a vulnerability to alcohol survives within individuals even when they are sober and after the overt symptoms of dysfunction have disappeared. Since Alcoholics Anonymous maintains that the disease is "cunning, baffling, and powerful," alcoholic tendencies are believed to be always waiting in the wings for a chance to reassert them.

The Handsome Lake program, expanding beyond Alcoholics Anonymous and the 12 Steps, focuses upon the fact that (1) the traditional culture may be under attack and (2) many Native people are estranged from their heritage. This model goes on to affirm that individual dysfunction is often directly linked to a weakening and undermining of the traditional culture. Self-help activities based on the expectation that (1) cultures can be strengthened, (2) that people can connect with this heritage, and (3) that recovery from alcoholism can be based, in part, upon the clients' embracing their culture and the strength and stability it provides. These are very real and achievable expectations and they can be easily articulated to clients.

INTERVENTION OR RITUAL

Not only do clients need to possess the expectation that their therapy will be effective and that it can help relieve their dysfunction in some way, progress is viewed as resulting from some special activity; "Our forth common factor is conceptualized as interventions, rituals, or techniques that are believed by... [participants] to have healing potential. Thus, an intervention that is relevant and effective for one ... [alcoholic] may not be as relevant or effective for another..., depending on the degree of relationship, shared worldview, and positive expectations"(Fischer, Jobe, & Atkinson, 1998).

Other groups of recovery, such as Alcoholics Anonymous have established a wide range of interventions and rituals. One only has to attend Alcoholics Anonymous 12 Step meetings to see a whole series of ritualistic routines that are intended to facilitate recovery. Those aspiring towards recovery, furthermore, are told that they must confess their shortcomings to themselves, to God and to another person. It is often predicted that those who hold back from formally practicing this ritual will be vulnerable to relapse.[1] Since recovery is often linked to humility, it is recommended that newcomers take on some menial task (such as making coffee before meetings or cleaning up the meeting room afterwards) and that doing so is a significant component of recovery.

One difference between the 12 Step Program and the model presented by Fischer, Jome, & Atkinson is that Alcoholics Anonymous tends to center upon the fact that all people are united by their malady and that one basic program of recovery is suitable for all alcoholics while Fischer, Jome, & Atkinson emphasize the differences between people and the need to adjust interventions accordingly. The Handsome Lake program, agreeing with Fishcher, Jome, & Atkinson, affirms that strategies of treatment need to be appropriate for specific participants and that what works for one person may not work for everybody. Indeed, this book has emphasized that Native alcoholics may need alternatives to the Alcoholics Anonymous/12 Steps Program because that program may not sufficiently address cultural stress/alienation and the dysfunction that is often triggered by them. As a result, this book has suggested that while the 12 Steps Program may be useful in many contexts and for many individuals, it does not deal with all of the issues that many Native alcoholics need to address.

This book also emphasizes that special interventions are needed that allow people to more fully embrace their cultural traditions and to mitigate the attacks that militate against this heritage (as well as the possibility that people may become alienated from their cultural background). In this way, the Handsome Lake program provides an array of interventions/rituals that help Native alcoholics to better deal with their culture. These activities can serve as catalysts for recovery in ways that transcend existing, mainstream programs.

Thus, the Path of Handsome Lake program of recovery meets the four criteria of therapy provided by Fischer, Jome, & Atkinson. Being flexible, furthermore, it can be implemented in a variety of self-help contexts ranging from a serving as a primary strategy of self-help to being used as a supplemental program. Examples of how the Handsome Lake strategy of recovery can serve in a variety of self-help contexts is provided below.

A PRIMARY PROGRAM

Programs of recovery that embrace the Handsome Lake approach may be used as a primary vehicle of self-help. This book has emphasized that many Native people are not adequately attuned to their cultural heritage and, as a result, they may be unaware of the impact of their culture upon their identity and upon their tendencies toward alcoholic drinking. Nonetheless, on many occasions, this heritage may covertly impact people in ways that lead to dysfunction. Where these tendencies of obliviousness exist, unmitigated stress, trauma, and anxiety can easily result. Alcoholic drinking and other dysfunctional behaviors have been known to arise under such circumstances.

Other self help methods, such as Alcoholics Anonymous and the 12 Step Program, do not overtly and forcefully deal with the weakening of cultural traditions and the alienation that it can trigger. They, in contrast, are likely to presuppose that a strong and vital society/culture remains for recovering alcoholics to rejoin once they embrace recovery. As a result of this focus and the assumptions inherent in it, little thought and effort is directed towards the culture, its health, and its impact upon individuals.

An unfortunate artifact of this mainstream vision is that it is not designed to help Native people cope with the fact that their cultures may be under severe attack and/or that they may have become alienated from their traditions and sunk into alcoholic drinking as a result. Nonetheless, many Native alcoholics face profound cultural trauma and alienation from their traditions and such experiences have often triggered alcoholic drinking. While mainstream methods are not designed to deal with these hurtful experiences, the Handsome Lake method is explicitly focused around them. This method, furthermore, can be adapted for either individual counseling or group therapy.

Structuring the Program/Setting the Stage

Specific Native alcoholics may or may not be aware that cultural decline and/or alienation from their culture heritage may trigger anxiety that can lead to a downward spiral of alcoholic drinking. Under such circumstances, a first step is to make clients aware of the possible negative impacts that can result from (1) attacks and pressures on their culture and (2) becoming alienated from the Native heritage. Some clients will immediately recognize these impacts while others will not.

As was the case for in our discussion of professional interventions in the last chapter, Harold Napoleon's analysis of cultural decline among the Yup'ik of Alaska and its impact (1996) may prove useful. This short and readable book chronicles how cultural decline, triggered by cultural disruption, can lead to personal dysfunction among Native people. The insights provided by Napoleon can pave the way for envisioning the value of the Handsome Lake program because Napoleon's account closely parallels the decline of the Iroquois and the resulting rise of alcoholism as chronicled by Handsome Lake. Once the hurtful impacts of cultural decline/alienation are understood and acknowledged, the value of a program of recovery that builds upon the cultural heritage can be more readily accepted.

When envisioning the example of Handsome Lake, it is useful for participants to recognize that he was a seemingly incurable alcoholic who recovered his personal life and went on to become an important leader of the Iroquois. By focusing on this example of personal success, the possibility of a positive and fruitful recovery for clients can be envisioned. Many Native alcoholics will identify with Handsome Lake's decline into alcoholism and, thereby, gain hope through his example of recovery.

Once Handsome Lake is recognized as a man who successfully recovered from alcoholism, his plan of recovery will gain credibility. Those embracing the program need to recognize how Handsome Lake combined personal recovery with cultural renewal. So envisioned, it can be presented in ways that provide the promise of personal recovery and point the way towards achieving it.

Those who are using the Handsome Lake program may need to view themselves as Native people who may have been injured and traumatized in a rapidly changing world where their heritage was ignored and devalued. They also need to be aware of a relationship between these experiences and their alcoholism. The Handsome Lake program provides these linkages.

Participants also need to remember that people are often unaware of their own identity and that their heritage influences behavior (including dysfunctional behavior). Due to this initial unawareness, clients may need to systematically think about who they really are. The process of gaining this insight is often complicated and difficult for people to follow. Nonetheless, doing so can be vital to recovery. If at all possible, participants should create their own personal record of building this awareness so that they can refer back to it later and recall how they felt and thought in an earlier stage of their lives. By having this personal document constantly available, they can refer back to it in days to come and, thereby, place their alcoholic drinking within a broader context.

This process of building a greater cultural awareness can be facilitated by the fact that many Native cultures are publishing lists of their values. These lists can be of great value to those engaged in a self-help program of recovery. If participants are from a Native culture that has compiled such a list, it can provide a useful point of departure for those seeking to build a greater degree of cultural awareness. If the specific culture has not created these documents, the codes and lists provided by other Native peoples may be able to trigger an understanding of similar traditions.

As has been emphasized throughout this book, if a program of recovery does not deal with cultural stress and alienation, it is not equipped to deal with a major source of Native alcoholism. As a result, Native alcoholics often need programs and therapies that provide a strong cultural orientation and analysis.

In situations where the Path of Handsome Lake program is practiced, a vibrant and robust Native community may exist. Where this is true, the recovering alcoholic may have access to important elders and other carriers of tradition that can be an aid the process of recovery. As indicted earlier, embracing Native traditions within the process of recovery is a well-established principle. The significance of the Handsome Lake program is that it blends with these practices by providing a means of focusing upon cultural themes as well as individual recovery.

Primary Individual Self-Help

Among the mainstream population, self-help programs are typically group activities. This is due, in part, to the fact that opportunities often exist for people to band together for their mutual benefit. Native people, in contrast, are more likely to live in more remote areas and, therefore, they may not have access to group activities. In addition, new programs (such as the Handsome Lake method) are not yet well established and groups will probably not be available. As a result, those seeking to use the Handsome Lake Program may have to do so independently or on an individual basis.

When working alone, participants will not be able to gain the essentials of the program from "osmosis" through associating with others more experienced participants. As a result, those working in isolation may need to exert considerable effort in order to master basics of the program. Gaining this background can make progress painfully slow at first. But by keeping in mind that dysfunction may result from cultural stress and alienation, participants can constantly focus upon the major premise of the program.

In any event, participants need to be consciously aware of the Path and the Landmarks (they should be have copies of both). In situations where participants are familiar with other self-help programs, they may have preconceived ideas that may be inappropriate for the Handsome Lake program. The significant differences between the Path of Handsome Lake and other alternatives, therefore, need to be spotlighted.

Discussed in tabular form (Table 11.1), we find:

Table 11.1. Primary Individual Self-Help

	Overview	*Analysis*
Relationship	A relationship between the participant and the program helps participants explore their cultural heritage as a therapy for combating alcoholism	In primary individual self-help, the Handsome Lake program focuses upon issues concerning the participants' Native culture. In doing so, an effort is made to strengthen this relationship so it can play a role in combating alcoholism.
Worldview	The Handsome Lake program establishes a shared worldview between the program and the participant that emphasizes how (1)cultural stress can trigger individual dysfunction and (2) being comfortable with a Native heritage can be therapeutic.	The Handsome Lake model of recovery is different from other self-help programs because it deals with the Native culture and its impact upon people. This worldview provides a means of envisioning both dysfunction and recovery. So focused, it can provide strategies of combating alcoholism.
Expectation	Participants expect that developing a greater cultural awareness and becoming comfortable with their heritage will have a therapeutic value that can aid in recovery from alcoholism.	Participants expect to explore aspects of their cultural and heritage in ways that can help mitigate anxiety and , thereby, reduce dysfunction. There is an expectation that recovery can result from greater cultural awareness.
Intervention	The Path of Handsome Lake and the Landmarks of the Path are employed in order to make people more in touch with their heritage and less vulnerable to dysfunction resulting from anxiety related to cultural stress.	The intervention consists of practicing the Path of Handsome Lake and the Landmarks of the Path. Such activities build confidence in the ability to achieve sobriety, while introducing elements of the cultural heritage that are useful in recovery
Discussion	Participants who are involved in a program of therapy that is primarily based upon the Path of Handsome Lake/Landmarks of the Path model seek to combine recovery with a greater understanding of their cultural heritage. Although other programs (such as the 12 Steps program) may be addressed, they do not deal with cultural issues as the Handsome Lake method does. The Handsome Lake method, therefore, has a specific and unique contribution to make that is not duplicated by other self-help program.	

As discussed earlier, the Handsome Lake program centers on the alcoholic's culture and it encourages participants to remain conscious of their heritage. Affirming that recovery is likely to be linked to a vital cultural tradition, the Handsome Lake method emphasizes the process of cultural renewal and how it can serve as a foundation for recovery.

Besides serving as a source of strength and comfort, the cultural heritage can mitigate the tensions that can lead to dysfunctional behavior, such as alcoholic drinking. Cultures that are under stress will not be able to mitigate the stressed faced by their members. This will be especially true where people do not identify with their heritage. As a result, strengthening cultures and by helping individuals to relate more effectively to their heritage are tools that may be invaluable in reducing the stress and anxiety that triggers dysfunction.

Individual primary self-help activities can provide a means of helping people explore what triggers their alcoholic behavior. This process can take place within a private context.

Primary self-help involving the Handsome Lake model of treatment is not the only available program of recovery. Other possible options will be discussed below.

PRIMARY SELF-HELP GROUP ACTIVITIES

As indicated above, individual and independent self-help activities can address the participant's unique needs, but they take place largely in isolation. Group self-help activities, in contrast, are able to provide multiple perspectives. Groups, furthermore, take on a life of their own that often possesses a therapeutic value. While these are significant benefits, self-help groups also have their potential drawbacks. Lay people who probably have little professional training in helping alcoholics to recover, for example, tend to run self-help groups. As a result, these well-meaning individuals may not be as well versed in dysfunction and its therapy as a professional counselor would be. Some, furthermore, may dogmatically champion what worked for them. Nonetheless, a group composed of lay people working for their mutual benefit can provide impressive results. Those involved in self-help activities need to be aware of both the strengths and weaknesses of such programs.

In self-help groups, participants come and go and some members become better versed in the program than others. Nonetheless, everyone tends to be given as "equal voice" and individual participants must figure out for themselves who are good role models and what messages are worth remembering. When employing the Handsome Lake program, a basic consideration is that cultural stress and/or decline (coupled with the possible alienation of individuals from their heritage) can trigger anxiety and dysfunctional behavior. By rebuilding the strength of the culture and the participants' awareness of and respect for their heritage, participants can develop valuable tools vital to recovery. Although not all members will be equally aware of their culture and its impact, the various steps in the Path of Handsome Lake and the Landmarks constantly reinforce this theme and a focus upon the culture and the individual's relationship to it.

While cultural identity is a primary focus, a particular group may have members that derive from different cultural traditions.[2] The program needs to help all members of the group to recognize the power of their own particular cultural heritage. By doing so, each member can better understand how cultural decline and personal alienation from a cultural heritage might trigger alcoholism

Presented in tabular form (Table 11.2), we find:

Table 11.2. Primary Group Self-Help Activities

	Overview	*Analysis*
Relationship	A group of people creates a forum where they can explore their cultural heritages in order to combat tendencies towards alcoholism	In primary group self-help activities, discussions center around Native cultures, and trauma related to it. Self-Help groups lack a formal leader, although some members emerge as leaders and role models.
Worldview	The shared worldview emphasizes that cultural stress can trigger individual dysfunction and that strengthening the cultural heritage and building the group's cultural awareness and developing a comfort for the Native culture can be therapeutic.	The Handsome Lake program is distinct because it acknowledges that Native cultures are often under stress and centers upon how members may be vulnerable to (1) assaults on the culture and (2) personal alienation from a cultural heritage.
Expectation	Participating in a group setting as equals, members expect to explore each other's cultural traditions in order to overcome vulnerabilities that can lead to dysfunction. People expect a forum free of ridicule.	The group explores cultures and heritages in ways that help all to overcome dysfunction. There is an expectation that recovery can result from greater cultural awareness and becoming comfortable with one's traditions.
Intervention	The group employs the path of Handsome Lake and the Landmarks of the Path so participants can better relate to their heritage and become less vulnerable to dysfunction resulting from cultural issues.	The Path of Handsome Lake and the Landmarks of the Path create a forum for both personal and group problems. Discussions build confidence in the ability to achieve sobriety by strengthening the culture and the individuals' relationship to it.
Discussion	Self-help groups focus to a large degree upon (1) the native culture, (2) how to strengthen it, and (3) how individuals can cease being alienated from their traditions. As in all self-help groups, the fact that all are "equal" and no specific leader is in charge can be both strength and a weakness.	

In therapy that is primarily based on the Handsome Lake method, the Native culture and its role in recovery becomes a central focus. Valuable though this may be, many people will be simultaneously be involved in other more mainstream groups. This reality must be recognized.

As a result, the Handsome Lake program will often be used in conjunction with other methods or programs of recovery. In an era when alternative strategies of recovery are more firmly established within the self-help community, the Handsome Lake program will often function in a supplemental role. As a result, situations where the Handsome Lake method shares the stage (often serving in a subordinate role) need to be discussed.

A SUPPLEMENTAL SELF-HELP PROGRAM

In reality, of course, mainstream methods of recovery tend to dominate self-help strategies. And the most prevalent self-help method is the 12 Steps Program developed by Alcoholics Anonymous. Without question, these mainstream programs dominate self-help activities and, as a result, such programs will primarily serve many individuals. Nevertheless, as discussed above, the shortcomings of these methods when applied to Native recovery may be profound. The 12 Steps Program, for example, does not focus upon cultural stress and the potential decline of Native cultures, nor does the program meaningfully counter the alienation that many Natives feel towards their traditions (not to mention the fact that many Natives may be largely ignorant of their heritage). Thus, although the 12 Steps Program is not antagonistic to the Handsome Lake method (and other culturally centered programs), it fails to deal with a wide array of pressures and challenges faced by many Native people seeking recovery. Due to this void, the Handsome Lake model provides an invaluable alternative to mainstream programs.

In the case of the 12 Step Program, for example, the focus is typically upon individuals who are characterized as having "lost touch" with their culture. That culture, however, is depicted as vibrant, permanent, and ongoing. Conceiving the problem of alcoholism in this manner, it logically follows that those seeking to recover need to re-embrace their culture as they recover from their dysfunction. Under such circumstances, the strength and security offered by the culture are viewed as continuing to exist and, upon regaining sobriety, the recovering individual can rather easily reclaim them. Because mainstream programs tend to be structured in this way, the health of the culture is not addressed as a significant issue. Among many Native peoples, however, the culture has been significantly undermined and/or people have become distanced from it; mainstream programs, unfortunately, do nothing to relieve these triggers of anxiety and dysfunction.

By positioning the Handsome Lake program as a useful addendum of self-help that fills in the gaps left by mainstream programs, a tool of recovery emerges that can be simultaneously practiced along with other more conventional models of treatment and/or self-help.

When the Path of Handsome Lake is being used in conjunction with some other program of recovery, clients need to be conscious of (1) the similarities and (2) the differences in each program and how each can usefully supplement the other. The lack of conflict between these programs also needs to be emphasized. Acting in such a spirit, each program needs to be dealt with as an equally valid (but distinct and unique) component of recovery. A good point of departure is to observe that people are simultaneously members of their traditional Native culture and the mainstream world.

Discussions in self-help meetings can seek to establish specific ways in which members identify with the mainstream world versus their traditional culture and vise versa. Because these two worlds may be in significant conflict with each other, such self-revelation is important and can be a significant component of recovery. These revelations are especially important when members are focusing upon conflicts that cause anxiety and need to be mitigated.

Individual Supplemental Self-Help

Individual supplemental counseling has the same strengths and weaknesses as primary individual counseling (see discussion above). In short, it is centered on the needs of one person, but it doesn't benefit from the positive synergism of group participation.

In individual supplemental counseling, it is vital for participants to determine how their needs can be addressed via conventional therapy, versus the use of more culturally sensitive strategies, such as the Handsome Lake method. As indicated above, mainstream programs (such as the 12 Step Program) are neither strongly attuned to cultural stress/cultural decline nor do they deal with the possibility that people have become alienated from their traditional culture. The participant needs to determine the role that each program should play in their recovery.

Determining how the Handsome Lake method can best be applied and how it can be most effectively integrated with other programs of recovery should be a goal of such thought. What benefits will the particular client get from each program? How can these benefits be blended with each other in a positive and synergistic way?

The Path of Handsome Lake should be viewed as a special program that has the potential to provide useful reflection and growth for some people. The ability to deal with issues of stress and alienation from the perspective of a cultural heritage provides the Handsome Lake program with a unique ability to aid the process of recovery. The Alcoholics Anonymous/the 12 Step Program, in contrast, is not equipped to deal cultural stress and decline and with the stress triggered by cultural alienation. The respective strengths and limitations of each program, provides each with a valuable role in the therapeutic process.

Those using the Handsome Lake program need to envision it as a supplement that helps completes the total equation of recovery. A tabular overview (Table 11.3) of such thinking is as follows:

Table 11.3. Supplemental Individual Self-Help Therapy

	Overview	*Analysis*
Relationship	The Handsome Lake program provides a stronger relationship between participants and their cultures	In situations where other programs are being employed along with the Handsome Lake program, participants need to determine the appropriate role of each program. There is no universally "right" or "wrong" strategy because different people have their own needs and vulnerabilities.
Worldview	Both the Handsome Lake method and conventional strategies of treatment possess strengths and weaknesses. Participants need to determine how each method can aid in their recovery. The resulting decision crates a worldview regarding the participants' needs.	Although the therapeutic relationship may employ two different methods or strategies, this does not mean that they are in conflict in any way. Instead, each method is able to serve participants in a specific manner. After determining participant's needs, the role of each method can be determined in an appropriate manner.
Expectation	Participants work toward recovery in the manner that coincides with their worldview. They will expect results to reflect the orientations of the Handsome Lake method and their personal needs.	Because the expectations will, to a large extent, be a function of a worldview that is a melding of the program and the visions of participants, the expectations will be unique. Formally establishing a list of expectations is a good strategy.
Intervention	Participants can use the program to intervene in a life that has gotten out of control. Components of both the Handsome Lake method and conventional self-help programs may provide valuable clues to recovery. The final formula will be based on participant's needs.	The intervention consists of combining the Handsome Lake and conventional methods of recovery in a way that suits the specific participant. To whatever degree participants have been impacted by cultural decline and/or have been alienated from their heritage, the Handsome Lake method will be of vital importance. Nonetheless, there is no inherent conflict between the different methods used.
Discussion	Participants who employ both the Handsome Lake method and other programs need to remember that they are not in conflict, but are merely different tools to be used as required. Since each participant will typically have a unique set of needs and expectations, it is a good idea to create a written list of expectations and a formal menu of how various methods will be implemented.	

When using the Handsome Lake model within a supplemental capacity, a complex situation develops because individual needs must be addressed. Striking a proper balance between various programs can be difficult and doing so cannot be applied in a routine and unthinking manner.

Group Supplemental Self-Help Activities

In-group self-help groups, as discussed earlier, the group has an ambience that transcends individual members. The resulting synergism serves both the individual and the entire body of participants.

In a supplemental capacity involving self-help groups, the Path of Handsome Lake may be used in conjunction with a variety of other self-help programs. Typically, these other programs will be mainstream self-help strategies such as the 12 Step Program. As discussed earlier, such programs usually fail to deal with cultural stress and alienation.

Under these conditions, two specific programs of self-help are dealt with simultaneously. This fact makes the situation complex. The fact that multiple cultures are likely to be represented in any group adds to this complexity.

During meetings, a wide number of participants can be expected to deal with their cultural issues and the stresses that result from them. When specific examples of cultural stress, conflict, and anxiety are discussed, they need to be discussed in ways to which the entire group can relate. By doing so, the specific needs of individual participants, as well as the universal issues they reveal, can be more readily appreciated

As has been emphasized, the Handsome Lake method is not in conflict or in competition with any other strategy of recovery. By using it, the distinctiveness of various cultural traditions can be emphasized. In such a manner a supplemental program of value to many valued participants can emerge. An overview is provided in Table 11.4.

On many occasions, it can be expected that the Handsome Lake method will be used in a supplemental capacity. After all, other programs of recovery dominate. But, as we have seen, these programs do not adequately deal with a wide range problems facing many members of Native and traditional cultures. The Handsome Lake method, in contrast does so.

CONCLUSION

According to Fischer, Jobe, & Atkinson (1998), multicultural therapy consists of at least the following components: (1) a therapeutic relationship exists, (2) those involved in this relationship have some kind of a shared world-view, (3) The person receiving help has certain expectations, and

Table 11.4. Supplemental Group Therapy

	Overview	*Analysis*
Relationship	The group develops a relationship that seeks to explore the advantages of the Handsome Lake and other models of recovery. The group and its members understand that different people have different needs and that each member will practice a unique program of recovery.	Where other programs are being employed along with the Handsome Lake model, the group needs to understand that different members will have their own unique needs. Members must respect the programs of recovery practiced by others and understand that there is no inherently "right" strategy, because different members have their own needs and vulnerabilities.
Worldview	Both the Handsome Lake method and the conventional strategy of treatment have their strengths and weaknesses. The group needs to understand that each program has its own role and that different people will employ them in their own ways.	Although the therapeutic relationship may employ two different methods or strategies, this does not mean that they are in conflict in any way. Instead, each is able to serve various group members in a unique manner. By allowing all group members to structure their own strategy of recovery, they will benefit from both self-determinism and the benefits of group solidarity.
Expectation	The group will work towards recovery in the manner agreed upon by the group. Nonetheless, the structure will allow for individual differences and all members will expect this kind of activity.	Because various strategies are combined, the shared worldview of the group will acknowledge individual variations. As a result, the expectations of each member will be somewhat unique. Formally establishing a list of expectations is a good strategy.
Intervention	An appropriate intervention will be based upon the worldview and expectations of the group and the needs of individual members. Components of both the Handsome Lake method and the conventional therapy will fit into the final formula chosen by individual members.	The intervention consists of practicing the Handsome Lake and conventional methods in a way that conforms to the group consensus and meets the needs of individuals. To whatever extent group members have been impacted by cultural decline and/or be alienation from their heritage, the Handsome Lake model will prove useful. Nonetheless, there is no inherent conflict between that method and any other.
Discussion	Groups using the Handsome Lake model need to remain conscious of the needs and vulnerabilities of specific members. The Handsome Lake model and other strategies of recovery are not in conflict, but are merely different tools to be used as required. Since specific members will typically possess their own unique set of needs and expectations, each member needs to keep track of their own needs, goals, and vulnerabilities.	

(4) some kind of ritual or intervention occurs. In this chapter, the Path of Handsome Lake/Landmarks of the Path method was viewed according to these criteria. So viewed, it clearly met the criteria of therapy and was applied to self-help activities.

While the Handsome Lake model provides a specific self-help strategy, it can be applied in many ways. On some occasions, the method may emerge as the primary self-help activity. In other contexts, it may serve in a supplemental program. As a result, the Handsome Lake program can be applied in at least four distinct ways, (1) individual primary self-help activities, (2) individual supplemental programs of self-help, (3) Primary group self-help efforts and (4) group supplemental self-help therapy. By providing guidelines for each use, the flexibility of the program has been demonstrated.

NOTES

1. This is a matter of debate among many members. Some, more conservative members, assert this step is part of the program and needs to be practices as outlined by Bill W. Others affirm that doing things in this ritualistic way is unnecessary as long as the individual deals with the issues involved in a thoughtful manner
2. Even among members of the same Native culture there are often many groups that are unique in their own distinctive ways. Among the Athabascan people of Alaska, for example, the culture is made up of many subsets each having their own traditions and distinctions. As a result, establishing a self-help group of Native people who are culturally "identical" is almost impossible.

REFERENCES

Fischer, A.R., Jome, L.M., & Atkinson, D.R. (1998). Reconceptualizing multicultural counseling: Universal healing conditions in a culturally specific context. *The Counseling Psychologist,* 26(4), 525–588.

Napoleon, H. (1996). *Yuuyaraq: The way of being human.* Fairbanks, AL.: Alaska Native Knowledge Network.

Sue, D. W., Arrodondo, P., & McDavis R. J. (1992). Multicultural counseling competencies and standards: A call to the profession. *Journal of Counseling and Development, 70*(4), 477–486.

CHAPTER 12

CULTURAL SENSITIVITY AND ALCOHOLISM THERAPY

A Conclusion

This book draws attention to the fact that many mainstream alcohol recovery programs fail to address a range of issues and anxieties that face Native people. Responding to this void, a more culturally sensitive alternative is offered.

In specific, most mainstream programs and strategies of recovery do not adequately deal with the fact that Native cultures tend to be under attack and that the resulting stress and unmitigated social change can lead to anxieties that can trigger alcoholic drinking. As a result of this hurtful environment, alcoholism among Native populations has reached epidemic proportions. Although this book primarily concerns Native American alcoholics, many other Native peoples have been impacted in a similar manner. Comparisons of the Maori of New Zealand and Native Hawaiians were provided in order to expand the range of applicability of the book. These similarities suggest that the program offered here can be applied to Native people worldwide.

In a nutshell, this book provides a strategy for recovering from alcoholism that is based upon the life and teachings of Handsome Lake, a late 18th/early 19th century Iroquois who personally recovered from seemingly

The Path of Handsome Lake: A Model of Recovery for Native People, pages 185–187

incurable alcoholism and, having done so, designed a program to help others do the same.

Documenting how the plight of Native alcoholics tends to be significantly different from that experienced by more mainstream people, the need for a special strategy of therapy is demonstrated. While mainstream people know they can return to their culture when they recover, rapid and unmitigated social change has often weakened or destroyed the cultural foundations of Native people. The resulting alienation and cultural disruption (1) often trigger alcoholism in the first place and (2) create a situation in which people entering recovery do not necessarily have a strong and vital culture to support them when they seek recovery.

Now that this overview has been provided, discussions of cultural stress, the anxieties that result from it, and the role that such disruptions play in triggering alcoholism are analyzed. A theoretic perspective, largely based on sociological theory, explains Native alcoholism in terms of cultural change and decline that leads to individual stress and anxiety and trigger dysfunction. Such is the fate of many Native people worldwide.

Besides being rooted in sociological theory, modern terror management theory (a school of social psychology) is embraced as complementary tool of analysis that provides parallel insights regarding the dysfunctional responses of Native people. In recent years, terror management has documented that people often identify with their cultural heritage and use it as a buffer against anxiety. Recently, theorists such as Michael Salzman, furthermore, have observed that in situations where the culture has been weakened, it may not be able to nurture and protect them from stress. Under these circumstances, we can expect anxieties to rise; this has been the case among many Native people experiencing cultural collapse. Melding terror management theory with social theories (such as Robert Merton's theory of anomie) that are largely parallel but derive from other intellectual traditions, a more robust theory is provided that straddles social and psychological theories in relevant and powerful ways.

Using this theoretic foundation, the life and contributions of Handsome Lake are placed in a framework that can serve Native alcoholics and provide them with a foundation for personal recovery. Just as Handsome Lake helped the 19th century Iroquois culture to stem its decline while providing individuals with the tools of recovery, his example remains ready to serve Native alcoholics today.

Thus, besides his historic significance, Handsome Lake developed a method by which Native alcoholics can recover and live a life of sobriety. Handsome Lake's recommendations involve combining a personal recovery with a strengthening of the Native culture. By updating and generalizing the suggestions of Handsome Lake, a model inspired by his teachings is provided to Native alcoholics seeking recovery.

The strength and power of the Handsome Lake program are reinforced by the fact that contemporary Native people have independently realized that the insights provided by Handsome Lake 200 years ago continue to be relevant today. Native Alaskan Harold Napoleon (1996), for example, has written an analysis of cultural decline, alienation, and alcoholism that almost completely mirrors what Handsome Lake had to say in the early years of the 19th century. These parallels demonstrate how the methods proposed by Handsome Lake are equally applicable in the 21st century.

From a more scholarly and theoretic point of view, Handsome Lake and his suggestions are clearly explainable in terms of modern terror management theory. That theory argues that cultural decay and decline can trigger anxieties that lead to dysfunctional behavior, such as alcoholic drinking. Expanding this theory, it logically follows that by strengthening the culture and by helping people to embrace their traditions, these anxieties and the dysfunctional behaviors they spawn will decrease. This is exactly what Handsome Lake proposed and his suggestions completely fit the theory and practice of modern terror management theory.

After providing these historical and theoretical discussions regarding Handsome Lake, discussions of the method's actual applications are provided. In specific, Chapter 10 discusses using the program within the contexts of professional counseling while Chapter 11 concerns self-help applications of the method. Each of these chapters provides insights regarding (1) both individual and group activities/therapy and (2) situations where the Handsome Lake program is the primary strategy of therapy vs. situations where it is applied in a supplemental fashion.

By updating and codifying Handsome Lake's strategies of recovery, Native people are provided with tools of recovery that are culturally sensitive and easy to apply, both in counseling and in self-help situations. The result is a systematic strategy of recovery that acknowledges the significance of culture and, in doing so, transcends other programs of recovery (such as Alcoholics Anonymous) that do not focus upon cultural issues or specifically deal with the anxiety that arises when people become alienated from their heritage. In view of the fact that these are significant issues for many Native people, the Handsome Lake program has an important contribution to make to Native recovery programs.

REFERENCES

Napoleon, H. (1996). *Yuuyaraq: The way of the human being.* Fairbanks, AL.: Alaska Native Knowledge Network.

APPENDIX A

THE PATH AND THE LANDMARKS IN POSTER FORM

Those employing the Handsome Lake method may wish to display the Path and the Landmarks. Doing so is a tradition among self-help groups; thus, Alcoholics Anonymous programs routinely display copies of their "12 Steps" and "12 Traditions."

In addition, participants in the program may benefit by having copies of the Path and the Landmarks readily available.

Therapists who own this book are given permission to duplicate the following "poster versions" of the Path and Landmarks. They may be placed in offices and meeting rooms and may be reproduced to be given to clients of counselors who own a copy of the book.

Individuals who own the book may reproduce these posters for their own use.

The Path of Handsome Lake: A Model of Recovery for Native People, pages 189–191

The Path of Handsome Lake

1. I possess a culture and a tradition. Embracing them is sacred, meaningful, and joyful.
2. All cultural traditions change and are under attack. I will strive to help my culture evolve and flourish.
3. I will break the cycle of personal and cultural decay by ceasing to abuse alcohol.
4. I recognize my past errors and I will remember them when choosing a more noble and fulfilling path.
5. Having chosen a more noble and fulfilling path, I will strive to keep my errors in the past and correct them as soon as the occur.
6. My heritage and my traditions give me a spirituality. By denying them, I deny my own self and become vulnerable to relapse. By embracing them, I can better succeed in recovery and in life.

Landmarks of the Path

1. We recognize who we are.
2. We acknowledge that our heritage, culture, and traditions are our strengths.
3. We reject the vulnerability that comes from ignoring our roots.
4. We realize that our brothers and sisters may have their own traditions and we respect them.
5. We understand that strength comes not in retreating from challenges, but from embracing ourselves.
6. While Handsome Lake was an American Indian, his example may be useful to others who face cultural and personal disruptions in their lives.

APPENDIX B

SUGGESTIONS FOR SESSIONS AND MEETINGS

INTRODUCTION

Being newly developed, no lore and grassroots suggestions have grown up around the Handsome Lake program of recovery. As a result, those who want to apply this tool of recovery may experience difficulty because they will have access to little practical advice. Due to that reality, providing a variety of "hands on" tactics regarding how to get the method "up and running" is an essential component of the book. By discussing an array of practical guidelines, I hope that both practitioners and lay people can better envision how this method can be usefully applied within a variety of contexts.

This discussion begins with a general consideration of how to apply the Handsome Lake program of recovery, what it can accomplish, and how it can help stem the tide of alcohol abuse among Native people. These discussions will be followed by advice regarding specific suggestions for both group meetings and one-on-one sessions that employ the Handsome Lake method. A number of suggestions regarding "specialty" meetings/sessions and how they can be conducted are also provided. Hopefully, the advice contained in these discussions will help those who are interested in the Handsome Lake program to gain the tools they need to begin using this tool of recovery in an organized and productive manner.

The Path of Handsome Lake: A Model of Recovery for Native People, pages 193–208

GENERAL OBSERVATIONS

As discussed throughout this book, many Native cultures are under stress and this situation often has the potential to trigger anxiety that can result in dysfunctional behavior, such as alcoholic drinking. Given this reality, a key to reducing anxiety lies in helping people develop a means of developing a positive and productive relationship with their heritage. As discussed above, Alcoholics Anonymous, the most popular program of recovery for alcoholics, does not actively focus upon the stress to which cultures (especially Native cultures) are subjected. As a result of this gap, that program is not well equipped to deal with issues that are related to the individual's cultural heritage and the fact that when legacies and heritages are under attack and/or subjected to profound change and tension, dysfunctional behavior among its members can easily result.

Because dominant strategies of recovery, such as Alcoholic Anonymous, do not deal with these issues of cultural stress, anxiety, and dysfunction they can cause, alternative methods of self-help and therapy are needed so Native people can focus upon their heritage and more effectively cope with whatever changes and stresses their cultures are experiencing.

Handsome Lake was an historic Native leader who recognized this need and he struggled to create a program that simultaneously dealt with restoring the culture to health, on the one hand, while helping individual people to overcome their alcoholic tendencies, on the other. Even though Handsome Lake created this method in the early 19th century, his work clearly reflects the orientations of modern social scientists and psychologists, on the one hand, coupled with the responses of contemporary Native people (such as Harold Napoleon who also seek to overcome alcoholic drinking by embracing their cultural identity) on the other. Given the validity, usefulness, and timeliness of Handsome Lake's wisdom, bolstered by parallel thinking from our era, this book has developed a program of recovery that is based upon such principles.

MEETINGS: AN OVERVIEW

Therapeutic meetings possess the advantages of (1) serving several individuals simultaneously (2) coupled with the power of group dynamics. Meetings provide a popular and proven method of both self-help and professionally managed therapy. The group method has proved itself within a variety of contexts and it has been usefully applied within both mainstream and Native cultural contexts. Examples will be discussed below:

The Alcoholics Anonymous Legacy

The methods associated with Alcoholics Anonymous are classic and widely known tools of recovery. Most basically, Alcoholics Anonymous is a program of group dynamics by which people collectively seek to overcome their common malady: alcoholic drinking. The method largely relies upon the benefits that can be derived from participation within a group context. Alcoholics Anonymous meetings are designed to (1) provide a reference group that encourages participants to find counsel and comfort in the company of others as they (2) work together to overcome their common problem: alcohol abuse. Since the earliest days of the organization, group meetings have been the bedrock of the Alcoholics Anonymous method. The basic strategy employed involves afflicted people banding together for their common benefit and, in the process, gaining a collective strength that, individually, they lack.

Many alcoholics seeking recovery, furthermore, have some prior experience with Alcoholics Anonymous and, therefore, they are familiar with its group dynamics and the patterns and structures of typical meetings. Even though the orientation of Alcoholics Anonymous is not well equipped to deal with the problems associated with cultural stress, the program is well known and many people have grown accustomed to it. As a result, other therapeutic organizations and strategies of recovery can easily build upon this strategy of treatment.

The Talking Circle Legacy

While the particular meeting format of Alcoholics Anonymous was forged by Bill Wilson in the 1930s and refined in the millions of meetings that have occurred since he developed the program and its strategies, Native peoples possess their own traditions of managing group responses and doing so in powerful and therapeutic ways. One such strategy is commonly known at the "Talking Circle." Basically, a talking circle is a group of people who meet in a largely unstructured and democratic forum. Those participating within a talking circle context agree that the person who currently "has the floor" has the freedom to discuss anything that he or she deems important and can do so without censure or interference from others. Typically, the speaker holds some object from nature (such as a feather), which grants the right to speak. After a person has finished talking, the object (and the right to speak) is passed to the next person who can either speak or pass it along in silence. While holding the object a person has the freedom to say anything on whatever topic without interference, censure, and without the threat of retaliation once the meeting is over. In addition, what is said within the context of a talking circle is viewed as confidential and people are forbidden to repeat or discuss what was said once the talking circle ends. Thus, the talking circle provides an open forum that facilitates talking about issues that are troubling, but cannot be comfortably or appropriately addressed within other contexts.

This kind of communication has proved to be very useful in many circumstances and it is a commonly used technique among many Native American peoples. In addition, many Native people have developed strategies of using the talking circle concept within the context of alcohol abuse therapy and many programs of recovery that are designed to assist Native alcoholics make good use of the talking circle method.

Discussion

Both of these tools allow participants to speak their mind without interference; thus in Alcoholics Anonymous meetings "cross talk" (responding directly to someone's comments, especially in confrontational ways) is forbidden. In both Alcoholics Anonymous meetings and talking circles, what is discussed is expected to remain confidential. Thus, significant parallels exist between the strategies of Alcoholics Anonymous and the talking circle method of Native people.

SPECIFIC TYPES OF MEETINGS

Using meetings within a therapeutic context has long been practiced within alcohol abuse therapy and special tools have been developed to serve within specific contexts. Meetings have an important role in both self-help activities and in professionally managed therapy involving counselors or therapists. Each option will be discussed.

Self Help Meetings

Alcoholics Anonymous, of course, is a self-help organization that is independent of any formal structure (such as a therapeutic organization or clinic). Using the context of self-help Alcoholics Anonymous has created a meeting format that is the province of lay people who are personally struggling for recovery from alcoholism. As a result, Alcoholics Anonymous meetings possess an air of being a democratic, open forum. In reality, however, many meetings are clearly influenced by a particular individual who may have founded the particular meeting and exerts great power upon it. In addition, some strong willed and dominant people put their personal stamp upon everything they do (including the meetings in which they participate).

Many recovering alcoholics prefer self-help meetings to professionally provided therapy because they believe (and sometimes vocally assert, typically in error) that professional therapists are probably only "in it for the money." Other participants may point to the fact that the members who participate in self-help groups are "real drunks" like themselves and, therefore, "over-intellectuals" with a lot of book learning, but little "real-world experience" will not control the discussions. Potential weaknesses in self-help meetings stem from the same phenomena that give them strength: they are run by lay people. Since a professional counselor does not manage self-help meetings, they may "get off the track" and/or some questionable ideas may be championed because no professional facilitator or authority figure is in charge who can challenge such thoughts. Nonetheless, these meetings are free to the public, populated by well meaning individuals who possess experience in fighting alcoholism, and most attendees take what is said with a grain of salt. Indeed, one of the classic and often repeated slogans of Alcoholics Anonymous is "take what you need and leave the rest."

By the same token, self-help meetings that revolve around the Handsome Lake model can, likewise, possess these same strengths and weaknesses. Learning from earlier examples of self-help, those who seek to establish Handsome Lake self-help meetings need to consider these issues in order to create the most effective forum.

Facilitator Managed Meetings

While Alcoholics Anonymous is a self-help group consisting of lay people, the ambience of the program and many of its techniques have been adapted for use within a professional therapeutic context. Under such circumstances, meetings are managed by a professional facilitator, social worker, or counselor and provided within the context of professional treatment. These meetings, by their very nature, tend to be more formal in structure and although the facilitator may allow and encourage a degree of flexibility, meetings are usually orchestrated or directed by the leader in some kind of overt or covert manner. In these meetings, there is a greater chance that the topic being discussed will be chosen by the facilitator. And the facilitator tends to have the authority to cut off participants when their contributions become offensive, drag on too long, or get off the point. While self-help meetings are purely voluntary (even if some attendees may be court mandated), attendance in facilitator-managed meetings tends to be formally scheduled and obligatory.

While the Handsome Lake method is unique in that it focuses around the cultural heritage and the stress that specific people are facing due to cultural stress, many of the tactics and structures inherent in Alcoholics Anonymous meetings can be adapted and adjusted for use within the Handsome Lake program of recovery. Instead of reinventing the wheel, those applying proven techniques from Alcoholics Anonymous can benefit from employing relevant strategies, even though the many of the specific concerns of the Handsome Lake program are very different from those of Alcoholics Anonymous. Since many participants in the Handsome Lake program will probably be familiar with the Alcoholics Anonymous format, furthermore, these veterans of recovery can more easily adjust to the new program.

SPECIALITY MEETINGS AND THEIR PURPOSES

Particular meetings, either as part of a self-help program or within the context of a professionally managed regimen of therapy, can be discussed in terms of their particular context or ambience. Some meetings just occur on a regular schedule, but the topic or tone of the meeting is not preordained in any way. In these meetings, whatever develops or comes to mind dictates the tact that the particular meeting will follow. At these meetings, a leader or some other participant will, typically, spontaneously throw out a topic for discussion and the theme for the hour is set in this informal manner. Or, perhaps, there may a call for a meeting topic and any member can suggest a theme. Other meetings, in contrast, may have a structure, purpose, or topic that is a regular and ongoing feature of that group. Pressing circumstances (such as a newcomer) may dictate adopting a special format for a specific meeting. Some of the possible varieties of meetings that fit well within the Handsome Lake program of recovery include the following.

Path Meetings

A common feature of Alcoholics Anonymous is that various meetings are known to be "12 Step" and "12 Tradition" meetings. Thus, those meetings typically deal with one of the 12 Steps or the 12 Traditions that are the principles that provide the foundation of the program. Typically, these meetings are held at a particular time (possibly on a special night once a week). This method has proven to be useful, constructive and enjoyable for many members. And these meetings provide a recurring reinforcement of key principles of the program.

Borrowing from the proven strategies of Alcoholics Anonymous, a Path Meeting can provide a way of focusing upon key elements of the Handsome Lake method. In order to do so, specific path meetings cans deal each of the particular steps, revolving in order in an endless circle. By doing so, the main issues in the program can be discussed and re-discussed on a regular schedule. Doing so provides an introduction to the program for newcomers while reinforce the essence of the program for ongoing members. As with 12 Step meetings, Path Meetings can be useful in helping individuals to begin internalizing the program, such a format can be useful for that reason. Various techniques for managing and structuring a Path meeting can be devised. A meeting may begin with some sort of reading with discussions being upon it or the meeting might focus on a particular aspect of the particular step under discussion. Perhaps a talking circle format will be chosen in order to discuss a particular part of the Path, etc. Typically, a particular meeting will adopt an ongoing format so participants will know what to expect.

Landmark Meetings

Just as Path meetings can reinforce the essence of the program, Landmark meetings can remind participants of strategies and tactics that can be employed when working the program. As with path meetings, landmark meetings can be scheduled at a special time and they can discuss the landmarks in some type of rotating order. And like path meetings, landmark meetings can help new members learn the essence of the program while serving as a useful reminder to veterans.

Qualifying Meetings

One popular category of meeting from Alcoholics Anonymous is generally known as a "qualifying meeting." These meetings feature a guest speaker (or the member) who provides a discussion regarding why he/she is "qualified" to be a member of the group. In general, this involves some kind of discussion of the problems that were experienced due to drinking and how the qualifier has been able to forge a long-term path towards sobriety (or, perhaps, why this has not occurred). Thus, the leader provides proof that they are "qualified" to discuss alcoholism. Typically the leader of a qualifying meeting will spend between 20 and 30 minutes providing some type of monologue; the remaining time is devoted to group discussions that, ideally, resonate from the theme of the qualification talk.

There is no reason why this kind of meeting cannot be a useful part of the Handsome Lake program, although it is good to have those who are leading discussions to attempt to remain focused upon cultural themes, if at all possible.

Talking Circle Meetings

Although any meeting can embrace a talking circle format in an impromptu sort of way, some meetings may be designated as talking circle meetings and will always be structured in such a manner. Other meetings may embrace the talking circle format as circumstances dictate.

Talking circle meetings are particularly useful when certain issues need to be discussed in an open forum and/or when certain members tend to dominate to the point where the opinions and feelings of the entire group (or some non-forceful members) can be overshadowed. The talking circle format can also emphasize the fact that the participants are Native people, because the talking circle format is a Native tradition of communicating. Because the talking circle format offers parity to all, it is especially helpful if certain shy or more reserved participants need to air an issue; this is especially true when controversy is involved.

Cultural Diversity Meetings

A key element of the Handsome Lake program is that a person's cultural heritage is both valuable, in its own right, and it serves as a strong buffer against anxiety and adversity. At the same time, this background can create vulnerabilities that need to be addressed.

On many occasions, however, people have trouble understanding the heritage of others and, as a result, confusions can arise when people lack the skills and knowledge that are needed to empathize with and provide support to each other. In view of the fact that many Native people suffer trauma due to assaults on their cultures, Native people seeking to recover from alcoholism often need the support and understanding of their fellows. The distinctiveness of particular cultures also needs to be recognized.

In addition, since many people have been exposed to generic modes of therapy that attempt to provide a general and universal program of treatment, Native people often need to be reminded of cultural diversity and how it can simultaneously provide strength and create vulnerabilities to particular people.

In order to best serve participants, special meetings can deal with and celebrate cultural diversity. By doing so, participants can learn to accept themselves (and others) for who they are and, as a result, they can better understand each other. Such an atmosphere can help relieve the anxiety that can result when people fail to acknowledge who they really are and/or when, due to misunderstanding, they are not treated in appropriate ways.

Achievement Meetings

One of the frequent types of meeting in Alcoholics Anonymous involves celebrations of personal achievements. Many of these meetings mark a milestone in a participant's recovery, such as the anniversary of sobriety.

Achievement meetings are valuable because people who are recovering from alcoholism often have a past track record of failure and disappointment. The path to a healthy sobriety, therefore, can be long and discouraging. Given this situation, individuals seeking recovery need to be constantly reminded of the fruits of their hard work. Celebrating the achievements of others, furthermore, can build confidence. As a result, achievement meetings are a meaningful addition to any program of recovery. Some groups may have regularly scheduled achievement meetings (on the first Monday of every month, for example). And when an especially significant achievement occurs in the life of some participant, it is often possible to have an impromptu achievement meeting to celebrate the event. Many people in recovery affirm that achievement meetings are of profound importance in maintaining their confidence and motivation. As a result, opportunities to celebrate personal achievements should be viewed as good therapy for those being recognized and an excellent example for the meeting as a whole.

Relapse Meetings

A sad reality of recovery from alcoholism is that many people backslide. This often happens even when people are making good progress and moving towards a healthy recovery. As a result of the importance of dealing with relapse and getting people back on the road to recovery, special meetings often deal with the topic of relapse when a member resumes drinking but then returns to a program of sobriety. If a member, for example, states that he/she has experienced a relapse, meetings typically restructure themselves in a spontaneous way to deal with that event, its implications, how the person should relate to the lapse, etc. Many groups and their members have the structure of a relapse meeting in the back of their minds and they can act accordingly on a moment's notice.

When people relapse, care must be taken so that they do not become so discouraged that they give up on themselves and their program of recovery. While relapse should not be encouraged, easily excused, argued away, or ignored, we all know that most recovering people often experience episodes of relapse before their recovery takes hold. As a result, relapse meetings need to walk that thin line between being overly permissive, on the one hand, and harshly judgmental, on the other. In addition, talking about relapse provides a means of underscoring how easy it can be to "let one's guard down" and make unwise choices. Thus, a well-orchestrated relapse meeting can comfort the relapse and provide a warning to the other attendees.

Concluding Statement

Meetings are an important component of programs of recovery from alcoholism. The benefits of group dynamics can be useful both within a self-help context and within the framework of professional therapy. The tactics used to manage group meetings derive from a variety of sources, including self-help organizations (such as Alcoholics Anonymous), the various helping professions, and tools of communication that have been developed by Native people (such as the talking circle method).

In order to provide suggestions on how to use group meetings, various specific suggestions were applied to both self-help and professionally managed meetings. It is hoped that these ideas will suffice until more tailored methods are developed by those who embrace the Handsome Lake method. Thus, what is stated here should be viewed as very elementary suggestions that will need to be expanded upon when people attempt to use the Handsome Lake method within their own communities.

PRIVATE SESSIONS: AN OVERVIEW

Alcohol abuse counselors or often another professional from one of the helping professions professionally conduct individual one-on-one private sessions. On some occasions, however, one-on-one sessions may involve two lay people. This kind of nonprofessional private therapeutic relationship has a long tradition in the fight against alcoholism and the results have often been impressive.

The Alcoholics Anonymous Legacy

While Alcoholics Anonymous is best known for its structure of meetings, the organization also has a strong tradition of one-on-one interactions and the pairing of two people for their mutual benefit. The Alcoholics Anonymous sponsorship program best showcases these therapeutic relationships. A basic principle of Alcoholics Anonymous is that each member should have a special relationship with a sponsor, who is typically an individual possessing extensive experience in recovery, some other area of life, and/or is someone with whom the individual can develop a special relationship.

When an individual is first becoming involved in Alcoholics Anonymous, the sponsor is expected to provide the newcomer with counsel, be a special advocate and mentor, and help the novice learn how the program works. In addition, sponsors are expected to be available in case the individual experiences a serious crisis or is in fear that a relapse is imminent. The whole idea behind the sponsorship relationship is to provide the one-on-one assistance that can help to prevent relapse and can lead to a healthy and stable recovery. Often sponsors and sponsees spend many hours in places like all night diners and/or hang out together before or after meetings, talking about whatever helps reduce the desire to drink. In the process, they develop a better understanding of the disease while enjoying human companionship. Although sponsors and sponsees typically develop a strong bond and friendship, care is taken to insure that the relationship remains therapeutic, at least during the early months of recovery when the threat of relapse is high.

One of the basic principles of Alcoholics Anonymous is the assertion that any hidden secret a person holds back is apt to exert a covert power that can help trigger a relapse to alcoholic drinking. As a result, participants are urged to reveal to the sponsor (or to some other person) everything that might be shameful or hurtful. Thus, Alcoholics Anonymous clearly affirms that one-on-one relationships are crucial to the program and to long-term sobriety.

The influence of Alcoholics Anonymous is even greater than this because many professional alcohol abuse counselors are themselves alcoholics whose recovery is largely based upon the Alcoholics Anonymous program that includes the 12 Steps and a sponsor/sponsee relationship. As a result, many counselors who provide one-on-one therapy are themselves veterans of the Alcoholics Anonymous sponsorship program, feel profoundly indebted to it, believe it is the most affective strategy of recovery, and have adopted various of Alcoholics Anonymous techniques for their professional therapeutic work.

The Professional Therapy Tradition

Although many counselors are significantly influenced by the techniques of Alcoholics Anonymous, they also tend to be influenced by the traditions of the counseling profession. Modern counseling theory and practice strongly emphasize that people often repress and thereby ignore the hurtful aspects of their lives that can lead to dysfunction. As a result, the one-on-one counseling relationship provides a forum where these issues can be forcefully addressed. Counselors recognize that finding the root of psychological problems can be a long and painful process and that individuals in therapy often need leadership in order to understand themselves and what triggers their dysfunctional drinking. As a result, personalized treatment is a commonplace tactic, even while group therapy continues to be an important tool in the recovery process. On many occasions, group activities cannot totally substitute for individual attention; as a result, one-on-one programs are often tailored around the needs of specific clients.

In addition, as was discussed above, the counseling profession is increasingly acknowledges and responds to cultural differences. Thus, the profession has become actively involved in dealing with cultural diversity and how cultural differences create a need for specific types of therapy that dovetail with the heritage of the individual and the special stresses that Native people (in general and in specific) face.

The Native American Respect for Elders

While the mainstream culture of the United States tends to revolve around youth, many Native people exhibit a special respect for tribal elders: the senior members of society who have mastered their culture and its insights and who seek to transmit these traditions to the next generation. As a result, elders are honored within many Native cultures and the special place in society these people occupy is determined by their experience, knowledge, and dedication to their heritage.

Elders are often viewed as master communicators who are able to help people to strengthen themselves and to better understand their cultural legacy, that may be fragile and under attack. As we saw in earlier chapters, a weakened culture can trigger anxiety and dysfunction. By honoring and learning from elders, some of the negative impacts of living in a modern and changing society can be mitigated. In any event, many Native people honor the bearers of their heritage and they look to them for guidance and leadership. The elders, furthermore, are often careful to interact with other members of the culture in a one-on-one manner in order to preserve the heritage of the people. Thus, many Native people are aware of the value of providing a dialogue regarding the cultural heritage and they are comfortable serving in such a capacity.

Discussion

One-on-one meetings are a valuable tool of therapy. And the methods of one-on-one meetings have roots in self-help tactics, the strategies of the counseling profession, and in Native American traditions. By combining the various techniques available and applying them in relevant ways, an effective formula of intervention can be developed.

SPECIAL TOPICS AND THEIR PURPOSES

A private session or meeting may deal with either general or specific issues. As a result, those involved in these meetings can benefit by envisioning an array of ideas that can serve as meeting topics. These concerns can be embraced, as required, in order to serve the needs of those involved. Below an array of options is provided:

Cultural Heritage Sessions

A strong cultural heritage is a powerful tool that can help people to mitigate the anxieties that people face and the pressures that can trigger dysfunction. On some occasions, clients may have a limited understanding of their culture and/or they might not perceive how important their culture might be and the power of the impacts it can exert. Thus, on some occasions, one-on-one sessions might focus on general discussions regarding the cultural heritage and its impact upon specific people. In such sessions, individuals can be exposed to a variety of cultural traditions other than their own. The example of Handsome Lake, of course, can be a good starting point for such therapy. In addition, if the individual is a reader, any number of novels about Native American life may prove useful. Especially recommended is F. Scott Momaday's work, especially his novel *House Made of Dawn*. These generic sessions can help individuals to understand the impact of the cultural heritage upon their lives and how nurturing and protecting these assets and tools can protect individuals protected from dysfunction.

Besides generic discussions that deal with the concept of "cultural heritage" and its importance, individuals often benefit by connecting, in a very personal manner, with their own specific cultural heritage. Many Native peoples have developed a significant literature regarding their cultures. This material should be sought out, if at all possible. Those who deal with a significant number of individuals from the same cultural tradition, may want to assemble their own private library of relevant materials. It is a good idea to have materials that are suitable for people with a variety of reading skills so something will be available for everyone. And where a person will be dealing with various members of the same cultural group, they will inevitably become knowledgeable of those traditions. Contacting Native elders or leaders, furthermore, might result in their aid or collaboration. Thus, elders might occasionally "sit in" on a one-on-one meeting, functioning as honored and knowledgeable guests.

Cultural Stress Sessions

Cultural stress is a major force impacting the lives of Native people. As the example of Handsome Lake demonstrates, cultural stress caused by the intrusion of outsiders, economic reversals, disease, etc. has the ability to undercut people, trigger anxiety, and lead to dysfunction. If individuals deal with this reality "head on" in a concrete manner, they may come to better understand a major force that contributes to their alcoholic drinking.

As with cultural heritage meetings, discussions of cultural stress can be either generic or specific. Besides discussions of Handsome Lake, The work of Harold Napoleon can be a useful tool when initially addressing the stress that faces Native cultures and the dysfunction the resulting anxiety can cause. When discussions move from general overviews to an analysis of specific cultures and traditions, the discussions need to become focused around the unique history of specific cultures and groups. Perhaps local histories and the memories of elders can prove to be a valuable point of departure. And perhaps the individual is well aware of the stresses that are impacting the local culture and they might be able to articulate what has happened and the implications of these experiences. In both cases, these discussions can help the individual to understand the pressures that are faced and the dysfunction they can trigger.

Path and Landmark Sessions

As with group meetings, a useful topic of one-on-one meetings can be the various components of the Path of Handsome Lake and the Landmarks of the Path. Within the context of one-on-one meetings, these topics may be scheduled in advance as required. Since the time available for individual sessions is often severely limited, several or all of the steps and landmarks may be discussed at once. If the individual is attending group sessions, such discussions can be scheduled after the individual has become familiar with these topics, thereby streamlining the process and making more efficient use of one-on-one time.

By doing so, the main issues in the program can be discussed in a manner that makes economical use of the time available while helping individuals to mold the Handsome Lake program around their own individual needs. Techniques, such as preparing a written document to be discussed during the session may help keep sessions focused and, thereby, increase the benefits derived from the meetings. These meetings can reinforce the essence of the program and help individuals to understand how the program can be an effective part of their personal recovery.

Relapse Sessions

Relapse is a common occurrence among recovering alcoholics. And if properly managed, relapse can be an important component of the process of recovery. All too often, however, relapse is viewed as a shameful failure and no benefits can be derived from reflecting upon what happened and why it occurred. Even worse, relapse can undermine the recovering alcoholic's confidence and result in a pattern of apathy and unwillingness for the individual to continue to work towards recovery.

If relapse is discussed in terms of the issues and tensions that contributed to it, benefits can derive from an analysis of what happened. From a Handsome Lake perspective, a key aspect of relapse is often related to the fact culture is under attack and creates anxieties that trigger dysfunction. By examining this process, debriefing sessions that analyze the relapse can provide a valuable service to those who seek recovery. As a result, special sessions that deal with relapse in an organized and thoughtful manner can be invaluable. Those involved in one-on-one meetings need to have a ready plan in mind that can deal with relapse at a moment's notice, because relapse is both a fact of life and unpredictable. If a relapse occurs, the next meeting (or meetings) typically needs to deal with that reality and do so in an organized manner. While no easy excuses should be given, relapse meetings need to go beyond judgmental evaluations and get down to the hard work of understanding how and why people made the choices they did.

A good place to start this discussion is by acknowledging that the relapse may have been triggered by the stress facing the culture and/or the individual being unable to relate in a healthy way to his/her heritage. Other causes, of course, might also exist. Thus, if a romantic relationship ends, people might get drunk as a result. This event was probably not triggered by cultural stress; instead it is likely to be an artifact of personal loss.

Discussion

One-on-one sessions are invaluable tools that can profoundly help those who seek to recover from alcoholism. They can be used in both self-help and in professional counseling situations. While group sessions have their values, on many occasions, people need specific and tailored help. One-on-one sessions can provide it.

CONCLUSION

Although the Handsome Lake program has a significant potential, it is new and those who want to use it need practical suggestions on how it can be applied within a therapeutic context. The discussion provided here suggests a number of practical applications that can be used to facilitate the use of the Handsome Lake method as a functioning program of recovery. I hope these ideas will suffice until a "folklore" regarding the programs arises from those who have used this tool of recovery.

Those seeking to recover from the ravages of alcoholic drinking can be served either by group meetings or by individual one-on-one sessions that employ the Handsome Lake method. Each of these options has both strengths and weaknesses; they were discussed as required above. Strategies for applying the Handsome Lake method were suggested that made use of both options.

Meetings and sessions, furthermore can be managed either by laymen by professionals. The benefits of both options are presented. In doing so, a wide variety of options are presented and analyzed in strategic ways.

This discussion provided here is only preliminary and it is merely intended to fill a void until the program becomes well enough established that others have developed methods and techniques that are useful and applicable in specific contexts. As a result, those who use the program are encouraged to forge new tactics and to share their successes and challenges with others. To be truly effective, methods of dealing with dysfunction (1) need to mesh with the personal style of those who use them and (2) reflect the needs and heritages of those who are involved. Doing so should be the goal of attempts to combat dysfunction; it is especially recommended here.

It is hoped, however, that by expanding the program it will come to extend beyond the core of basic suggestions that have been provided here. The resulting collective effort will work on behalf of Native people who employ the Handsome Lake method. Doing so is important both because (1) programs need to continue to evolve and grow and (2) each person in recovery and every self-help and therapeutic group needs to develop its own solutions to the problems that are faced. By tailoring the Handsome Lake program accordingly, it full benefits can be developed.

INDEX

The Path of Handsome Lake: A Model of Recovery for Native People, pages 209–213

V

Y

Z

www.ingramcontent.com/pod-product-compliance
Lightning Source LLC
LaVergne TN
LVHW052315200926
848481LV00002B/570